Discussion-Worthy Readings in Child Developmental Psychology

First Edition

Edited by Carrie Lane

Southwestern College (Kansas)

cognella®
academic publishing

Bassim Hamadeh, CEO and Publisher
Michael Simpson, Vice President of Acquisitions
Jamie Giganti, Managing Editor
Jess Busch, Graphic Design Supervisor
Becky Smith, Acquisitions Editor
Monika Dziamka, Project Editor
Natalie Lakosil, Licensing Associate

First published in the United States of America in 2014 by Cognella, Inc.

Cover image: Copyright © 2011 by Depositphotos Inc./monkeybusiness

Printed in the United States of America

ISBN: 978-1-62131-744-9 (pbk)/ 978-1-62661-866-4 (br)

cognella
academic publishing

www.cognella.com   800-200-3908

Contents

4/18 Exam
4/25 Presat
5/2 Presat

Attachment - Class 3

SECTION II: COGNITIVE PROCESSES   53

Language, Emotions, Temperament, Suicide, and Death

outdated

This is for Nate, who makes all dreams possible.

Acknowledgments

Special thanks to my family and friends, especially those who helped with revisions and cover color choices.

Section I: Biological Process

Childhood History, Teratogens, Birth, Breastfeeding, and Early Experience

Conclusion

Childhoods from Past Toward Future

By Peter N. Stearns

Here's an important and tantalizing debate, applying to childhood the kind of discussion that models of modernity have provoked in other aspects of contemporary life. For many children still in the labor force, rather than primarily focused on schooling, key experiences resemble what children in Western Europe, the United States and Japan encountered a century or a century and a half ago. Traditional family economies are eroding, if only because of rapid urbanization and the incapability of rural families to provide. In this context a good bit of children's work becomes novel, even though the fact of child labor is not; and this sometimes involves increased exploitation and new vulnerabilities. Many girls in India or Africa are today working as domestic servants in the cities, just as in Paris or New York in the 1850s; some are also sexually exploited on the job, as in the West before. Street trades, begging and petty crime draw many children, as in Charles Dickens's London. In the West and Japan, of course, conditions later changed, after this long and often painful transition; the modern model came largely to predominate even for most children in the lower classes, though it brought its own problems. Will further economic development and protective legislation, including pressures by global standards, move the poorer children of India or East Africa, or their descendants, into the more standard model over the next decades? Or are local traditions or permanent economic inequalities, often worsened by the new effects of disease and war, going to sustain a durable division in childhood around the globe, not only by social class but also by region?

Pulling together the strands of a global history of childhood is no easy task. This book has emphasized three major versions of childhood: hunting and gathering, agricultural, and modern. Childhood in this argument depends first and foremost on economic systems—and this is still true today, amid schooling and consumerism (children trained as consumers are vital to sustain this particular system). However, cultures and family structures enter in, which is why there is no *one* traditional agricultural childhood and, in addition to economic variables, no single modern childhood either. There are, nevertheless, two basic questions that spring from the world history of childhood, particularly of course the modern history, as we think about where childhood may head in the future.

Does what we've called the modern model of childhood, embellished by growing consumerism, describe the near future of childhood around the world, with an increasing number of societies moving closer to the model while other societies extend its implications? (Another way to put this question: should we expect the frameworks of childhood to become more similar from one region to another over the next few decades?)

And question number 2: should we want this to happen?

Recent history, in its diverse implications for childhood, certainly complicates any predictive effort. Depending on place and social class, we have seen growing numbers of older children sold into what amounts to sexual slavery. From Africa, the most common image of children seems to involve their presence in refugee camps, fleeing ethnic or religious conflict, sometimes maimed in the process, with the bloated stomachs and empty eyes of the starving; or, in southern Africa, lying on beds as AIDS victims, the disease contracted from parents at birth. Contrast this with the overbooked teenagers in the suburbs of the United States or Western Europe, cramming for exams that will determine college entrance, the day apart from school parceled out among so many activities that it will take some later years, in early adulthood, to regain a sense of spontaneity. Or, with overloaded, fashion-conscious California-style "valley girls," or Japanese teenagers trying to figure out the latest must-have good. Or, in yet another place, with the older children volunteering as suicide bombers, with the encouragement not only of local militants but often of proud parents as well. It seems impossible to fix on a single pattern of childhood.

There is the contemporary reality of child soldiers, not only in Africa but in parts of Southeast Asia, armed with weapons more deadly than children have ever possessed before. Reality in this case is complicated by the fact that, as we have seen, child soldiers used to form a significant part of many armies. While global outrage at use of child soldiers may be quite appropriate, particularly in light of the guns involved, it also reflects some new standards.

Quite recently, experts have begun to worry that huge gaps in economic standards and political instability are jeopardizing one of the most precious parts of the modern model of childhood, the decline of death rates. During the 1990s death rates worsened or stagnated in over a third of all sub-Saharan African countries, while in war-torn Iraq 10 percent of all children were now dying before five years of age (double the 1990 rate). More generally, malnutrition and AIDS were the worst villains in the slowing of gains in terms of global averages.

Current childhoods are, obviously, deeply divided by values, by affluence or poverty, by political chaos or relative stability. An anthropologist recently captured one aspect of diversity by the image of the fenced-in school, seemingly a common symbol of modern childhood virtually anywhere. But in Africa, the fence is largely designed to help keep children out who want schooling, who see it as a key to their future, but for whom there are simply not enough places given the limited resources available. On the other hand, in the United States the fence is partly intended to keep students in, who find school a boring trap, a site of bullying and social tension that seems unrelated to any meaningful future.

The kaleidoscope of childhoods in the contemporary world offers almost endless variety, with dramatically different sets of opportunities and sorrows. Yet without denying this aspect of reality, there is also a reality of some overriding trends. The trends may seem familiar, but they constitute real change for many of the societies involved, and they do largely point to the applicability of the modern model.

There was no country, not even the most impoverished and disease-afflicted, where infant and early child mortality had not continued to decline during the last third of the twentieth century, despite recent stagnation and valid new concerns. Sierra Leone, with the world's worst rate in 1998, with 316 children per 1,000 dying before five, nevertheless had experienced a 20 percent drop since 1960, along with a doubling of female literacy and a 50 percent increase in male literacy between 1980 and 1995. The world's poorest countries collectively, with 282 children per 1,000 dying before five in 1960, had seen rates drop to 172, while the world as a whole dropped from 193 to 86—a truly astonishing rate of change by any historical standard. The rise in literacy rates, though less dramatic, showed similar movement, reflecting the increased presence of schooling in global childhoods. It was certainly appropriate to note the huge gaps between rich countries and poor, and the equally huge differences in childhood experience these gaps reflected; but the directions of change were widely shared, at least into the early twenty-first century.

Infant mortality by world region, 1950–2000			
	Infant mortality rate (deaths before age one per 1,000 births)		
Region	1950–1955*	1980–1985*	2000
World	156	78	54
Africa	192	112	87
Asia	181	82	51
Europe	62	15	11
Oceania	67	31	24
Northern America	29	11	7
Latin America and the Caribbean	125	63	32

*Probability of dying before age one.
Source: *Mortality* 1988, table A.2; U.S. Census International Database 2000, <http://www.census.gov/ipc/www/idbnew.html>

Any world history with a strong modern focus faces the inevitable tension of balancing regional and global characteristics, and this is obviously true of childhood. Shared overall patterns coexist with sharp differences. Growing numbers of people and governments are agreeing that the principal focus of childhood should be schooling, not work—the global statistics for the past two decades bear this out clearly. Despite deeply troubling pockets of disease, hunger and strife, it seems plausible to predict that the school—work balance will continue to shift in favor of education—but plausibility is not certainty, which is one reason that scholars often object to the presentation of models of modernity. Not only are many societies still too poor to afford widespread access to education, but also significant groups remain who are not yet convinced that schooling makes any sense.

Kailash Satyarthi, a lifelong crusader against child labor in India and a successful mobilizer of world opinion, tells a story about his own childhood that dramatizes the problem. He went to school regularly in the town of Vidisha (and ultimately would graduate from university), but he always saw a cobbler sitting with his son outside the school, cleaning and repairing shoes. He could not understand why the man didn't let his boy join him in class, and when he finally summoned up the courage to ask, the answer was straightforward: "Young man, my father was a cobbler and my grandfather before him, and no one before you has ever asked me that question. We were born to work, and so was my son." Obviously, the answer did not satisfy Satyarthi, who went on in adulthood to chair the Global March Against Child Labor, the South Asian Coalition on Child Servitude, and the Global Campaign for Education, winning both Indian and international support in the process and rescuing as many as 66,000 children from work in manufacturing, domestic service and circus performance. But the clash of values should not be ignored, nor the fact that child labor has been increasing on Satyarthi's home turf despite reform efforts. Why is this particular region such an exception to the global trend? And is there any assurance that the exception will end any time soon?

The questions involve social class as well as geography, for the debate over making the transition to the more modern model of childhood has been immensely complicated by variations in outlook and resources within individual societies. In 2004, entertainer Bill Cosby openly berated many African-American parents and children for, among other things, not taking school seriously, including the training it offered in language and manners—they attended, but they did not really buy into the model. What most British working-class parents mean by an educational commitment for their children differs markedly from the more gungho devotion of their middle-class counterparts, another version of the divide within apparently modern societies. And while both groups maintain birth rates far below traditional levels, their average family sizes still vary in ways that suggest different attitudes toward children and toward parental responsibilities. It is vital to note the common surface trends, including birth rate reductions and transitions toward schooling, while going beneath the surface as well.

Furthermore, the modern model of childhood—quite apart from variations in meanings and huge differences in stages of change from one part of the world to the next—is only part of the story. It says nothing, even under the heading of schooling, about whether children are encouraged to think of themselves as individuals or are urged to find identities in family or religion. It says nothing about learning styles and their impact, between memorized rote lessons (quite successful for certain purposes) or a commitment to often chaotic self-expression and assurances for self-esteem. Even exposure to common aspects of global consumerism hardly assures a similar basic experience or outlook.

In 1994 an American teenager residing with his family in Singapore committed an act of vandalism, spray-painting parked cars. He was arrested and sentenced to a caning, with thirty blows to be administered across his bottom. The incident provoked a furor in the United States and other parts of the West: the punishment itself seemed barbaric, and the offense seemed trivial. The whole episode occurred at a time when several East Asian leaders were emphasizing their commitment to community values and discipline, as against excessive Western individualism and sloppy permissiveness, and of course the arguments about the American offender seemed to dramatize precisely these divisions. Here were two clearly modern, successful societies pitted against each other when it came to defining key standards for childhood. There is simply no escaping the messy need to recognize the mixture of common patterns that move childhood away from traditional bases, and sweeping diversities regarding the deeper meanings of childhood. The boy was caned, not seriously damaged according to accounts at the time, but he quickly left the city-state to get back to Michigan.

Assessing childhood in world history involves more than the characteristic local–global complexity: it also requires some qualitative evaluation of the modern experience, both for historical and for comparative purposes. Granting that what is modern can be variously handled – between working class and middle class, or between East Asia and the West – surely these diversities pale before the achievement of modernity itself. Remember the crudely pioneering historians of childhood, a generation ago, who couldn't help but note the improvements of modernity over the constraints on childhood in the past. The same temptation surely applies to current comparisons: how can we fail to agree that childhoods are better in societies that have moved more fully toward modernity than to those in which childhood is more vulnerable to stark poverty and disease? There is no way to escape some confrontation with value judgments on this particular historical subject.

Who could want, to take the most obvious apparent gain, to go back to a situation in which 30 percent or more of all children would die within two years of birth, in which virtually no family could escape the experience of at least one child's death? We can grant some interesting medical-ethical issues concerning the particular Western (especially American) devotion to keeping some children alive at great expense and with uncertain prospects for a healthy adulthood, but surely the society that has successfully cast off traditional fatalism about children's survival has made undeniable gains.

But this is not the whole modern package, of course, and some of the other components are clearly more open to debate – not about returning to the past, which is an improbable quest, but about recognizing that something other than pure progress describes the relationship of present to past, or of the more modern societies to those still grappling with transition. It is vital to remember some of the strengths and clarities of more traditional, agricultural childhood as laid out in the early chapters of this book.

Indeed, judging by polling results, many American parents, if they could articulate their historical model, would probably prefer more complex alternatives from the outset. They might not want to go back to ancient Rome, though more obedience might sound nice, but they definitely don't associate recent trends with unbridled progress. They would grant the improvement of modernity over certain agricultural traditions, with lower death rates, fewer crowded families, and schooling instead of some of the physical hardships and indignities of traditional work. But they might be inclined to argue that once modernity was achieved – say, early in the twentieth century – actual American childhood began to slide downhill. Still modern, it became too undisciplined, too self-centered, too disrespectful, too removed from family obligation – even apart from the debatable absorptions of rising consumerism. This might be why every American poll since the 1930s sees childless parents happier than those with children, and why parents who defined themselves as modern – a steadily growing group – indicated more concern about children and their own responsibilities than did self-identified traditionalists. Why else would "modern" parents tend to argue that the "good old days" were better for children (they probably meant an idealized nineteenth century, not really premodern good days) while expressing nostalgia for "more traditional standards of family life and responsibility." Without taking a parental approach exclusively, and while noting that 90 percent of American parents, while griping a lot, say they would choose to have children were they to do it all over again, there are some drawbacks to modernity that deserve comment, as against a blithely optimistic historical view.

There are two kinds of uncomfortable facts, though neither set is surprising. First, converting to some version of modern childhood does not remove all the problems that attended more traditional patterns.

Take just one example: Abuse does not cease. It may be more clearly identified and attacked, as governments take a more active role; but there's a plausible argument that government monitoring does not match the kind of controls over abuse offered by tight-knit customary villages or neighborhoods. A historian of colonial America, well versed in childhood, notes how rare cases of child abuse were in New England, compared to more modern times. He admits that some punishments accepted then might be regarded as abusive today, and he certainly acknowledges the possibility of faulty records. But he argues that it was actually harder to conceal abuse in conventional villages than is the case today, which makes the absence of the kind of abuse crises encountered in more modern periods all the more impressive. Abuse, in other words, may have gotten worse; it certainly has not ended. Changes in definitions of abuse may not have kept pace with the problem.

The second set of facts involves issues that seem to attach distinctively to modernity itself. Declining birth rates have drawbacks, quite apart from transitional periods when parents are confused about proper targets and also have to adjust to the decline of sibling care. In contemporary India and China, birth control combined with customary preferences for boys has led to practices that create a considerable surplus of young men reaching sexual maturity—several million more young men than young women, in each giant nation. Lots of men are, as a result, going to have trouble finding normal outlets and satisfactions, and the situation could produce wider social tensions as well. This is a particularly dramatic instance, and it's always easier to identify problems in societies other than one's own.

Downsides of modern childhood go beyond distinctive implementations in distant parts of the world. Closer to home, the decline of close sibling relations certainly makes it easier for children to be lonely. New gaps between adulthood and childhood create new barriers of understanding. While lots of adults in traditional societies like classical Rome once lamented the decline of youth—reflecting more about their own ageing than about actual youth—there is no precedent for the anxieties and divisions that surround modern adolescence. Psychological depression among children has almost certainly increased, granting that comparison with the past is difficult and that we have become more attuned to the problem and so more likely to perceive it. Attention Deficit Disorder is another new and growing malady, though particularly widely identified in the United States where patience with "overactive" children may have worn thin. Japan has its own categories. Early in the twenty-first century, several thousand Japanese schoolchildren suffered from a malady called *hikikomari*, an inability easily to leave home and function normally. In the West and Japan alike, youth suicides went up: 22 percent in 2003 alone, in Japan. Changes in family life, including greater marital instability, plus pressures associated with schooling and with finding identity and meaning create a context for rising problems in these categories, in all the advanced industrial societies. Also troubling, in these same societies, are acts of gruesome violence by children under 12, infrequent but dramatic and apparently on the rise. Eating problems have increased even more definably, ranging from the severity of anorexia nervosa to the more common if less dramatic escalation of childhood obesity. Given the changes in food availability and work and leisure patterns for young people, modern societies have not figured out the proper means to regulate children's eating habits, and the results are getting worse.

The point in all this is not to claim some dramatic deterioration of childhood from the past, but to note that change has brought drawbacks as well as gain, along with some outright continuity added in, where patterns didn't change one way or the other. And this complex package is worth grasping not just for the sake of historical accuracy, but as a means of helping modern societies, and societies moving toward the modern model, more clearly to identify areas that need attention, rather than celebrating progressive triumphs alone. We may well hope that more and more societies will make the turn to low birth and death rates and to schooling rather than demanding work; but we should strive for more besides, to palliate some of the common problems associated with modern childhood. Quite properly, to take the now-familiar example, the World Health Organization has moved in recent years to seek new means of combating excess weight in children, along with its established historic mission against hunger and infant mortality. There is more to dealing with the issues of contemporary global childhood than pushing the modern agenda alone.

Many people are deeply committed to helping children; Kailash Satyarthi is one example, as are the many dedicated relief workers dealing with children in refugee camps around the world. It is legitimate, however, to raise two concerns about the attention available for children today, without claiming that, on a global basis, we face some unprecedented crisis. The first concern involves the tendency of most international movements to assume the validity of modern standards of childhood and urge that the rest of the world catch up. This approach minimizes the drawbacks of the modern model itself, while encouraging a patronizing tone towards the more traditional societies, which may not produce a constructive response. The approach is undeniably humanitarian in intent, but charity does not always enhance mutual under-standing. And at the same time, some of the problems in the more modern societies risk winning insufficient notice. The second concern, noted in Chapter 11, springs from the declining importance of childhood itself in the societies where the modern model has gone farthest—precisely the societies that still take the lead in modern global pronouncements. Increasing numbers of families either have no children or have aged past the stage of active parenting. A provocative book by Muriel Jolivet describes Japan, admittedly with some exaggeration, as the first "childless" society; a British study of modern marriage, Young and Willmott's *The Symmetrical Family*, describes the fulfillment of relationships where both spouses work and jointly enjoy rewarding consumerism—and children are not mentioned at all. For increasing numbers of people in influential societies, in other words, most children at home and abroad are "other"—someone else's responsibility, neither seen nor thought about very often. They are poor, inner city or remote rural, or immigrant, or foreign; they do not provide active, daily encounters in societies that steadily become less child-centered. Factors of this sort warrant attention, for contemporary children's issues are quite real and far more complicated than some well-meaning rights pronouncements manage to convey.

Change, in the meantime, continues. New diseases, like the impact of AIDS on children, and new patterns of violence among children, whether youthful suicide bombers or kids in Britain or the United States who turn guns on each other, mark new issues in the history of childhood in the late twentieth and early twenty-first centuries.

Implications of the further implementation of the modern model cause change as well. Many observers note a global trend toward the expansion of childhood or preadulthood, whether because of economic dislocations that extend youth dependency or the extension of educational requirements, or both. Lower birth rates also explain why parents, however reluctantly, can accept this expansion as well. China makes a new commitment to send 15 percent of its huge population to university, in the relevant age groups, a decision that will keep millions out of the labor force for a more extended period of time. American families note the number of college graduates who return to the family home for a period of post-adolescence youth, while they experiment with careers or maybe take on a bit more education. A Harvard admissions officer argues that a period of post-college youth is becoming psychologically essential as well, given the hothouse pace of successful childhood itself. Reasons for the extension of childhood may vary, and the phenomenon is not yet firmly established as a durable trend, but it seems to be cropping up in several different settings around the world.

Gender differences among children decline, though this is still fiercely disputed in some societies. Declining birth rates mean that a growing number of families have only a son or two, or a daughter or two—and those with only daughters inevitably pay more attention to girls than their traditional counterparts once did, even in places like China. Education continues to equalize: from Iran to the United States, 55–60 percent of all university students are women. Some observers even argue that, with their greater interest in education and their ability to take advantage of jobs in the global economy that sometimes marginalize male youth, young women are beginning to reap distinctive benefits from modern childhood, compared to their male counterparts. Not enough to rectify traditional overall gender inequality yet, but sufficient to bear watching.

Recurrent change in childhood is not a modern monopoly. Childhood changed massively in the conversion from hunting and gathering to agriculture. Later shifts in social organization and religious beliefs brought more modest alterations, but significant ones. The advent of modern ideas and conditions for childhood, spread by imitation, by international pressure and by the sheer requirements of trying to build industrial economies and modern states, heightened the pace of change once again—always amid great variety. The shifts are fundamental and they are still, in historical terms, very recent, even in the societies that pioneered the first versions of modern childhood. It is small wonder that difficult adjustments continue; that adults and children continue to debate what childhood should entail, whether explicitly or implicitly; and that further change is inescapable. The beauty of the history of childhood, for all its complexities and debates, is that it provides a roadmap of where this human experience is coming from, as it barrels through the present on its way from past to future.

Discussion Questions

1. What are the drawbacks and gains of the traditional, agricultural model of childhood and the modern model of childhood?
2. Is it right to push the modern model of childhood on others around the world?
3. Do you think extending childhood or preadulthood is beneficial to our society? Beneficial to you? What are the reasons for why this is happening around the world?

Assignment

Using what you learned in the reading, describe your childhood experience using the modern model. Now create and describe what your life would have been like as a child growing up with a traditional, agricultural model of childhood. Choose similar milestones in childhood for each description to make comparison possible.

Incidence of Major Malformations in Infants Following Antidepressant Exposure in Pregnancy

Results of a Large Prospective Cohort Study

By Adrienne Einarson, Jacquelyn Choi, Thomas R. Einarson, Gideon Koren

S elective serotonin reuptake inhibitors (SSRIs) were developed and released on the market in the United States in 1988 and in Canada in the early 1990s with fluoxetine as the prototype. Subsequently, other classes of antidepressants have been developed and introduced, such as serotonin norepinephrine reuptake inhibitors (for example, venlafaxine), aminoketones (bupropion), phenylpiperazine (nefazodone, an updated version of trazodone that was released in the late 1970s), and noradrenergic and specific serotonin antidepressants (for example, mirtazapine).

More women than men suffer from depression with up to 20% of women of childbearing age diagnosed with the condition, most prevalent between the ages of 25 and 44 years.[1] About 10% to 15% of these women experience depression during pregnancy and in the postpartum period.[2] Therefore, a substantial number of women are likely to be taking antidepressants when they become pregnant.

Prior to late 2005, there was no evidence that the newer antidepressants, as a group, increased the incidence of major malformations above the 1% to 3% found in the general population.[3,4] However, in 2005 and 2006, GlaxoSmithKline published on their website preliminary results of a study documenting an increased risk for cardiac malformations (2/100, compared with 1/100) in infants whose mothers took paroxetine in early pregnancy. The type of cardiac defects were not

Adrienne Einarson, Jacquelyn Choi, Thomas R Einarson, and Gideon Koren, "Incidence of Major Malformations in Infants Following Antidepressant Exposure in Pregnancy: Results of a Large Prospective Cohort Study," *Canadian Journal of Psychiatry*, pp. 242–246.

specified and some could have been minor and might have resolved spontaneously.[5] Later, they reanalyzed the data and revised the incidence to 1.5% and published the results in a peer-reviewed journal.[6] These data were supported by 2 other studies,[7,8] where researchers also found a small increased risk for cardiovascular defects associated with only paroxetine, and not with other SSRIs. However, a recent study from Motherisk, with more than 1100 prospectively collected cases of women exposed to paroxetine in the first trimester of pregnancy, did not find an increased risk for cardiac defects.[9]

In addition, in 2007, 2 case–control studies were published and in neither study was there an increased risk for most birth defects documented with the use of SSRIs in pregnancy. However, after performing numerous analyses, thereby creating a high probability of false positives owing to alpha slippage, each of those studies documented small increased risks for specific birth defects, craniosynostosis, omphalocele, or heart defects but with contradictory results. It would appear that if these drugs did cause birth defects, the same defects would have been found in both groups, and they were not. The authors did state that it should be recognized that the specific defects implicated are rare and the absolute risks are small.[10,11]

Subsequently, based on the 3 reports on paroxetine, the US Food and Drug Administration[12] and Health Canada[13] posted warnings on their websites advising women to avoid paroxetine if possible during pregnancy. In December of 2006, the American College of Obstetricians and Gynecologists published a similar advisory.[14] In addition, the National Institute for Health and Clinical Excellence guidelines from the United Kingdom stated that if a woman taking paroxetine is planning a pregnancy or has an unplanned pregnancy, she should be advised to stop taking the drug. They also stated that when choosing an antidepressant for pregnant or breast-feeding women, prescribers should, while bearing in mind that the safety of these drugs is not well understood, take into account that tricyclic antidepressants, such as amitriptyline, imipramine, and nortriptyline, have lower known risks during pregnancy than other antidepressants.[15] This last statement does not appear to be based on published evidence, as there are no studies in the peer-reviewed literature to corroborate this information.

When warnings, especially about adverse effects of exposures in pregnancy are published, they are almost always widely cited by the media and subsequently make their way to the Internet. A recent Google search, using the key words antidepressants, pregnancy, and birth defects, revealed 563 000 results, mostly describing how dangerous and harmful antidepressants are to take during pregnancy and warning women not to take them if they are pregnant. In addition, there are numerous websites that have been developed, inviting women to join a class action suit against GlaxoSmithKline if they had taken paroxetine during pregnancy and delivered a baby with a cardiovascular birth defect.

Following review of this information, much of it contradictory, it is obvious that for a physician to prescribe, and for a woman to take an antidepressant during pregnancy, it has become a complicated process. Our objective was to analyze pregnancy outcomes of women exposed to antidepressants during pregnancy in our large prospective cohort, calculate the incidence of major malformations, and compare the results with a matched comparison group.

Methods

The Motherisk Program at the Hospital for Sick Children in Toronto is a teratogenic information service. We provide evidence-based information on the safety and risks associated with exposures to drugs, chemicals, radiations, and infectious diseases during pregnancy and lactation to pregnant women, lactating mothers, and their health care providers. Women call us for information regarding the safety of a drug, usually early in pregnancy, most often following recognition of the pregnancy. During the initial telephone contact, demographics, medical, and obstetrical histories as well as details of exposure and concurrent exposures are recorded on a standardized questionnaire. Details about the exposure include duration, timing in pregnancy, dose, frequency, and indication for drug use. At the follow-up interview, gestational findings, fetal outcomes, and neonatal health are documented on a structured form by telephone interview with each mother, following a detailed explanation of the study and with her consent. The details are then, with her permission, corroborated with the report of the physician caring for the baby, which is sent out to the physicians caring for the child in question. This study protocol was approved by the Hospital for Sick Children Research Ethics Board.

We used this method to ascertain pregnancy outcomes of women who called us regarding the use of antidepressants during pregnancy and entered the details in an electronic database. We used data from women who contacted us for the antidepressant exposure and compared them with an equal number of women who were not exposed to antidepressants and who had called Motherisk for information regarding nonteratogenic drugs, such as acetaminophen. To assess the number of major malformations, we only included women who were exposed to the antidepressant during the first trimester. The 2 groups were matched for maternal age, smoking, and alcohol use. We ascertained the number of major malformations in each group in percentages and then calculated the risk ratio and 95% confidence interval between exposed and nonexposed women.

Results

We were able to analyze 928 women in each group who fulfilled the inclusion criteria. Owing to the matching, there was no difference in maternal characteristics, 20% of the women smoked and less than 1% used alcohol. The antidepressants included in the analysis were: bupropion (113), citalopram (184), escitalopram (21), fluvoxamine (52), nefazodone (49), paroxetine (148), mirtazepine (68), fluoxetine (61), trazodone (17), venlafaxine (154), and sertraline (61).

There were 24 (2.5%) major malformations in the antidepressant group and 25 (2.6%) in the comparison group. The risk ratio was 0.96 (95% CI 0.55 to 1.67). There was no pattern of defects or clusters within any particular body system. An analysis of the malformations attributed to each antidepressant did not reveal an increased risk for any specific malformation associated with an individual antidepressant. Table 1 lists all of the defects documented in our cohort of exposed women. There were no defects reported associated with bupropion ($n = 113$), escitalopram ($n = 21$), or trazodone ($n = 17$).

Discussion

To our knowledge, this is the largest prospective cohort of women ($n = 928$) exposed to an antidepressant during the first trimester of pregnancy, with a matched comparison group ($n = 928$). In this cohort, details of pregnancy outcomes, gathered prospectively and personally from each individual woman, were corroborated by the infant's physician. We did not detect an increased risk for major malformations higher than expected in the general population (that is, 1 % to 3%) in the group overall, or with any individual antidepressant.

Table 1. Antidepressant exposure (*n* = 928)[a] and major malformations (*n* = 24) (2.5%) in the antidepressant group

Citalopram *n* = 184	Fluvoxamine *n* = 52	Fluoxetine *n* = 61	Mirtazepine *n* = 68	Nefazodone *n* = 49	Paroxetine *n* = 148	Sertraline *n* = 61	Venlafaxine *n* = 154
Umbilical hernia	Atrial septal defect	Pulmonary valve stenosis	Trachomalacia	Hirschsprung disease	Bilateral pulmonary hypoplasia	Hiatus hernia	Hypospadias
Duplex kidney	Umbilical	Hypospadias	Vesicoureteral reflux		Ventricular septal defect		Club foot
Duplex kidney	Umbilical hernia	Hypospadias			Clinodactyly		
Club foot		Ventricular septal defect			Clinodactyly		
Pyloric stenosis					Cleft lip and palate		
Neural tube defect					Omphalocele		
Atrial septal defect							
Congenital pneumothorax							
Hypsospadias							

[a]No major malformations reported with the use of: bupropion (*n* = 113), escitalopram (*n* = 21), or trazodone (*n* = 17)

The main strength of this model is the personal interview with the individual, which includes a detailed history. Our pregnancy registry is designed specifically for collecting pregnancy outcome, consequently we are able to collect details of alcohol, tobacco, and concurrent drug use, as well as other important potential confounders of pregnancy outcome. This information is usually not possible in studies that analyze data from prescription or administrative databases, which are examples of data collection that were not designed for this purpose, but are used. Importantly, because all of the women called us early in their pregnancy, and the details of their pregnancy and drug exposure were recorded at that time, the possibility of a recall bias was eliminated. It also allows for a comparison between exposed and nonexposed groups (that is, baseline rates) of major malformations.

The major limitation of this model is most often the sample size, which is usually less than 200 women. As about 800 women are needed to rule out a 2-fold increase, we can usually only rule out a 4- to 5-fold increased risk, at best. However, in this study, by combining the antidepressants, there were 928 women, which was more than enough power to detect a 2-fold increased risk in commonly occurring malformations. In this field, it is considered a benchmark owing to the nonrandomized nature of the studies that are possible to conduct. We were not able to rule out a 2-fold increased risk of each individual antidepressant owing to the small samples sizes. However, regarding paroxetine, we were able to rule out a 2-fold increase, specifically for cardiovascular defects (1/48) as this is a relatively common defect and is known to occur in about 1 in 100 of all births.[16] As well, we were not able to rule out an increased risk of more rare malformations, as one would need thousands of cases, or alternatively conduct a case–control study, which other groups have. Another limitation is the samples are not randomly selected, as women calling a teratogenic information service do not necessarily reflect the general population. Women who participate in this type of research generally have a higher socioeconomic status and are more motivated and want to do the right things to have a healthy baby.

In summary, depression in pregnancy cannot be ignored and may require treatment with pharmacotherapy. The decision to continue or discontinue antidepressants should be made on a case-by-case basis after a careful discussion of the evidence-based information between the woman and her physician. Untreated depression during pregnancy appears to carry substantial perinatal risks, which may be direct risks to the fetus and infant, or risks secondary to unhealthy maternal behaviours arising from depression. These risks include suicidal ideation, an increased risk for miscarriages, hypertension, preeclampsia, and lower birth weight.[17] In addition, it has been documented in published studies in the peer-reviewed literature that untreated depression in pregnancy carries a 6-fold increased risk for postpartum depression.[18]

We hope that the reassuring results from this study (about having a child with a relatively common major malformation) will assist women and their health care providers in making an evidence-based decision as to whether to continue antidepressant use during pregnancy.

Funding and Support

No funding was provided for this study.

In the past, Dr Koren and Ms Einarson have both received unrestricted educational research grants from Wyeth and Janssen-Ortho. Ms Einarson has also received unrestricted educational research grants from Organon and GlaxoSmithKline. Dr Koren has also received unrestricted educational research grants from Duchesnay, Novartis, Apotex, and Pfizer. Dr Einarson has received research support from Bristol Myers Squibb, Lundbeck, Eli-Lilly, Novo Nordisk, and also from Organon and Janssen-Ortho. Ms Choi has not received any financial support.

References

1. Grigoriadis S, Robinson GE. Gender issues in depression. Ann Clin Psychiatry. 2007;19:247–255.
2. Bennett HA, Einarson A, Taddio A, et al. Prevalence of depression during pregnancy: systematic review. Obstet Gynecol. 2004;103:698–709.
3. Einarson TR, Einarson A. Newer antidepressants in pregnancy and rates of major malformations: a meta-analysis of prospective comparative studies. Pharmacoepidemiol Drug Saf. 2005;14:823–827.
4. Malm H, Klaukka T, Neuvonen PJ. Risks associated with selective serotonin reuptake inhibitors in pregnancy. Obstet Gynecol. 2005;106:1289–1296.
5. GlaxoSmithKline. GlaxoSmithKline Advisory October 2005 [Internet]. Middlesex (GB): GlaxoSmithKline; 2005 [cited 2008 Feb 15]. Available from: http://ctr.gsk.co.uk/welcome.asp.
6. Cole JA, Ephross SA, Cosmatos IS, et al. Paroxetine in the first trimester and the prevalence of congenital malformations. Pharmacoepidemiol Drug Saf. 2007;16:1075–1085.
7. Källén BA, Otterblad-Olausson P. Maternal use of selective serotonin re-uptake inhibitors in early pregnancy and infant congenital malformations. Birth Defects Res A Clin Mol Teratol. 2007;79:301–308.
8. Diav-Citrin O, Shechtman S, Weinbaum D, et al. Paroxetine and fluoxetine in pregnancy: controlled study (Abstract). Reprod Toxic. 2005;20:459.

9. Einarson A, Pistelli A, DeSantis M, et al. Evaluation of the risk of congenital cardiovascular defects associated with use of paroxetine during pregnancy. Am J Psychiatry. 2008;165(6):749–752.

10. Louik C, Lin AE, Werler MM, et al. First-trimester use of selective serotonin-reuptake inhibitors and the risk of birth defects. N Engl J Med. 2007;356:2675–2683.

11. Alwan S, Reefhuis J, Rasmussen SA, et al. National Birth Defects Prevention Study. N Engl J Med. 2007;356:2684–2692.

12. US Food and Drug Administration. FDA Public Health Advisory: paroxetine [Internet]. Rockville (MD): US FDA; 2005 [cited 2008 Feb 15]. Available from: http://www.fda.gov/cder/drug/advisory/paroxetine200512.htm.

13. Health Canada. Health Canada Advisory: paroxetine [Internet]. Ottawa (ON): Health Canada; 2005 [cited 2005 Oct 06]. Available from: http://www.hc-sc.gc.ca/dhp-mps/medeff/advisories-avis/public/paxil_3_pa-ap_e.html.

14. ACOG Committee on Obstetric Practice. Committee opinion no. 354: treatment with selective serotonin reuptake inhibitors during pregnancy. Obstet Gynaecol. 2006;108:1601–1603.

15. National Institute for Health and Clinical Excellence. Antenatal and post natal mental health, clinical and service guidance [Internet]. London (GB): NICE; 2007 [cited 2008 Feb 17]. Available from: http://www.nice.org.uk/nicemedia/pdf/CG045NICEGuidelineCorrected.pdf.

16. Hoffman JI, Kaplan S. The incidence of congenital heart disease. J Am Coll Cardiol. 2002;39(12): 1890–1900.

17. Bonari L, Pinto N, Ahn E, et al. Perinatal risks of untreated depression during pregnancy. Can J Psychiatry. 2004;49:726–735.

18. Beck CT, Records K, Rice M. Further development of the Postpartum Depression Predictors Inventory–Revised. J Obstet Gynecol Neonatal Nurs. 2006;35:735–745.

Discussion Questions

1. This study suggests that untreated depression during the pregnancy is risky. What are some of the risks to the fetus and how might they develop?
2. Do you think that based on the study results that if your friend had depression you would encourage them to take anti-depressants while they were pregnant? If not, why?
3. Why do you think that with evidence that antidepressants taken in pregnancy lead to similar malformations as those who haven't taken antidepressants that the mainstream societal beliefs are still that they are dangerous to take during pregnancy?

Assignment

Search online for the following terms: antidepressants, pregnancy, and birth defects. Based on what you find, think of ways we can use information from the study to combat the inaccuracies you may encounter on the internet.

Laboring On

Birth in Transition in the United States

By Wendy Simonds and Barbara Katz Rothman

When it comes to motherhood, we live in a world that makes no sense.

We have seen the return of the midwife. And the rise of the cesarean section. For fifty years there were almost no midwives to be found in most of the U.S. Then during the same period in which nurse-midwives began practicing in U.S. hospitals, while hospitals introduced "birthing rooms" to replace operating-roomlike delivery rooms and the "natural childbirth" movement flourished, we also saw the cesarean section rate rise from 5% in 1970 to an astonishing and unprecedented 31.1% in 2006; it increased by a full 50% between 1996 and 2006 (Curtin and Kozak 1998, DeClercq et al. 2006, Hamilton et al. 2007, Martin et al. 2005).

Since the development of modern obstetrics, there has never been more talk of birth as a "healthy natural event," yet each individual birthing woman is now acquainted with her personal "risk factors," factors that doctors tell her make *her* birth less than healthy and far less than "natural." Eighty-five percent of women who birth in hospitals are strapped to fetal monitors (Martin et al. 2003), despite evidence that such monitoring produces unnecessary interventions (see Goer 1999, 244–47, for a summary of the medical literature on this issue).

How did we come to this strange paradoxical position regarding childbirth in this country? Understanding these contradictions of contemporary U.S. maternity care is the goal of this reading.

Constructing the Meaning of Procreation

Pregnancy and birth have different meanings to different people. What after all is a pregnancy?

Pregnancy is, sometimes, a contraceptive failure, a side effect of a not very reliable method of birth control. Pregnancy is the effect of a successful treatment for infertility. Pregnancy is a condition of a woman's body, to be distinguished from ovulation, menstruation and menopause. Pregnancy is the presence of a man's baby in a woman, as when a man wants a woman to bear him a son to carry on his name. W.I. Thomas famously said, "Situations defined as real are real in their consequences." How do we define, how do we give meaning to pregnancy, to birth? Who has the power to define?

The meaning of pregnancy is, like everything else, in the eye of the beholder, and in the U.S., the foremost "beholder" of pregnancy is the obstetrician. The obstetrical perspective on pregnancy and birth is held to be not just one way of looking at it, but to be the truth, the facts, science: other societies may have had beliefs about pregnancy, but we believe our medicine has the *facts.* But obstetrical knowledge, like all knowledge, comes from *somewhere,* it has a social, historical and political context. Medicine does not exist as "pure," free of culture or free of ideology. The context in which knowledge develops and is used shapes that knowledge. Doctors see pregnancy, childbirth, and women's entire procreative lives, from their perspective. Home-birth advocates and midwives offer a radically different—in some ways diametrically opposed—view. It is in the conflict between these two perspectives that the contradictions surrounding birth in this country arise.

The primary characteristic of the modern medical model of health and illness in general is that it is based on the ideology of technology, that ideology appropriate to technological society, with its values of effciency and rationality, practical organization, systematizing, and controlling. The application of a technological model to the human body can be traced back to Rene Descartes' concept of mind-body dualism. For Descartes, the body was a machine, the structure and operation of which fell within the province of human knowledge, as distinguished from the mind, which God alone could know. Even though the Hippocratic principles state that the mind and body should be considered together, most physicians, whatever their philosophical views on the nature of the mind, behave in practice as if they were still Cartesian dualists (Dubos 1968, 76). The Cartesian model of the body as a machine operates to make the physician a technician, or mechanic. The body breaks down and needs repair; it can be repaired in the hospital as a car is in the shop; once "fixed," a person can be returned to the community. The earliest models in medicine were largely mechanical; later models worked more with chemistry and newer medical writing describes computer-like programming, but the basic point remains the same. Problems in the body are technical problems requiring technical solutions, whether it is a mechanical repair, a chemical rebalancing, or a "debugging" the system.

A second major ideological basis of the medical model comes from its history as a men's profession, growing out of a patriarchal history. Its values are those of men as the dominant social power; medicine sees pregnancy and birth through men's eyes—even now, as more and more women are trained in obstetrics, that history continues to cast its shadow. Medicine treats all patients, male and female, as "machines," in conformance with the ideology of technological society. The treatment of women patients is further affected by the ideology of patriarchal society. We mean something more subtle here than just "men rule." In a patriarchy, it is men *as fathers* who rule, and families take their name and their identity through fathers. Our society is not of course a simple patriarchy. But the history of patriarchy continues to color our understandings of birth and family.

One important consequence of its patriarchal history is that medicine has fared no better than other disciplines in arriving at a working model of women that does not take men as the comparative norm. Medicine has treated and in many instances overtly defined, normal female reproductive processes as diseases. Certainly U.S. medicine is disease oriented, and has been since its early formal organization. Yes, doctors are illness oriented, and yes they did and sometimes still do treat pregnancy, birth, menstruation and menopause as diseases. But knowing that is not enough. We must go beyond that and ask *why*. Medicine does not, after all, treat all of our biological functions as diseases: the digestive system, for example, is usually considered well unless shown otherwise. Neither a full nor an empty colon has been seen as a disease-like state, and normal bowel movements are not medically monitored. Why then were female reproductive processes singled out to make women "unwell," in a "delicate condition," constantly moving from one disease-like state to another?

The source of the pathology orientation of medicine toward women's health and reproduction is a body-as-a-machine model (the ideology of technology) in which the male body is taken as the norm (the ideology of patriarchy). From that viewpoint, reproductive processes are stresses on the system, and thus disease-like.

Until the middle of the 1900's, doctors used the language of illness when discussing women's reproductive systems, with pregnancy seen as a disease, menopause as a deficiency disorder, childbirth as a surgical procedure. Contemporary physicians do not usually speak this way any more, regularly asserting that female reproductive functions are normal and healthy. However, they make these statements within the context of teaching the medical "management," "care," "supervision" and "treatment" of these "conditions." From the "diagnosis" of pregnancy, through the "management" of its "symptoms," on to "recovery" from childbirth, the disease imagery remains and continues to influence obstetric thinking and practice.

The contemporary midwifery model of birth grew in response to this medical approach. Coming together out of the "back to nature," movements of the 1960's, "hippy" communal life, the feminist movement, the patient's rights movement, religious fundamentalism, radical individualism—from a variety of strangely interrelated and sometimes apparently unrelated sources, a new midwifery began to appear in the U.S. Where the obstetric approach was "technological," the midwives were "holistic," where the obstetricians were patriarchal, the midwives were "women centered." In home births, birth centers, in midwifery practices in and out of hospitals all over the United States, midwives worked to redefine birth, to offer a different place to stand, a new—and maybe a very old—perspective on pregnancy, birth, mothers and babies.

We've done interviews with over 100 midwives and midwifery students—both direct-entry midwives who mostly practice home birth, and nurse-midwives, who mostly practice in hospitals—around the U.S., as well as with a smaller groups of women obstetricians (ten who were recommended to us by midwives) in Atlanta. In the rest of this article, we will offer brief a summary of the history of birth work in the U.S., and compare how members of these groups talked about one particular birth practice.

Birth in the U.S. in Historical Perspective

Midwives came over with the Pilgrims, and indeed the native peoples had their midwives before that. What is different about the United States, compared to other countries, is that it was virtually unique in the world in largely abolishing midwifery before reinventing it in a new form, as a branch of nursing. Other developed countries, like France, Germany, Japan, and the Netherlands, each maintained a form of midwifery. In some the midwives had more power, and in some less, but all have a continuous history of practicing midwives. There are continuing midwifery traditions all over the world, but their independence and their relationship to medical practice directly reflects the history of imperialism and colonization. The history of midwifery reflects world history: America won World War II and Japanese midwives lost status and power as Americans restructured Japanese hospitals; East and West Germany went separate ways in birth practices; countries colonized by the Dutch show a different midwifery than those colonized by the British. But it is in the United States that we see an attempt to simply abolish midwifery completely.

The beginning of the end of American midwifery goes back before the establishment of the United States, and has its roots in British and European history. The earliest sign of encroachment on midwifery came from the development of the barber-surgeons guilds. In England, for example, under the guild system that developed in the thirteenth century, the right to use surgical instruments belonged offcially only to the surgeon. Thus, when giving birth was absolutely impossible, the midwife called in the barber-surgeon to perform an embryotomy (crushing the fetal skull, dismembering it in utero, and removing it piecemeal) or to remove the baby by cesarean section after the death of the mother. It was not within the technology of the barber-surgeon to deliver a live baby from a live mother. Not until the development of forceps in the 17th Century were men involved in live births, and so became a genuine challenge to midwives. Interest in abnormal cases increased throughout the 17th and especially the 18th centuries; this may have been due to rapid urbanization and the resultant increase in pelvic deformities caused by rickets. (For a history of American midwifery, see Donegan 1978; Donnison 1977; For a history of European midwifery, see Bullough 1966).

In the early 17th century, the barber-surgeon Peter Chamberlen developed the obstetrical forceps, an instrument that enabled its user to deliver a child mechanically without necessarily destroying it first. The Chamberlen family kept the forceps secret for three generations, for their own financial gain, and only let it be known that they possessed some way of preventing the piecemeal extraction of an impacted fetus. The right to use instruments resided exclusively with men, and when the Chamberlens finally sold their design (or the design leaked out) it was for the use of the barber-surgeons, and not generally available to midwives.

It has frequently been assumed that the forceps were an enormous breakthrough in improving maternity care, but on careful reflection that seems unlikely. The physicians and surgeons did not have the opportunity to observe and learn the rudiments of normal birth, and were therefore at a decided disadvantage in handling diffcult births. And unlike in the pre-forceps days, when a barber-surgeon was called in only if all hope of a live birth was gone, midwives were increasingly encouraged and instructed to call in the barber-surgeon prophylactically, whenever birth became diffcult.

The midwives of the time expressed their concerns. Sarah Stone, an 18th century midwife and author of *The Complete Practice of Midwifery*, alleged that more mothers and children had died at the hands of raw recruits just out of their apprenticeship to the barber-surgeons than through the worst ignorance and stupidity of the midwife (Donnison 1977, 31). The noted midwife Elizabeth Nihell, author of *A Treatise on the Art of the Midwife,* in 1760 questioned the value of instrumentation as a result of her training in France at the Hotel-Dieu, where midwives practiced without male supervision or intervention (Donnison 1977, 33). Instruments were, in her opinion, rarely if ever necessary. The forceps of that time were of a primitive design, not originally curved to fit the birth canal, and so went high up into the birth canal; and were not sterilized. Injuries and infections were common. A journalist of the time, Philip Thicknesse, agreed with Elizabeth Nihell that the growing popularity of the man-midwife, the barber-surgeon, and his instruments was not because of his superior skills but because of the power of men to convince women of the dangers of childbirth and the incompetence of the midwives. The men were aided by the growing prestige of male birth attendants as a symbol of higher social status, possibly because of their higher fees. Not only did the men use their instruments unnecessarily, resulting in maternal and infant mortality and morbidity, puerperal fever and extraordinary birth injuries, but, Nihell complained, were so adept at concealing errors with "a cloud of hard words and scientific jargon" that the injured patient herself was convinced that she could not thank him enough for the mischief he had done (Donnison 1977, 34). "Meddlesome midwifery," as it was called at the time, was the forerunner of what later became known as "interventionist obstetrics."

Spurred on by the development of basic anatomical knowledge and increased understanding of the processes of reproduction, surgeons of the 1700s began to develop formal training programs in midwifery. Women midwives were systematically excluded from such programs. Women were not trained because men believed women to be inherently incompetent. The situation was far from simple however, and some men surgeons did try to provide training for the midwives, sharing with them the advances made in medical knowledge. Such attempts failed in the face of opposition from within medicine, supported by the prevailing beliefs about women's abilities to perform in a professional capacity. The result was a widening disparity between midwives and surgeons. As men developed newer and more sophisticated technologies were developed, they kept them from the women.

We cannot assume that midwives would have been incompetent to use these technologies. Rather, their basic experience with normal birth probably made them eminently more capable than the inexperienced men. For example, some historians believe that the first cesarean section recorded in the British Isles in which both mother and child survived was performed by an illiterate Irish midwife, Mary Dunally (Donnison 1977, 49). The training, experience and competence of the midwives of the 17th and 18th centuries varied enormously, and went largely unregulated. And the same was true of the training, experience and competence of the physicians and barber-surgeons.

As physicians gained near-complete ascendancy, the midwife was redefined from being a competitor of the physician-surgeon to being, in her new role, his assistant. Midwives lost autonomy over their work throughout most of Europe and in England, to a greater or lesser degree losing control over their own licensing, training requirements and the restrictions under which they functioned. Once physicians came to be *socially defined* as having expertise in the management of diffcult or abnormal birth, midwifery effectively lost control over even normal birth. The deleterious results of the new obstetrics outweighed its benefits, particularly for normal and healthy pregnancies. The rise of obstetrics in the U.K., in Europe, and in cities throughout the U.S., was not associated with improved outcome for mothers and babies.

But once the surgeon or physician is held to be necessary "in case something goes wrong," then the midwife becomes dependent on the physician and his goodwill for her "backup" services. When physicians want to compete with midwives for clients, all they have to do is withhold backup services, that is, refuse to come to the aid of a midwife who calls for medical assistance. This is a pattern that began in the earliest days of the barber surgeon and continues right through to today.

Even when physicians are not in competition with midwives, but really need midwives to handle the cases that they, the physicians, wish to avoid—such as the rural poor or the tediously normal births—physicians still control midwives by setting the standards for training and regulating which instruments and procedures they may use, and for which they must call on their backup doctors. While these decisions are ostensibly made to bring about best possible health care for mother and child, by preventing "unqualified" persons from providing particular services, that is certainly not the way it always worked out. And again, this is a problem that repeats itself over and over in different eras.

The U.S. Situation

The balance of power that has been achieved between medicine and midwifery varies across the world. It is only in the United States however, that midwifery actually failed to survive.

In the 19th and early 20th centuries, midwives and physicians in the U.S. were in direct competition for patients, and not only for their fees. Newer, more clinically oriented medical training demanded "teaching material," so that even immigrant and poor women were desired as patients (Ehrenreich and English 1973). Doctors used everything in their power to stop the midwives from practicing. They advertised, using racist pictures of "drunken, dirty" Irish midwives, and of hooked-nose, witch-like Jewish midwives. They played on immigrant women's desire to "become American," linking midwives with "old country" ways of doing things. The displacement of midwives can be better understood in terms of this competition than as an ideological struggle or as "scientific advancement." Physicians, unlike the unorganized, disenfranchised midwives, had access to the power of the state through their professional associations. They were thus able to draw women in with their advertising, but also to control licensing legislation, in state after state restricting the midwives' sphere of activity and imposing legal sanctions against them (Brack 1976, 20).

What did the medical takeover of birth mean for women and babies? Medicine would have us believe that it meant above all a safer birth. The profession of medicine claims the decline in maternal and infant mortality that we experienced in the 20th century was a result not so much of women's hard-won control over their own fertility, or even of better nutrition and sanitation, but rather of medical management per se. Medical expansion into the area of childbirth began, however, *before* the development of any of what are now considered to be the contributions of modern obstetrics: before asepsis, surgical technique, antibiotics, anesthesia. At the time when physicians were taking over control of childbirth in the U.S., the noninterventionist, supportive techniques of the midwife were safer for both the birthing woman and her baby.

In Washington, D.C., as the percentage of births reported by midwives shrank from 50% in 1903 to 15% in 1912, infant mortality in the first day, first week, and first month of life all increased. New York's dwindling corps of midwives did significantly better than did New York doctors in preventing both stillborns and puerperal sepsis (postpartum infection). And in Newark a midwifery program in 1914–1916 achieved maternal mortality rates as low as 1.7 per thousand, while in Boston, in many ways a comparable city but where midwives were banned, the rates were 6.5 per thousand. Infant mortality rates in Newark were 8.5 per thousand, contrasted with 36.4 in Boston (Kobrin 1966, 353). The situation was similar in England, where an analysis of the records of the Queen's Institute for Midwives for the years 1905–1925 found that the death rate rose in step with the proportion of cases to which midwives called the doctors (Donnison 1977, 120).

In sum, during the course of the late 1800's through the early 20th century, medicine gained virtually complete control of childbirth in U.S., beginning with the middle class and moving on to the poor and immigrant population. And it did this without any indication that it was capable of doing it well. Midwifery almost ceased to exist in this country, and for the first time in history, an entire society of women was attended in childbirth by men.

Medicalized Birth

What did this medically attended birth look like, feel like, to the women who experienced it?

The standards for obstetrical intervention that gained acceptance in the 1920's and 30's remained in place through the 1970's, and shadows of those practices remain with us today. These practices can be traced back to a 1920 article in the *American Journal of Obstetrics and Gynecology*, "The Prophylactic Forceps Operation," by Joseph B. DeLee. DeLee's procedure for a routine, normal birth required sedating the woman through labor, and giving ether for the descent of the fetus. The baby was to be removed from the unconscious mother by forceps. An incision through the skin and muscle of the perineum, called an episiotomy, was to be done before the forceps were applied. Removal of the placenta was also to be obstetrically managed rather than spontaneous. Ergot or a derivative was to be injected to cause the uterus to clamp down and prevent postpartum hemorrhage.

Why were DeLee's procedures, rather than allowing the mother to push the baby out spontaneously, so widely accepted by the 1930's? On one level, we can answer this in terms of the needs of the still developing profession of obstetrics: the need for teaching material; the need to justify both the costs and the prestige of obstetrics by providing a special service that midwives and general practitioners had not provided; the need to routinize patients in a centralized facility. Consider, however, the medical rationale, the reasons doctors themselves gave. They thought that what they were doing was a reasonable response to the demands of labor. Just how did they understand labor, and what is this medical model of birth?

The use of forceps was to spare the baby's head, DeLee having famously compared labor to a baby's head being crushed in a door. The episiotomy was done to prevent tearing of the perineum, something that is almost inevitable with the use of forceps. Even without forceps use, however, U.S. physicians were finding tearing to be a problem, most likely owing to the use of the American-style delivery table, which required the supine position, with legs in stirrups (Haire, 1972). The clean cut of the episiotomy was held to be easier to repair than the jagged tear. DeLee further claimed that the stretching and tearing of the perineum resulted in such gynecological conditions as prolapsed uteri, tears in the vaginal wall, and sagging perineums. It wasn't until 1976 that an empirical study was done to determine the long-term effectiveness of episiotomies, and the results indicated that episiotomies caused rather than prevented these conditions (Brendsel, Peterson, and Mehl 1979). Episiotomies are still one of the most widely performed surgical procedure on women and every few years another study comes forth showing that they do not work (most recently, Hartmann et al, 2005). Most intriguingly perhaps, DeLee claimed that the episiotomy would restore "virginal conditions," making the mother "better than new." All through the 1970's obstetricians were heard to assure husbands, who were just then starting to routinely attend births, that they were sewing the woman up "good and tight."

For the baby, according to DeLee and his many followers, the labor was a dangerous, crushing threat, responsible for such conditions as epilepsy, cerebral palsy, "imbecility" and "idiocy," as well as being a direct cause of death. For the mother, birth was compared to falling on a pitchfork, driving the handle through her perineum. Using these analogies, DeLee was able to conclude that labor itself was pathological (DeLee 1920, 40).

The implication of the DeLee approach to birth for the mother is that she experienced the birth as an entirely medical event, not unlike any other surgical procedure. At the beginning of labor she was brought to the hospital and turned over to the hospital staff . The sedation most commonly used from the 1930s through the 1970s was "twilight sleep," a combination of morphine for pain relief in early labor, and then scopolamine, believed to be an amnesiac. A woman under twilight sleep can feel and respond to pain; the claim is only that she will not remember what happened. Women in twilight sleep therefore had to be restrained, or their uncontrolled thrashing could cause severe injuries, as the drugs left them in pain and disoriented. Obstetrical nursing texts offered warning pictures of women with battered faces who were improperly restrained and threw themselves out of bed.

The birth itself was not part of the mother's conscious experience, because she was made totally un-conscious for the delivery. Such women required careful watching as they recovered from anesthesia. They were in no way competent to hold or even see their babies; it might be quite some time before they were told the birth was over (Guttmacher 1962). The babies themselves were born drugged and required careful medical attention. That drugged, comatose newborn was the source of the popular imagery of the doctor slapping the bottom of the dangling newborn, attempting to bring it around enough to breathe. It was several hours, or even days, before the mother and baby were "introduced."

While women were sometimes co-conspirators with doctors in the development of twilight sleep, so-called "painless" labors, and medicalization, other women fought this turn of events. When the DeLee approach developed in the 20's and 30's became dominant throughout the United States by the 1950's, a counter voice was raised, calling for a return to a more "natural" childbirth.

Making Pain the Issue

"Natural childbirth" is a slippery concept: one would be hard put to claim that anything people do is "natural." In the world of birth, "natural" is used for anything from a vaginal (as contrasted to a cesarean) birth, whether or not the woman was conscious, to a completely "non medicated" birth. "Prepared childbirth" is a more useful concept for viewing U.S. hospital births; it has come to mean the use of breathing and/or relaxation techniques, and particularly, taking some "childbirth preparation course," perhaps six evenings, perhaps one or two days over a weekend, to learn about birth. Or perhaps, to be more accurate, to learn about the medical management of birth: Most of the preparation courses, many offered by the hospitals themselves, are designed to prepare women for the hospital experience they are expected to have.

And what is that experience? Largely it is understood in terms of pain: pain experienced and pain avoided. There are a number of reasons why pain became a central issue in hospitalized births. For one thing, birth in hospitals is almost certainly experienced as more painful than birth outside of hospitals. Before the pressures of the prepared-childbirth movement brought husbands or other companions into the labor room, laboring women were routinely left alone. Their only companionship might have been another laboring woman on the other side of a curtain. A nurse would stop in now and again, but for hour upon hour the woman lay alone, with no one to comfort her, hold her hand, rub her back, or just talk to her, and nothing to do to take her mind off her pain. Consider what a toothache feels like in the middle of the night, when you're all alone and just lying there, feeling it ache and watching the clock tick away hours.

Second, the physical management of birth made it more painful. Confinement to bed prolongs labor, and the comparatively ineffcient contractions in the horizontal position may make it more painful. When a woman is upright, each contraction presses the baby down against her cervix, opening up the birth passage. When she is lying down, the weight of the baby presses on her spine, accomplishing nothing except to increase her discomfort.

Third, the mother's experience needed to be conceptualized as pain in order to justify medical control. Conceptualizing the mother's experience as *work* would have moved control to the mother. This was clearest in the medical management of the second stage of labor, pushing the baby out, in which the woman was so positioned as to make the experience as painful as possible and at the same time to minimize the value of her bearing-down efforts. In the lithotomy position, the baby must be moved (pushed or pulled) *upward* because of the curve of the birth canal. Doctors felt that this position gave them the most control, with total access to the woman's exposed genitals. But doctors' control came at the expense of mother's control. The lithotomy position rendered her totally unable to help herself, feeling like "a turtle on its back," or a "beached whale."

This is not to say that labor, even under optimal conditions, is not painful. It is. But there is a difference between experiencing pain and defining the entire situation only in terms of pain. Pain may be one of the sensations people experience in sexual activity, for example, but most do not take it as the key element in sex. Any particular stimulation or pressure produces many complex sensations, and pain may be part of what one feels. And birth does have much in common with orgasm: the hormone oxytocin is released; there are uterine contractions, nipple erection, and, under the best circumstances for birth, an orgasmic feeling (Gaskin 2003). But the lithotomy position, like the "missionary" position, put women flat on their backs and made attaining an orgasm—or any pleasurable feelings—a lot less likely.

What Happens at Home?

Midwifery focuses on pregnancy and birth as processes. Labor is *labor*, diffcult *work*, but it is beautiful, normal, "natural" as midwives see it. They work to help women have birth experiences that are spiritual, beautiful, and worthwhile. Pain may be part of labor, risk may be part of giving birth, but they are not the central elements around which midwifery practice is built. When discussing what they're all about, the dominant theme for midwives is facilitating one of life's most meaningful events. Doctors, in contrast, with their risk-orientation, focus much more on the outcome: healthy baby, healthy mom.

To illustrate the differences in their philosophies, we will focus here on participants' views about the topic of home birth. (For an extended discussion of many more aspects of maternity care and birth attendants' discussions of their motivations and practice ideals, see Simonds, Rothman, and Norman 2007.) Home birth is, according to most studies, safer than hospital birth, but doctors in this country have continuously raised opposition to—and political leverage against—home birth.

The smear campaigns against home birth midwifery that U.S. doctors have orchestrated at various times in U.S. history have not, and do not, rely on data that show hospital birth to be safer than home birth, because such data are lacking. One study out of dozens recently showed a higher infant death rate in home births than in other settings (Pang et al. 2002), but critics of that study refute the claim because the authors did not clearly distinguish between intentional (planned) and unintentional home births (see, e.g., MANA press release 2003 and Vedam 2003). All other studies show superior outcomes in terms of maternal and infant morbidity for home births, and equivalent outcomes in terms of mortality (see, e.g., Goer 1999; Johnson and Daviss 2005; and Olsen 1997).

Discussion Questions

1. Explain the contradiction that exists in the labor and delivery process.
2. Do you think our current system is flawed and if yes, what could be done to make it better?
3. Based on what you have read does it change what you want to do with your own labor and delivery? Why or Why not?

Assignment

Create a timeline that will represent the historical changes in the process of labor and delivery. A complete timeline will address the following components:

1. Location of birth
2. Birth facilitator (doctor, midwife, etc.)
3. Process of birth based on facilitator (what was used, like forceps, birth methods, etc.)

Editorial

Is the Breast Always Best? Balancing Benefits and Choice?

By Colin R. Martin and Maggie Redshaw

C hoice is not always about choosing between equals and this point needs to be held in mind when discussing breastfeeding. There exists little controversy regarding the significant benefits of this method of infant feeding, both in terms of nutritional and immunological advantages to the infant (Fisk et al., 2007; Oddy et al., 2011; Quigley, Kelly & Sacker, 2007) and the psychological benefits to the mother in terms of the developing mother–child relationship (Field, Hernandez-Reif & Feijo, 2002). The huge weight of evidence in support of breastfeeding and the positivity bias towards this type of infant feeding implicit within contemporary Western culture currently frame desirable maternal attributes and underpin social policy (Marshall, Godfrey & Renfrew, 2007), although this position is not without its critics (Schulze & Carlisle, 2010). During the booking appointment, at which women are usually given their pregnancy notes, occurring at around 10–12 weeks of pregnancy, a key question is invariably asked regarding intention to breastfeed. Increasing the proportion of breastfeeding new mothers has represented an explicit clinical indicator for acute and primary care trusts providing maternity care in the UK and an objective in terms of interventions to support breastfeeding. What then of maternal choice? Since 'Changing Childbirth' (Department of Health, 1993), the choice of the mother has been emphasised in terms of where and with whom antenatal appointments take place and in options for place of birth and birth plans and also in relation to postnatal care and support. Given the incontrovertible evidence for the desirability to breastfeed, how does the maternal choice agenda sit with the dominant 'breast is best' position? What of mothers who try to breastfeed and, for a range of reasons, find this difficult or not possible for them? What also of mothers who choose not to breastfeed, perhaps based on previous experience, personal views or convenience (Skafida, 2011)? There are tensions and sometimes stresses and strains between the different policies at individual and organisational level. Yet, there is clear recognition of the public health benefits of breastfeeding and consequently the expression and support of maternal choice are clearly not in conflict where a woman chooses to breastfeed. While many women breastfeed their baby at least once after birth, significant proportions give up in the early days or weeks following (Henderson & Redshaw, 2011). Women may not initiate or continue to breastfeed either through difficulty or through choice and in the case of choice, this can represent a clash of policies and individual expression, giving rise to negative attributions regarding the mother (Hausman, 2009) and, in the case of mothers who cannot breastfeed, a perception of 'having failed'. There is a view that egalitarian and broad cultures should embrace choice, yet what pressures does a mother who chooses not to breastfeed experience in terms of mechanisms of conformity to breastfeed, while orientated to an expectation of choice in their infant feeding decisions? It has been suggested that mothers who do not breastfeed may experience psychological burden and disadvantage. However, it is likely that disadvantage influences breastfeeding uptake, rather than being caused by not breastfeeding per se, and needs to be explored further in light of possibly conflicting policies and the social construction of breastfeeding as being central to the conceptualisation of the 'good new mother'. Dispassionate research which looks at the needs and wishes of all women at what is a really important time in the lives of them, their infants and families, including women who do not breastfeed, may provide new insights into the mechanisms associated with disadvantage, perhaps even illuminating how such mothers could be disenfranchised by social policy and political correctness. A huge amount of research has been conducted on the impact of breastfeeding on the mother and infant; however, investigating what factors play a part in both the positive and more negative outcomes for children following quite different early infant feeding practices is critical (Hay et al., 2001; Sharp et al., 1995). Greater understanding of the psychological and emotional costs and benefits for women and their babies could only contribute to the promotion of exemplary evidenced-based practice which supports the needs and choices of all mothers, those who breastfeed and those who do not.

References

Department of Health. (1993). *Changing childbirth*. London: HMSO.

Field, T., Hernandez-Reif, M., & Feijo, M. (2002). Breastfeeding in depressed mother–infant dyads. *Early Child Development and Care*, 172(6), 539–545.

Fisk, C.M., Crozier, S.R., Inskip, H.M., Godfrey, K.M., Cooper, C., Roberts, G.C., et al. Southampton Women's Survey Study Group. (2011). Breastfeeding and reported morbidity during infancy: Findings from the Southampton Women's Survey. *Maternal and Child Nutrition*, 7(1), 61–70.

Hausman, B.L. (2009). Motherhood and inequality: A commentary on Hanna Rosin's 'The case against breast-feeding'. *Journal of Human Lactation*, 25, 266–268.

Hay, D.F., Pawlby, S., Sharp, D., Asten, P., Mills, A., & Kumar, R. (2001). Intellectual problems shown by 11-year-old children whose mothers had postnatal depression. *Journal of Child Psychology and Psychiatry*, 42(7), 871–889.

Henderson, J. and Redshaw, M. (2010). Midwifery factors associated with successful breast-feeding. *Child Care Health and Development*, 2010 Dec 9. doi: 10.1111/j.13652214.2010.01177.x. [Epub ahead of print].

Marshall, J.L., Godfrey, M., & Renfrew, M.J. (2007). Being a 'good mother': Managing breastfeeding and merging identities. *Social Science and Medicine*, 65(10), 2147–2159.

Oddy, W.H., Robinson, M., Kendall, G.E., Li, J., Zubrick, S.R., & Stanley, F.J. (2011). Breastfeeding and early child development: A prospective cohort study. Acta Paediatrica 2011 Feb 7. doi: 10.1111/j.1651-2227.2011.02199.x. [Epub ahead of print].

Quigley, M.A., Kelly, Y.J., & Sacker, A. (2007). Breastfeeding and hospitalization for diarrheal and respiratory infection in the United Kingdom Millennium Cohort Study. *Social Science and Medicine*, 119(4), e837–842.

Schulze, P.A. and Carlisle, S.A. (2010). What research does and doesn't say about breastfeeding: A critical review. *Early Child Development and Care*, 80(6), 703–718.

Sharp, D., Hay, D.F., Pawlby, S., SchmŸcker, G., Allen, H., & Kumar, R. (1995). The impact of postnatal depression on boys' intellectual development. *Journal of Child Psychology and Psychiatry*, 36(8), 1315–1336.

Skafida, V. (2011). Juggling work and motherhood: The impact of employment and maternity leave on breastfeeding duration: A survival analysis on growing up in Scotland data. *Maternal and Child Health Journal*, 2011 Jan 28. [Epub ahead of print].

Discussion Questions

1. Do women really have a feeding choice if research shows breastfeeding is the best option for the baby?
2. Is it still important for women to have a feeding choice?
3. What are the negative effects of saying that breastfeeding is the best and only choice?

Assignment

Watch the video *Latching On: The Politics of Breastfeeding in America* by Katja Esson (A Women Make Movies Release) and read the article for this assignment.

1. Please summarize the main ideas in the film.
2. Are any of these main ideas surprising or new information? What do you think about them? Do they impact how you understand breastfeeding and other infant feeding practices?
3. Describe any other comments or reactions to the film.
4. Please summarize the main ideas in the article.
5. How are these two pieces of information (film and article) connected? How do they relate to breast-feeding experiences for women?

Designing Research to Study the Effects of Institutionalization on Brain and Behavioral Development

The Bucharest Early Intervention Project (Excerpt)
With an introduction and conclusion by Carrie Lane

By Charles H. Zeanah, Charles A. Nelson, Nathan A. Fox, Anna T. Smyke, Peter Marshall, Susan W. Parker, And Sebastian Koga

Editor's Introduction

Normal brain development is crucial for biological, cognitive, and socio-emotional growth. Researchers have found that the infant's environment can play a very important role in how the brain develops. In a deprived environment where the infant doesn't receive enough physical stimulation and human contact, the infant's brain doesn't properly develop. Between conception and three years of age, children grow at a rapid rate. Many key body structures, like the brain, continue to develop.

A specific environmental situation where children aren't receiving enough physical stimulation and human contact is an orphanage. Children housed in orphanages suffer from delays in physical growth, cognitive development, and poor quality of attachment. There are many places in the world that still use this child-rearing system. Romania is one of the countries using orphanages to deal with their large numbers of orphaned children. Historical factors have led to the abandonment and overabundance of children without families. After WWII, Nicholae Ceausescu became the head of Romania, and in order to further the prosperity of the country at that time, he ordered families to have 4–5 children; he punished those who did not comply. The economy failed and these families couldn't take care of all the children. A large number of these children were abandoned and ended up in orphanages. Between 1989 and 2002, as a result of media attention around the world, outside adoptions lowered the number of children in institutions from 170,000 to 40,000 (Zeanah, et al., 2003).

Over the past 70 years, many studies have examined possible interventions to reverse or prevent the developmental delays that result from orphanages. Researchers have tried educational programs, adoptions, non-random assignment foster care, and one study where they were able to randomly assign children into foster care situations to determine if any could positively impact the child's development (Bakermans-Kranenburg, et al., 2008). The ability to randomly assign children into either foster care or into an orphanage gives researchers more confidence that their findings are due to their intervention and not some characteristic of the children. This evidence could be used to encourage countries to move away from an orphanage model to deal with abandoned orphaned children.

The Bucharest Intervention Project was designed as a scientific and humanitarian project. Researchers hoped to move past animal model research to find human evidence that the deprived environment of an orphanage leads to poor development and long-lasting damage. The hope was that the experimental manipulation of placing some children into foster care would demonstrate improved brain development and could even in some cases lead to recovery. Researchers also wanted to know if recovery was possible, and if there was a time frame where recovery was no longer possible. Finally, the humanitarian aspect was to help use this information to convince the government in Romania that a foster care system would be advantageous for their country.

Project Design and Methods

Feasibility Phase

In the fall of 2000, we began an initial feasibility phase of the study. The goal of this phase of the research was to establish feasibility of measures, procedures, training, and administration. We constructed a full-scale scientific laboratory in Bucharest's oldest and largest institution for young children, St. Catherine's. We recruited research assistants and provided them with training in the United States and Romania. We tested all of the proposed procedures and measures with 30–50 children who were living in the institution that housed our lab but who were not available for the longitudinal study, usually because their legal status made them available for imminent adoption. We also established methods of recruiting, training, and monitoring foster families and set up protocols and methods of working collaboratively with our administrative partners at SERA Romania.

In March 2001, we concluded that the intervention study was scientifically, logistically, and administratively feasible, and we launched the intervention phase in April 2001. In the sections that follow, we detail our experimental methods, including setting, design, participants, and measures, and then describe the intervention.

Intervention Phase

This phase of the project comprises a randomized, controlled trial of foster care as an intervention for institutionalized young children.

Study design. Baseline assessments prior to randomization assured comparability of intervention and control groups and therefore increased confidence that outcome differences reflect true effects of the intervention. Randomization prior to intervention addressed two important issues. First, it addressed the concerns about previous studies of adopted children that have the potential of selection bias with regard to who is adopted and therefore included in studies. Second, randomization prior to intervention increased the likelihood that prenatal risk factors, which cannot be ascertained, were evenly distributed across the intervention and control groups. The inclusion of a Romanian never-institutionalized comparison group allowed for use of measures that have not been standardized on Romanian children. This permitted us to evaluate whether our measures would yield the same findings in a Romanian comparison sample as in a U.S. sample and to reveal potential ethnic differences. Because we predicted that foster care would enhance the development of formerly institutionalized children, inclusion of a never institutionalized comparison group allowed us to have a basis of evaluating the degree of developmental recovery that resulted from the intervention.

The study was designed to vary both length of time in institutions and months of intervention at each time of assessment. That is, if we assess a group of children aged 17–20 months, for example, some of the children would have baseline assessments only, whereas others would have had 1–15 months of intervention, depending upon the age at which they entered the study. This may allowed us to assess the effects of timing of intervention on remediation.

Setting: Institutional environment. Although there is considerable variability in Bucharest's placement centers, with significant differences seen even between different units of the same institution (see Smyke et al., 2002), they share several features in common. These include a regimented daily schedule, a high ratio of children to caregivers, and a management structure led by medical personnel.

A standard unit at St. Catherine's Placement Center houses 36 children: 12 infants and 24 toddlers/preschoolers. Infants and toddlers have different daily schedules, but all children share a 6:30 am wake-up, a 1–3 pm afternoon nap, and an 8 pm bedtime. Children in both age groups are fed meals in small groups seated in high chairs or around small tables. Multiple children are fed a bite at a time in turn by a caregiver who rarely speaks during the meal. "Hygiene" periods for washing and changing are scheduled before and after meals. Each morning the younger age group has 90 min of "stimulation" scheduled while those over 36 months of age attend educational activities or a kindergarten equivalent. Before lunch and before dinner, two times (totaling 3.5 hr) are scheduled for outdoor free play in pleasant weather and TV/ playroom time in bad weather. Children are confined to bed when they are ill. Quarantines and staff shortages also can keep children indoors.

Since the early 1990s, an infusion of humanitarian aid has equipped most institutions with toys and playgrounds. Caregivers, however, most commonly supervise children at play rather than engaging with them. Physical punishment is not condoned officially, but it occurs in many institutions (Stativa, Tabacaru, Stanescu, & Simion, 2000).

Since all children are fed, bathed, changed, and put to bed at the same time, each child interacts only briefly with caregivers as they complete instrumental tasks. During the course of a day, a child has contact with three shifts of caregivers, a physician, a nurse, and a psychologist. In a given week, a child may come in contact with 17 caregivers rotating in 8-hr shifts: 3 housekeepers, 4 nurses, 2 educators, 1 physician, 1 psychologist, and 1 physical therapist.

Participants. Participants are 208 children and their parents, foster parents, or institutional caregivers (see Figure 1). As noted, 136 children were recruited from all six institutions for young children in Bucharest.

These children ranged in age from 5 to 31 months at the time of recruitment and had spent more than half of their lives in institutional care.

Institutional group. Inclusion criteria included all children in institutions in Bucharest who were 31 months or younger and who had spent at least half of their lives in an institution. Screening for inclusion in the study consisted of pediatric (including neurological) examination, growth measurements, and assessment of any physical abnormalities. Exclusion criteria included genetic syndromes (e.g., Down syndrome), definite signs of fetal alcohol syndrome, and microcephaly (more than 2.5 standard deviations [SD] below the mean for occipitofrontal circumference), using standards from Tanner (1973). Subjects selected for inclusion fell within 2.5 SD from the mean for occipitofrontal circumference, using standards from Tanner (1973).

Of the 187 institutionalized children screened for participation in the study, 51 cases were excluded on medical grounds, including fetal alcohol syndrome, microcephaly, Down syndrome, and related conditions. Four subjects who were included in the study had suffered congenital syphilis but had and received timely treatment. None of the subjects tested positive for HIV infection. The remaining 136 children were in fair health and suffered no known genetic abnormalities or signs diagnostic of fetal alcohol syndrome.

Hearing was also tested using an AuDX Bio-logic Systems Corp. otoacoustic emissions measurement system. Of the 187 subjects who were screened, 23 (12%) were untestable, 90 (48%) passed in both ears, 35 (19%) failed in both ears, and 39 (21%) failed in one ear. The high rate of failure was most likely due to the high incidence of acute and chronic middle ear disease noted with tympanometry and otoscopy.

Of the 136 institutionalized children included in the study, 78 are of Romanian ethnicity (57.4% of sample), 36 are Rroma Gypsy (26.5%), 1 is Turkish (0.7%), 1 is of subcontinent Indian extraction (0.7%), and the remaining 20 (14.7%) cannot be classified. At the time of baseline assessment, all subjects had spent between 51 and 100% of their lives in the institution ($M = 89\%$). Of the total of 136, 70 children (51.5% of sample) have spent all of their lives in an institution (see Figure 2).

Gestational age data were available only for 112 subjects, and many of these estimates were of uncertain reliability. There was a range of 30–42 weeks ($M = 37.2$ weeks, $SD = 2.2$ weeks). Birth weight (available for 117 cases) ranged from 900 to 4150 g ($M = 2767$ g, $SD = 609$ g) and was significantly different from the community control group ($M = 3338$ g, $SD = 467$ g). The average age at baseline assessment for the institutionalized group was 21.6 months.

The 136 institutionalized children were randomly assigned either to the foster care intervention group (FCG) or to the continued institutional care group (IG). Because siblings were randomized together, 69 children were assigned to foster care and 67 children were assigned to continued institutional care. Following random assignment, no differences were observed between the resulting groups in gender distribution, age, birth weight, or percentage of life spent. There were delays ranging from days to 13 weeks ($M = 6$ weeks) between completion of baseline assessments and actual placement in foster care. At the present time (24 months postbaseline) only 5 of 136 participants have dropped out of the study (2 adopted out of the FCG and 3 adopted from the IG).

Foster parents. Of 60 foster families recruited to participate, 27 (46%) were single parent families (11 widowed, 11 divorced, and 5 never married). The age of the foster mothers ranged from 30 to 66 years ($M = 47.7$ years). All foster mothers had a high school education: 37 (63%) had completed vocational training, 11 (19%) had specialized skills, and 4 (7%) had completed college. In addition, 16 (27%) were retired, and 3 (5%) had never been employed. Of the 60 families recruited originally, 50 are currently employed, caring for 62 children. The income per household (including their salary but not the child's supplement) ranged from $63 to $355 monthly ($M = \$165$ monthly).

Community comparison group. Another 72 children who had never been institutionalized were recruited using birth records at the same maternity hospitals where the FCG and IG had been born, and they are included as a community comparison group. Their parents were approached by personnel from the IOMC (directly or through their family physician) at the children's routine clinic visits and invited to participate. They were matched to the other groups by child age and gender. The screening included pediatric examination, physical growth measurements, and psychosocial interview with the family. All participants fell within 2 *SD* from the mean for physical growth (weight, length, occipitofrontal circumference). The group comprises 42 males and 31 females. Of the 72 who consented to participate, 66 children (91.7%) were Romanian, 4 children (5.6%) were Rroma, 1 child was Spanish, and 1 child was Turkish. To date, families of 12 children have dropped out (9 in the first 3 months of the study), generally citing time pressures.

Of the 60 community comparison children currently in the study, 6 are being raised in single-parent families. Of community mothers participating in the study, 29 (46%) have high-school level education whereas 21 (33%) hold university degrees. Fifteen (24%) are homemakers, 9 (4%) are unskilled laborers, 15 (24%) are skilled laborers, and 24 (38%) are professionals. In keeping with Romania's negative population growth, 39 (61%) families have only 1 child. The number of children per household ranges from 1 to 7, but the mean is 1.5. Fathers' levels of education mirror those of their spouses: only 6 (9%) are unemployed. Household income ranges from $76 to $606 per month (*M* = $200), which is close to the national average.

Procedures. For all subjects enrolled in the study, informed consent was obtained from biological parents and/or the Commission for Child Protection. Videorecording consent was obtained from all parents and caregivers.

Following baseline assessment, all subjects are evaluated at 9, 18, 30, and 42 months of age. Thus, the youngest subjects to enter the study (6–8 months) undergo five assessments, whereas the oldest undergo three assessments. At 42 months, the age of final data collection, the youngest children at the time of study initiation will have received 37 months of intervention (i.e., foster care placement) whereas the oldest children in the study will have received 11 months of intervention.

Each assessment consists of up to 14 procedures (depending on age) and is usually divided into three visits at the laboratory and one home/institutional observation. Additionally, physical growth measures of all children in the institutional and foster care groups are obtained monthly.

Each child's principal caregiver accompanies the child during evaluations. In lieu of a parent, institutionalized children are accompanied by their "favorite" caregiver, as determined through interviews and observations. When the staff was unable to identify a favorite caregiver, we included the person who had spent the most time with the child and knew the child best.

Measures. The measures included in this study and the constructs they are intended to assess may be found in Table 1. These include a range of structured and unstructured procedures, in laboratory and naturalistic settings, as well as elicited and observed behaviors in the child. Because the most important deficits documented in children adopted out of institutions involve abnormalities of cognitive functioning, social communication and social relatedness, and attachment (Ames, 1997; Chisholm, 1998; Johnson, 2000; O'Connor, Marvin, Rutter, Olrick, & Britner, 2003; O'Connor, Rutter, & the ERA Study Team, 2000; O'Connor, Rutter, Beckett, et al., 2000; Zeanah, 2000), these were all included as central measures.

Caregiving environment. This will be the most extensive study ever conducted on the caregiving environment of the institution. Further, we will use the same measure (Observational Record of the Caregiving Environment) to assess similarities and differences in caregiving environments in the institution, foster care homes, and homes of the never institutionalized children. No previous study has attempted to demonstrate that individual differences in outcome are related to individual differences in the "dose" of intervention, in this case, the quality of the caregiving environment.

Physical growth. Physical growth is assessed using standard measures of weight, length/height, occipito-frontal circumference, midarm circumference, and triceps skinfold. Height is measured using a stadiometer.

Cognitive level. The Bayley Scales of Infant Development—second edition (BSID-II) are used to assess developmental level. The BSID-II was selected because it was in use by psychologists at St. Catherine's Placement Center before the project began.

Language. Language development was assessed with the Receptive–Expressive Emergent Language (REEL) scales (Bzoch & League, 1972) and the Reynell Developmental Language Scales III (Edwards, Garman, Hughes, Letts, & Sinka, 1997). The REEL and the second edition REEL (REEL2) are parent/caregiver interviews that have been used in clinical practice in a Romanian language version for many years. The revised Reynell is a 62-item scale emphasizing vocabulary and connected speech, which is administered by a trained examiner directly to the child and can be used with children between 18 months and 7 years of age.

Social communication. The Early Social Communication scales (Mundy, Hogan, & Doehring, 1996) are administered by an examiner to assess the child's initiation of joint attention, response to joint attention, and behavior regulation. These skills are important components of social and emotional reciprocity, and their assessment in institutional children may reveal specific strengths and weaknesses related to subsequent outcomes (Morales et al., 2000; Mundy & Gomes, 1998).

Temperament. Individual differences in emotional disposition have been linked to a variety of outcomes in young children. They also have been shown to mediate the effects of caregiving environments on children's behavior. We selected two tasks from a standard laboratory battery for the assessment of temperament (Goldsmith & Rothbart, 1999) to assess positive affect: the peek-a-boo and the puppet interview tasks. For peek-a-boo, the child's caregiver/mother participated; for the puppet interview, a female experimenter performed the task. We decided to attempt to elicit positive affect during this part of the assessment because we predicted that individual differences in positive affect reactivity might relate to general social relatedness.

Interactional behavior. Patterns of social interaction with familiar caregivers are established in the first few months of life, under ordinary circumstances. These patterns are somewhat stable over time and have been associated with a variety of risk and protective factors and shown to predict a variety of outcomes in young children. In the institutional setting, we were curious about whether individual differences in interactional behavior between young children and their caregivers would be associated with other characteristics of the children's development. We used the Crowell Procedure (Crowell & Feldman, 1988) to observe a variety of more and less structured episodes, including free play, clean-up, blowing bubbles, a series of teaching tasks and a separation and reunion between the child and a caregiver who knew the child well. Previously, this measure has differentiated clinic-referred and nonreferred children (Crowell & Feldman, 1989), maltreated and nonmaltreated children (Smyke, 2000), and relationship differences in maltreated children with foster and biological parents (Zeanah, Larrieu, Heller, & Valliere, 2001).

Attachment. The development of a hierarchy of preferred attachment figures is an important developmental task in the first year of life, and significant impairments in attachment in institutional settings have been demonstrated (Smyke, Dumitrescu & Zeanah, 2002; Tizard & Rees, 1975; Vorria, Papaligoura, Dunn, van IJzendoorn, Steele, Kontopoulou, & Sarafidou, in press). In order to assess attachment in the institutional setting, we use three different methods. First, we use the Strange Situation procedure (Ainsworth,

Blehar, Waters, & Wall, 1978), observing the child with his or her favorite caregiver. Second, we conduct naturalistic observations of the child in his or her unit and code these observations with the Attachment *Q*-set (Waters & Deane, 1985). Third, we use the Disturbances of Attachment Interview (Smyke & Zeanah, 1999) to assess attachment disorder symptomatology. This interview has been validated preliminarily in a sample of institutionalized Romanian children (Smyke et al., 2002; Zeanah, Smyke, & Dumitrescu, 2002).

Emotion recognition. As described, institutional care involves serious disruptions of caregiver–infant interactions. Moreover, in the first 1–1.5 years of life, infants have only limited face to face interactions with their caregivers, thus restricting their access to emotional information displayed on the face of the caregiver. This occurs primarily because infants spend most of their time in individual cribs and have only occasional views of their caregivers' faces (mostly during feeding and changing). Based on the assumption that face recognition is an experience-expectant and activity-dependent process (see Nelson, 2001), we posited that institutional care would lead to impairments in emotion recognition, possibly due to delays in the development of the amygdala and surrounding circuitry purported to be involved in this process (for review, see Nelson, 2001; Nelson & deHaan, 1996). Consistent with this view are recent studies by Pollak and colleagues, who demonstrated that maltreated and neglected children differ from typically developing children in their electrophysiological and behavioral responses to facial expressions of emotion (e.g., Pollak & Kistler, 2002; Pollak, Klorman, Thatcher, & Cicchetti, 2001; Pollak & Sinha, 2002).

We employ two tasks designed to examine the discrimination and recognition of facial expressions. The first involves the visual paired comparison procedure in which infants are first presented with pairs of identical faces (e.g., the same model posing the same expression; "happy") and then tested by presenting the familiar stimulus alongside a stimulus in which the facial expression has changed ("happy" vs. "fear"). Looking time is recorded, and longer looking at the novel stimulus permits the inference that the infant has discriminated the two emotions. In our second paradigm, we record event-related potentials (ERPs) while infants are presented with happy, fear, anger, and sad faces (25% probability each). Here, the goal is to examine whether the neural correlates of emotion recognition differ across our samples. Collectively, we hope to be able to specify some of the areas of neural functioning underlying social relatedness that are impacted by early social deprivation.

Electrophysiology. One of the prime goals of this project is to examine the effects of early deprivation on brain development. To accomplish this goal we acquire brain electrical activity via electroencephalogram (EEG) while the children participate in one of the assessments in the laboratory. The EEG hardware consists of a battery powered, optically isolated bioamplifier with 16 channels, a PC dedicated to stimulus presentation, a PC dedicated to EEG acquisition, and the additional equipment hardware required for precise auditory and visual stimulus presentation. This setup allows us to acquire ongoing EEG as well as to synchronize the presentation of visual or auditory stimuli to the EEG to acquire ERPs. Our intention is to examine the ongoing EEG during a number of different conditions, as well as acquire ERP data to both auditory and visual stimuli.

The EEG data are acquired using a lycra stretchable cap that has tin electrodes sewn into it. For a full description of similar EEG methods, see Fox, Henderson, Rubin, Calkins, and Schmidt (2001). Research assistants spent time at the laboratory of one of the investigators (N.A.F.) during which time they were trained on the equipment and acquisition of EEG with infants and young children.

There are four issues to be investigated with respect to the EEG data: (a) the patterning of EEG power in different frequency bands across the scalp, (b) the development of EEG power spectra, (c) intrahemispheric EEG coherence, and (d) frontal EEG asymmetry. More specifically, power spectra are computed for each of the 12 electrode sites to examine power in various frequency bands. In order to track the development of alpha peak frequency, the EEG is recorded under two conditions: lights on and lights off. Power spectra of the EEG during the lights on and off segments are compared to identify the alpha band for the different aged infants and children, since it is known that this band changes with normative development (Marshall, Bar-Haim, & Fox, 2002). In addition, within-hemisphere coherence between pairs of electrodes is computed. Coherence is a frequency-dependent cross-correlation that provides a measure of the degree to which the EEG signals at different electrode sites are in phase (working together) or out of phase with each other. A number of researchers have argued that with development and during cognitive activity the degree of coherence across the scalp decreases as different regions begin to work independently (Bell & Fox, 1994; Thatcher, 1994). Finally, we wish to examine the degree to which power recorded from scalp locations over the left and right prefrontal cortices is asymmetric. A variety of data from a number of clinical, neurological, and psychophysiological sources have indicated that the left and right prefrontal cortices are differentially specialized for the expression and experience of affects associated with approach or withdrawal. Specifically, the left prefrontal region appears to be associated with affects and motivation to approach novel stimuli whereas the right appears to be associated with affects and motivation to withdraw from novelty. Indeed, a number of studies suggest that the pattern of prefrontal EEG asymmetry may be a marker for the dispositon to express dysphoric affect: individuals displaying right frontal EEG asymmetry are more likely to express and experience negative affect and dysphoric mood. We thus decided to examine the pattern of frontal EEG asymmetry in infants and children in our study.

In addition to collecting EEG data during different stimulus conditions, we acquire EEG time locked to the presentation of auditory and visual stimuli. We are interested in the infants' and young childrens' physiological responses to novelty in the auditory channel. To examine this process we present an ERP protocol in which subjects are presented with a stream of 300 short (150 ms) stimuli, 76% of which are "standard" tones, and 12% of which are "deviant" tones of slightly different frequencies, and 12% of which are complex "novel" stimuli. Stimulus presentation is synchronized with EEG acquisition, which enables us to examine the ERPs to the three classes of stimuli. We are particularly interested in the ERP responses to the deviant and novel sounds in relation to the ERP response to the standard tones. The comparison of these ERP waveforms allows us to investigate electrophysiological reactivity to auditory novelty.

Face recognition. Given the important role that face recognition plays in caregiver–infant interactions prior to the onset of language, we are also evaluating the child's ability to recognize his or her caregiver's face and discriminate this from the face of a stranger. Building on previous work in one of our laboratories (C.A.N.) and recent extension to children with autism (Dawson, Carver, Meltzoff, Panagiotides, McPartland, & Webb, 2002), children are presented with digitized images of their primary caregiver's face and the face of a stranger while ERPs are recorded. From this project we intend to evaluate not only whether children show ERP evidence of discriminating caregiver from stranger but also whether the neural processes involved in such discrimination are the same across groups.

Theoretical Implications

This design allows us to determine within and across developmental domains, using multiple levels of analysis (see Cicchetti & Dawson, 2002), the implications of early experiences of extreme adversity for developmental processes. As indicated in Table 2, how results for each of the three groups of children compare will have implications for understanding the importance of early experiences and potential recovery from early adversity. Although one can argue that we have considerable data already about the importance of early experiences for development, it is rare to find a single study using an experimental design in which these questions can be addressed in multiple domains of development simultaneously. Obviously, the design also lends itself to evaluating the effects of various mediators and moderators of outcome.

Intervention

After selecting a design that focused on enhancing brain and behavioral development, it was important to include an intervention that was feasible within the context of Romanian social policy and within the context of our project. We chose foster care because, although it was quite limited in Romania throughout the 1990s, the government is now actively promoting alternatives to institutionalization and local authorities began to develop foster care programs in 1998. We designed the foster care intervention to be realistic within the constraints of logistics but to benefit from best practices approaches in the United States.

Recruiting Foster Parents

Over a period of 4 months, we recruited and trained 60 foster parents from the Bucharest community. We advertised through posters, brochures, and newspaper ads. In addition to a standard salary, we offered complete support for the children's material needs and a 3year employment contract. The limited foster care that existed in Romania before 2001 was sponsored primarily by international adoption agencies that used foster care to enhance development during the 6 months prior to adoption. Because of the moratorium imposed on international adoptions in June 2001, adoption agencies diminished and many foster parents lost employment. Nearly half the foster parents we recruited were already licensed and had previous work experience.

Training Foster Parents

Foster care is classified as a profession in Romania, requiring a license to practice and a full-time commitment. County and sector Commissions for Child Protection issue foster care licenses to qualified persons of both genders (although the overwhelming majority are female) who have fulfilled a series of criteria stipulated by law and have completed an accredited training course.

A Law of Maternal Assistance requires that all prospective foster parents submit a criminal background check, proof of adequate living space (including an extra room for the child), a high school diploma, a health certificate, and the written approval of all members of the household. Having fulfilled these, the prospective foster parent must complete 30 hr of coursework before applying to the commission for a license.

Initial Placement of Foster Children

BEIP social workers were charged with matching children to appropriate foster homes. To this end, they conducted visits at the institution with prospective foster parents to observe and interact with children there. The social workers placed children in the foster homes and visited these homes every 10 days for the first several months of placement and twice monthly thereafter. Maintaining close contact enabled the social workers to solidify their own relationships with foster parents, to monitor children's adjustment to the placement, and to document difficulties.

Monitoring Foster Parents

BEIP social workers distributed the caseload so that each social worker was responsible for no more than 20 cases. Within the first 2 weeks after placement, frequent telephone calls and visits occurred. Those cases presenting special problems received more attention and staff resources. For all families, case managers are available 24 hr each day to address concerns and emergencies.

Home visits allow social workers to check on children's status and to listen to foster parents' concerns. While many of the worries expressed by foster parents are related to problems of behavior, sleep, and illness, others concern material needs, rising prices, utility bills, and keeping a household functional in Romania's transitional economy.

Supporting Foster Parents

Support for foster parents in the challenging job of nurturing very young, deinstitutionalized children is provided in three interrelated ways. During the initial placement of the child in the foster family and continuing over time, the social workers provide personal support via visits and telephone calls and discuss issues regarding child behavior or other issues relevant to the foster parent. Developmental and behavioral interventions are provided to assist foster parents in the management of their children. These sessions allow foster parents to feel more successful in their jobs and also to have feedback from other foster parents whose children may have experienced similar problems. In addition, BEIP social workers conducted an 8-week foster parent support group that had as its goal both education and support for foster parents.

Behavioral Challenges

Although some children made a relatively smooth transition to placement, others posed more challenges for foster parents. Placement in a foster family represents a marked change for the deinstitutionalized child who may react with marked agitation and anxiety to the differences in food, sleeping arrangements, and demand for personal interaction. Concerns regarding children's behavior seemed to peak at approximately 1 month postplacement. We addressed these problems by assisting foster parents in the implementation of individually tailored behavioral interventions.

Developmental Challenges and Interventions

In order to encourage language development and caregiver–child interaction, a language stimulation group was introduced. Derived from a manualized approach to language facilitation (Schober–Peterson & Cohen, 1999), each session focused on such language support skills as turn taking, imitating, pretending, and focusing. In addition to providing information about, and opportunity to practice, specific language development skills, the group enabled foster parents to see the importance of getting down on the floor and playing with their foster children. Further, group facilitators noted that the sessions also gave children opportunities for supervised peer interactions, addressing an area of relative weakness. As language skills have improved, study personnel have proposed an intervention focused on the development of appropriate play skills.

Contributions to Developmental Science: Sensitive Periods and Neurobiological Development

As the first randomized, controlled trial of foster care for institutionalized children ever conducted, the BEIP will provide the most definitive test to date for the widely held belief that young children develop more favorably in families than in large group settings with rotating staff. Beyond informing social policy in Romania and in many other countries where institutional care is practiced, the study also stands to contribute to our understanding of how the experiences of children raised in adverse circumstances may yield insights relevant for understanding normal developmental processes, both behavioral and neurobiological.

Studies of children adopted out of institutions have suggested that cognitive and social domains of development are clearly compromised. Following adoption, recovery of cognitive abilities is a fairly linear process: the younger children are adopted and the longer they are in adoptive homes, the more they recover cognitively (O'Connor, Rutter, Beckett, et al., 2000). Social and emotional functioning, on the other hand, is less straightforward, as some significant socioemotional deficits have been identified even in early adopted children (O'Connor, Rutter, & the ERA Study Team, 2000). This suggests differential effects of deprivation on different domains of development. From a theoretical perspective, it is paramount to understand why some domains of development are more compromised than others and why some are more protected than others. It is our view that only by understanding the neurobiological mechanisms that underlie development will we truly understand behavioral development.

For many years, developmental science has argued that social deprivation in the first years of life has significant consequences for the cognitive and socioemotional development of the young child. The issue of the magnitude of these effects goes to the heart of a fundamental concern among developmental psychologists about the consequences of early experience for later behavior. The observations of Spitz (1945), Goldfarb (1945a, 1945b), and Bowlby (1952) regarding the consequences of early separation or loss of the mother and institutionalization suggested that lack of early social interaction had profound effects upon the social and emotional development of the child. These observations were supported by the work on isolation effects in nonhuman primates.

Scientists, such as Harlow (1971), provided dramatic evidence of the consequences of social deprivation for the young monkey's behavioral development, showing that early separation of the infant from mother had significant effects on the monkey's social and emotional development. Animals exhibited depressed affect and little social interaction with conspecifics even after they were placed back into a peer group. Raising the monkey with same aged peers had a similar outcome, in that these animals exhibit high degrees of anxious-like behaviors.

Although the behavioral aftermath of social isolation in the early months of life has been well documented, less is known about the underlying neurobiology of these effects. That is, even in nonhuman primate studies, where there is a good deal of description of the behavioral consequences of early social deprivation, there are few data on the effects of such deprivation on the developing central nervous system. What systems, for example, are compromised by lack of early social contact?

As well, there are few data that address the issue of sensitive periods for the effects of deprivation. While we know a good deal about developmental changes in the nervous system during early development, we know much less about the effects of timing of social deprivation on the processes involved in this development. This contrasts with ample data that exist on the effects of timing of certain types of sensory deprivation on developing perceptual systems, such as visual–perceptual development. Much less is known about the effects of timing of social deprivation during the first years of life on subsequent socioemotional development, although some effects of timing of maternal separations on Rhesus macaques (see Nelson et al., 2002) and of timing of maltreatment in humans have been documented (see Manly, Kim, Rogosch, & Cicchetti, 2001). Such information is important for interpreting the aforementioned results of studies that have found differential outcomes in cognitive and social domains in children adopted from institutions. Perhaps there are periods of development during which social interaction is critical for adaptive behavioral development. If so, when do they occur and how much recovery is possible if those periods are characterized by limited opportunities for interaction?

Questions about sensitive and critical periods in social and emotional development are among the most pressing in neuroscience. This will be the largest longitudinal investigation of institutionalized children less than 2 years old at the time that the intervention begins. This will allow a more fine-grained look at issues of timing of intervention and recovery than previous studies that have included children with histories of deprivation longer than 2 years. The BEIP will allow an examination of the issue of the effects of length of early social deprivation (infants and young children in the sample vary in the length of time they have spent in the institutional setting), and it will allow us to directly examine the effects of intervention on such early deprivation. Hopefully, it will provide answers to many of the critical questions that developmental psychopathologists have asked about the effects of early experience, the timing of deprivation, and the ameliorating effects of early intervention and provide clues to which underlying neurobiological processes are compromised by, and resilient to, dramatic changes in early experience. With regard to the neurobiological systems affected by such deprivation, we anticipate several such systems to be affected. For example, due to its prolonged developmental trajectory, a number of regions that lie within the prefrontal cortex (e.g., orbitofrontal, dorsolateral) may be affected. Similarly, if we construe the environment in which institutionalized children are raised as stressful, then the hippocampus likely will be affected. Finally, given the role of the amygdala in mediating emotional responses to environmental demands, we might also expect amygdala circuitry to be deleteriously affected.

Natural experiments, such as institutional care, provide an opportunity to enhance the ecological validity of experimental designs typical of neuroscience and to refine the observational designs typical of ethology in order to address vital questions about normal and pathological developmental processes. This investigation was actually designed with specific policy questions in mind, as recommended by Cicchetti and Toth (2000), who pointed out the inherent difficulties in post hoc application of scientific findings to policy questions. Questions posed by the BEIP are both theoretically interesting and practically important, especially in a setting in which the course of policies about how best to provide for abandoned children are being actively constructed. Results of studies such as this experiment in nature have the potential to inform scientific and policy questions in many related areas as well.

Editor's Conclusion

Researchers conducting the Bucharest Intervention Project found similar findings as previous research in that institutionalized children compared to their age-matched peers had lower IQs, more mental illness, were less likely to respond to social interaction, had stunted language skills and attachment abilities, and marked reduction in brain activities. The most impressive part of this study was that when children were placed into foster care, researchers found that emotional disorders and language improved. Complete recovery seems possible in children under the age of 2 years (Zeanah, et al., 2003).

The research that has been done on intervention and especially the intervention work done in Romania is uplifting and gives hope to a desperate situation. Research on deprived environments gives us evidence that children need more than food and shelter to development properly. They need human contact to flourish, and if they are able to get an adequate amount before age 2, they can develop normally.

Editor's References

Zeanah, C.H., Nelson, C.A., Fox, N.A., Smythe, A.T., Marshall, P., Parker, S.W., & Koga, S. (2003). "Designing Research to Study the Effects of Institutional Research to Study the Effects of Institutionalization on Brain and Behavioral Development: The Bucharest Early Intervention Project." Development and Psychopathology, 15, 885–907.

Bakermans-Kranenburg, M. J., van IJzendoorn, M. H., Juffer, F. (2008). "Earlier is Better: A Meta-analysis of 70 Years of Intervention Improving Cognitive Development in Institutionalized Children." Monographs of the Society for Research in Child Development, 73(3), 279–293.

References

Ainsworth, M. D. S., Blehar, M. C., Waters, E., & Wall, S. (1978). *Patterns of attachment: A psychological study of the Strange Situation procedure.* Hillsdale, NJ: Erlbaum.

Albers, L. H., Johnson, D. E., Hostetter, M. K., Iverson, S., & Miller, L. C. (1997). Health of children adopted from the former Soviet Union and Eastern Europe: Comparison with pre-adoptive medical records. *Journal of the American Medical Association, 278,* 922–924.

Ames, E. W. (1997). *The development of Romanian orphanage children adopted into Canada. Final report to human resources development, Canada.* Burnaby, Canada: Simon Fraser University.

Bachman, R. D. (1991). *Romania: A country study.* Library of Congress, Federal Research Division. Retrieved August 25, 2002, from http://memory.loc.gov/ frd/cs/rotoc.html

Bell, M. A., & Fox, N. A. (1994). Brain development over the first year of life: Relations between electro-encephalographic frequency and coherence and cognitive and affective behaviors. In G. Dawson & K. W. Fischer (Eds.). *Human behavior and the developing brain* (pp. 314–345). New York: Guilford Press.

Benoit, T. C., Jocelyn, L. J., Moddemann, D. M., & Embree, J. E. (1996). Romanian adoption: The Manitoba experience. *Archives of Pediatric and Adolescent Medicine, 150,* 1278–1282.

Bowlby, J. (1952). *Maternal care and mental health.* Geneva: World Health Organization.

Bzoch, K., & League, R. (1972). Receptive–Expressive Emergent Language (REEL) Scale. Baltimore, MD: University Park Press.

Calafteanu, I. (1998) *History of Romanians.* Government of Romania, Ministry of Public Information. Retrieved August 31, 2002, from http://domino.kappa .ro/govern/istoria-e

Cermak, S. A., & Daunhauer, L. A. (1997). Sensory processing in the post-institutionalized child. *American Journal of Occupational Therapy, 51,* 500–507.

Chisholm, K. (1998). A three year follow-up of attachment and indiscriminate friendliness in children adopted from Romanian orphanages. *Child Development, 69,* 1092–1106.

Chisholm, K., Carter, M. C., Ames, E. W., & Morison, S. J. (1995). Attachment security and indiscriminately friendly behavior in children adopted from Romanian orphanages. *Development and Psychopathology, 7,* 283–294.

Chisholm, K., & Savoie, L. (1992, June). Behavior and attachment problems of Romanian orphanage children adopted to Canada. In E. W. Ames (Chair), *Development of Romanian orphanage children adopted to Canada.* Symposium conducted at the meeting of the Canadian Psychological Association, Quebec City, Canada.

Chugani, H. T., Behen, M. E., Muzik, O., Juha´sz, C., Nagy, F., & Chugani, D. C. (2001). Local brain functional activity following early deprivation: A study of postinstitutionalized Romanian orphans. *NeuroImage, 14,* 1290–1301.

Cicchetti, D., & Dawson, G. (2002). Editorial: Multiple levels of analysis. *Development and Psychopathology, 14,* 417–420.

Cicchetti, D., & Toth, S. (2000). Editorial: Social policy implications of research in developmental psychopathology. *Development and Psychopathology, 12,* 551–554.

Crowell, J. A., & Feldman, S. S. (1988). Mothers' internal models of relationships and children's behavioral and developmental status: A study of mother–child interaction. *Child Development, 59,* 1273–1285.

Crowell, J. A., & Feldman, S. S. (1989). Assessment of mothers' working models of relationships: Some clinical implications. *Infant Mental Health Journal, 10,* 173–184.

Dawson, G., Carver, L., Meltzoff, A. N., Panagiotides, H., McPartland, J., & Webb, S. J. (2002). Neural correlates of face and object recognition in young children with autism spectrum disorder, developmental delay and typical development. *Child Development, 73,* 700–717.

Dennis, W., & Najarian, P. (1957). Infant development under environmental handicap. *Psychological Monographs: General and Applied, 71,* 1–13.

Edwards, S., Garman, M., Hughes, A., Letts, C., & Sinka, I. (1997). Assessing the comprehension and production of language in young children: An account of the Reynell Developmental Language Scales III. *International Journal of Language and Communication Disorders, 34,* 151–171.

Federici, R. S. (1998). *Help for the hopeless child: A guide for families.* Alexandria, VA: Author.

Fisher, L., Ames, E. W., Chisholm, K., & Savoie, L. (1997). Problems reported by parents of Romanian orphans adopted to British Columbia. *International Journal of Behavioral Development, 20,* 67–82.

Fox, N. A., Henderson, H. A., Rubin, K. H., Calkins, S. D., & Schmidt, L. A. (2001). Continuity and discontinuity of behavioral inhibition and exuberance: Psychophysiologial and behavioral influences across the first four years of life. *Child Development, 72,* 1–21.

Goldfarb, W. (1945a). Effects of psychological deprivation in infancy and subsequent stimulation. *American Journal of Psychiatry, 102,* 18–33.

Goldfarb, W. (1945b). Psychological privation in infancy and subsequent adjustment. *American Journal of Orthopsychology, 15,* 247–255.

Goldsmith, H. H., & Rothbart, M. K. (1999). *The Laboratory Temperament Assessment Battery* (Locomotor Version, Edition 3.1). Madison, WI: University of Wisconsin–Madison.

Government of Romania. (1991). *Constitutia Romaniei (The Romanian Constitution).* Retrieved September 2, 2002, from http://domino.kappa.ro/guvern/constitutiae.html

Groze, V., & Ileana, D. (1996). A follow-up study of adopted children from Romania. *Child and Adolescent Social Work Journal, 13,* 541–565.

Grupul Independent pentru Analiza Sistemului de Adoptii Internationale (GIASAI). (2002). *Reorganizarea sisemului de adoptii internationale si de protectie a copilului in dificultate (Final report, revised version).* Retrieved September 2, 2002, from Government of Romania press office, http://www.guv.ro/presa/rapoarte/ 200204/rap-020405-adoptii-internat.pdf

Gunnar, M., Bruce, J., & Grotevant, H. D. (2000). International adoption of institutionally reared children: Research and policy. *Development and Psychopathology, 12,* 677–693.

Harlow, H. F. (1971). *Learning to love.* San Francisco, CA: Albion.

Hodges, J., & Tizard, B. (1989a). IQ and behavioral adjustment of ex-institutional adolescents. *Journal of Child Psychology, Psychiatry, and Allied Disciplines, 30,* 53–75.

Hodges, J., & Tizard, B. (1989b). Social and family relationships of ex-institutional adolescents. *Journal of Child Psychology, Psychiatry, and Allied Disciplines, 30,* 77–97.

Iorga, N. (1970). *A history of Roumania: Land, people, civilization* (J. McCabe, Trans.). New York: AMS Press. (Original work published 1925)

Johnson, D. E. (1997). Medical issues in international adoption: Factors that affect your child's pre-adoption health. *Adoptive Families, 30,* 18–20.

Johnson, D. E. (2000). Medical and developmental sequelae of early childhood institutionalization in Eastern European adoptees. In C. A. Nelson (Ed.). *Minnesota Symposia on Child Psychology: Vol. 31. The effects of early adversity on neurobehavioral development* (pp. 113–162). Mahwah, NJ: Erlbaum.

Johnson, D. E., Miller, L. C., Iverson, S., Thomas, W., Franchino, B., & Dole, K. (1992). The health of children adopted from Romania. *Journal of the American Medical Association, 268,* 3446–3451.

Kreppner, J. M., O'Connor, T. G., Rutter, M., Beckett, C., Castle, J., & Croft, C. (2001). Can inattention/ overactivity be an institutional deprivation syndrome? *Journal of Abnormal Child Psychology, 29,* 513–528.

Manly, J. T., Kim, J. E., Rogosch, F. A., & Cicchetti, D. (2001). Dimensions of child maltreatment and children's adjustment: Contributions of developmental timing and subtype. *Development and Psychopathology, 13,* 759–782.

Marshall, P. J., Bar-Haim, Y., & Fox, N. A. (2002). The development of the EEG from 5 months to 5 years of age. *Clinical Neurophysiology, 113,* 1199–1208.

Morales, M., Mundy, P., Delgado, C. E. F., Yale, M., Messinger, D., Neal, R., & Schwartz, H. (2000). Responding to joint attention across the 6-to 24-month age period and early language acquisition. *Journal of Applied Developmental Psychology, 21,* 283–298.

Morison, S. J., Ames, E. W., & Chisholm, K. (1995). The development of children adopted from Romanian orphanages. *Merrill-Palmer Quarterly, 41,* 411–430.

Moskoff, W. (1980). Pronatalist policies in Romania. *Economic Development and Cultural Change, 28,* 597– 614.

Muhamedrahimov, R. (2000). New attitudes: Infant care facilities in Saint Petersburg, Russia. In J. Osofsky & H. Fitzgerald (Eds.), *WAIMH Handbook of infant mental health.* New York: Wiley.

Mundy, P., & Gomes, A. (1998). Individual differences in joint attention skills in the second year. *Infant Behavior and Development, 21,* 469–482.

Mundy, P., Hogan, A., & Doehring, P. (1996). *A preliminary manual for the abridged Early Social Communication Scales (ESCS).* Retrieved May 10, 2002, from http://www.psy.miami.edu/faculty/pmundy/manual .html

Nelson, C. A. (2001). The development and neural bases of face recognition. *Infant and Child Development, 10,* 3–18.

Nelson, C. A., Bloom, F. E., Cameron, J., Amaral, D., Dahl, R., & Pine, D. (2002). An integrative, multidisciplinary approach to the study of brain-behavior relations in the context of typical and atypical development. *Development and Psychopathology, 14,* 499–520.

Nelson, C. A., & deHaan, M. (1996). A neurobehavioral approach to the recognition of facial expressions in infancy. In J. A. Russell (Ed.), *The psychology of facial expression* (pp. 176–204). Cambridge: Cambridge University Press.

O'Connor, T. G., Bredenkamp, D., Rutter, M., & the English and Romanian Adoption Adoptees Study Team. (1999). Attachment disturbances and disorders in children exposed to early severe deprivation. *Infant Mental Health Journal, 20,* 10–29.

O'Connor, T. G., Marvin, R. S., Rutter, M., Olrick, J. T., & Britner, P. A. (2003). Child–parent attachment following early institutional deprivation, *Development and Psychopathology, 15,* 19–38.

O'Connor, T. G., Rutter, M., & the English and Romanian Adoptees Study Team. (2000). Attachment disorder behavior following early severe deprivation: Extension and longitudinal follow-up. *Journal of the American Academy of Child and Adolescent Psychiatry, 39,* 703–712.

O'Connor, T. G., Rutter, M., Beckett, C., Keaveney, L., Kreppner, J. M., & the English and Romanian Adoptees Study Team. (2000). The effects of global severe privation on cognitive competence: Extension and longitudinal follow-up. *Child Development, 71,* 376–390.

Pollak, S. D., & Kistler D. J. (2002). Early experience is associated with the development of categorical representations for facial expressions of emotion. *Proceedings of the National Academy of Sciences (USA), 99,* 9072–9076.

Pollak, S. D., Klorman, R., Thatcher, J. E., & Cicchetti, D. (2001). P3b reflects maltreated children's reactions to facial displays of emotion. *Psychophysiology, 38,* 267–274.

Pollak, S. D., & Sinha, P. (2002). Effects of early experience on children's recognition of facial displays of emotion. *Developmental Psychology, 38,* 784–791.

Provence, S., & Lipton, R. C. (1962). *Infants in institutions: A comparison of their development with family-reared infants during the first year of life.* New York: International Universities Press.

Romanian National Institute for Statistics. (2000). *Raportul dezvoltarii umane (Report on human development).* Bucharest, Romania: Author.

Romanian National Institute for Statistics. (2002). *Recensamantul populatiei si locuintelor 2002: Rezultate preliminare (National census of population and residences: Preliminary results).* Bucharest, Romania: Author.

Rosapepe, J. C. (2001). *Half way home: Romania's abandoned children ten years after the revolution.* Report to Americans from the U.S. Embassy, Bucharest, Romania.

Rutter, M., Andersen–Wood, L., Beckett, C., Bredenkamp, D., Castle, J., & Groothues, C., (1999). Quasi autistic patterns following severe early global privation. *Journal of Child Psychology and Psychiatry and Allied Disciplines, 40,* 537–549.

Rutter, M., & the English and Romanian Adoptees Study Team. (1998). Developmental catch-up, and delay, following adoption after severe global early privation. *Journal of Child Psychology and Psychiatry, 39,* 465–476.

Sanchez, M. M., Ladd, C. O., & Plotsky, P. M. (2001). Early adverse experience as a developmental risk factor for later psychopathology: Evidence from rodent and primate models. *Development and Psychopathology, 13,* 419–449.

Schober–Peterson, D., & Cohen, M. (1999). *Toddler talk: A family-centered intervention program for young children.* Oceanside, CA: Academic Communication Associates.

Smyke, A. T. (2000). *Effects of maternal maltreating status on maternal representation and mother–child interaction.* Unpublished doctoral dissertation, University of New Orleans.

Smyke, A. T., Dumitrescu, A., & Zeanah, C. H. (2002). Disturbances of attachment in young children: I. The continuum of caretaking casualty. *Journal of the American Academy of Child and Adolescent Psychiatry, 41,* 972–982.

Smyke, A. T., & Zeanah, C. H. (1999). *Disturbances of Attachment Interview.* Unpublished manuscript, Tulane University School of Medicine.

Spitz, R. A. (1945). Hospitalism: An inquiry into the genesis of psychiatric conditions in early childhood. *The Psychoanalytic Study of the Child, 1,* 53–74.

Stativa, E., Tabacaru, C., Stanescu, A., & Simion, B. (2000). *Cercetarea abuzului asupra copilului in institutiile de protectie sociala din Romania – 2000 (Child abuse research in social residential institutions in Romania – 2000).* CERAB report, preliminary version. Unpublished manuscript.

Tanner, J. M. (1973). Physical growth and development. In J. O. Forfar & G. C. Arneil (Eds.), *Textbook of pediatrics.* London: Churchill Livingstone.

Thatcher, R. W. (1994). Cyclic cortical reorganization: Origins of human cognitive development. In G. Dawson & K. W. Fischer (Eds.). *Human behavior and the developing brain* (pp. 232–266). New York: Guilford Press.

Tizard, B. (1977). *Adoption: A second chance.* New York: Free Press.

Tizard, B., & Hodges, J. (1978). The effect of early institutional rearing on the development of eight-year-old children. *Journal of Child Psychology, Psychiatry, and Allied Disciplines, 19,* 99–118.

Tizard, B., & Rees, J. (1974). A comparison of the effects of adoption, restoration to the natural mother, and continued institutionalization on the cognitive development of four-year-children. *Child Development, 45,* 92–99.

Tizard, B., & Rees, J. (1975). The effect of early institutional rearing on the behavior problems and affectional relationships of four-year-old children. *Journal of Child Psychology, Psychiatry, and Allied Disciplines, 16,* 61–73.

Treptow, K. W. (Ed.). (1997). *A history of Romania* (3rd ed.). Iasi, Romania: Center for Romanian Studies.

UNESCO. (2002). *The EFA (Education for All) 2000 Assessment Country Report: Romania–Part I.* Retrieved September 1, 2002, from http://www2.unesco .org/wef/countryreports/romania/rapport_1.html

United Nations. (2001, January). *Romania country briefing report.* Retrieved September 2, 2002, from http:// www.un.ro/briefing.html

Vorria, P., Papaligoura, Z., Dunn, J., van IJzendoorn, M. H., Steele, H., Kontopoulou, A. & Sarafidou, Y. (in press). Early experiences and attachment relationships of Greek infants raised in residential group care. *Journal of Child Psychology, Psychiatry and Allied Disciplines.*

Vorria, P., Rutter, M., Pickles, A., Wolkind, S., & Hobsbaum, A. (1998a). A comparative study of Greek children in long-term residential group care and in two-parent families: I. Social, emotional, and behavioral differences. *Journal of Child Psychology and Psychiatry, 39,* 225–236.

Vorria, P., Rutter, M., Pickles, A., Wolkind, S., & Hobsbaum, A. (1998b). A comparative study of Greek children in long-term residential group care and in two-parent families: II. Possible mediating mechanisms. *Journal of Child Psychology and Psychiatry, 39,* 237–245.

Waters, E., & Deane, K. E. (1985). Defining and assessing individual differences in attachment relationships: Q-sort methodology and the organization of behavior in infancy and early childhood. In I. Bretherton & E. Waters (Eds.), Growing points of attachment theory and research. *Monographs of the Society for Research in Child Development, 50* (1–2, Serial No. 209), 41–65.

Zeanah, C. H. (2000). Disturbances of attachment in young children adopted from institutions. *Journal of Developmental and Behavioral Pediatrics, 21,* 230–236.

Zeanah, C. H., Larrieu, J. L., Heller, S. S., & Valliere, J. (2001). Infant–parent relationship assessment. In C. H. Zeanah (Ed.), *Handbook of infant mental health* (2nd ed., pp. 222–235). New York: Guilford Press.

Zeanah, C. H., Smyke, A. T., & Dumitrescu, A. (2002). Attachment disturbances in young children. II: Indiscriminate behavior and institutional care. *Journal of the American Academy of Child and Adolescent Psychiatry, 41,* 983–989.

Discussion Questions

1. Why are there so many orphaned children in Romania? What about other places in the world? Why should we care about what happens to children outside of the United States?
2. There are quite a few criticisms of the American foster care system. Why are the researchers pushing this type of system in Romania?
3. Do you think the researchers' attempts to remain ethical were enough? Is it ever fair to randomly assign children to stay in an orphanage you know is damaging their development?
4. In Zimbabwe there is a child care system called Eden Children's Village. This childcare system takes children that would normally be in an institution like an orphanage and puts them into homes with a man, woman, and other orphans of varying ages. It is intended to model a typical family. Compare this system with the foster care system promoted in the article. Do you think it will have a better, worse, or similar result to the child's cognitive and socio-emotional development? Could this be done in the United States?

Assignment

Please carefully answer the following questions:

1. What is a hypothesis for the study?
2. Please explain what the feasibility phase is, when it occurred, and why it occurred.
3. Please list and explain the steps in the study design (be sure to adequately explain why they chose to do each step).

Please describe the typical day in the life of these industrialized children:

1. Describe the study participants.
   a. What made one likely to be chosen for the study?
   b. What kept one out of the study?
2. How were participants assigned to groups?
3. Describe the makeup of the foster parents and community comparison group.
4. Explain the steps in the procedure.
5. List five measures/constructs that were used, what they were, and why they were chosen.
6. Explain the intervention, with focus on foster parent recruitment, training, support, monitoring, and placement of children.

Section II: Cognitive Processes

Language, Emotions, Temperament, Suicide, and Death

The Development of Gesture

By Marion Tellier

Human beings gesture every day while speaking: they move their hands, their heads, their arms; their whole body is involved in communication. But how does it work? How do we produce gestures and in what purpose? How are gestures connected to speech? When do we begin producing gestures and how do they evolve throughout the lifespan? These are questions gesture researchers have been trying to answer since the second half of the 20th century.

This chapter will first define what a gesture is by describing the different kinds of gestures and by explaining some of the current theories about gesture production. Then the emergence of gesture along with language development will be exposed as well as its evolution during childhood. Finally, we will review studies about adults' gestures and what we know about their change across adulthood.

What Is a Gesture?

At first, gesture may seem easy to define: a movement of the hand or maybe of both hands produced by a human being. However, when one thinks more precisely about it, one may wonder if a gesture is only performed with hands or if it can involve other body parts such as head, face or arms. One can also wonder if there are different kinds of gestures: are nervous scratches, gestures accompanying speech and gestures used in deaf sign language the same kind of movements? Indeed, even if these are all called gestures, they differ. This first section will give a brief overview of the various types of gestures and of the main issues in gesture studies.

What Is a Communicative Gesture and What Is Not

If we look at two persons involved in a face-to-face interaction, we will notice that they move their bodies continuously. One of the participants may be performing practical actions such as taking notes, smoking, driving, etc.: these are not considered as communicative gestures. Similarly nonverbal behavior such as postures, crossing the legs and nervous gestures like scratching, playing with an object, stroking the hair are not regarded as communicative gestures either. Nevertheless, these movements can have an impact on the interaction. For instance, if one nervously plays with a pen or taps on the table with their fingers, their addressee might end the conversation earlier than planned. Thus, as Kendon puts it (2004, p. 8) "usually 'gesture' is not used to refer to those visible bodily expressions of thoughts or feelings that are deemed inadvertent or are regarded as something a person cannot 'help'". A gesture is rather considered as intended to communicate something. Now that we have put aside what movements are not regarded as gestures, we are left with the idea that a gesture is an action related to ongoing talk and that has the features of manifest deliberate expressiveness (Kendon, 2004). This includes a whole range of movements such as a thumb up for OK, a finger pointing to a place or an object, and even a gesture of sign language. Researchers have proposed several classifications of these gestures in order to differentiate them. Classifications can rely on semiotic or functional distinctions, sometimes a mix of both (for an overview of the various classifications, see Kendon, 2004, Chapter 6). A very efficient and practical classification is called Kendon's Continuum and will be detailed below for it is nowadays commonly used to explain the different kinds of gestures.

Kendon's Continuum

Based on Adam Kendon's work, Kendon's Continuum has been elaborated by David McNeill (1992 and 2000). McNeill placed four kinds of gestures on a continuum: gesticulation, pantomime, emblems, and sign language. Gesticulation refers to "idiosyncratic spontaneous movements of the hands and arms accompanying speech" (McNeill, 1992, p. 37); they are also called cospeech gestures and will be detailed below. Pantomime is used to define those gestures that mime an action or an object, a profession, etc., and that are mainly used when it is impossible to speak (because of the noise, distance, need to be discreet...) or in games of miming. Emblems are conventionalized gestures used in a specific community; they have a defined meaning. For instance, the thumb up meaning OK in some countries such as the USA, or the forefinger pulling down the skin under the eye, which means in the French culture: I don't believe it ("*Mon oeil*"). Emblems are most of the time associated with a fixed expression but can be used without speech. People belonging to the same cultural community understand these gestures because they have learned them along with their first language. Eventually, sign languages are "full-fledged linguistic systems with segmentation, compositionality, a lexicon, a syntax, distinctiveness, arbitrariness, standards of well-formedness, and a community of users" (McNeill, 1992, p. 38). Indeed, sign languages (no matter if they are languages used by the deaf or ritual and cultural languages used by the North American Plain Indians or by Central Australia Aborigines, for instance) are languages of their own and are mainly used without speech.

Originally, McNeill (1992) organized these four kinds of gestures on a continuum according to their link to speech and to their degree of convention (see Table 8.1). Thus, on the left-hand side, gesticulation is made of gestures that require the presence of speech, whereas on the right-hand side, sign languages are used without speech. On the left-hand side, gesticulation is made of spontaneous idiosyncratic gestures, and on the right extremity, sign languages are strongly conventionalized and socially regulated signs.

Table 8.1 McNeill's Continuum

Gesticulation ☐ Pantomime ☐ Emblems ☐ Sign languages ☐		
Obligatory presence of speech	☐ —————————— ☐	absence of speech
Not conventionalized	☐ —————————— ☐	conventionalized

In 2000, McNeill enriched this continuum by dividing it into four continua by using the original characteristics "relationship to speech" and "relationship to conventions" and by adding other characteristics such as "relationship to linguistic properties" and "character of the semiosis." See Continua 1, 2, 3 and 4.

Continuum 8.1 Relationship to Speech

Gesticulation ☐	Emblems ☐	Pantomime ☐	Sign Language ☐
Obligatory presence of speech	Optional presence of speech	Obligatory absence of speech	Obligatory absence of speech

Continuum 8.2 Relationship to Linguistic Properties

Gesticulation ☐	Pantomime ☐	Emblems ☐	Sign Language ☐
Linguistic properties absent	Linguistic properties absent	Some linguistic properties present	Linguistic properties absent

Continuum 8.3 Relationship to Conventions

Gesticulation ☐	Pantomime ☐	Emblems ☐	Sign Language ☐
Not conventionalized	Not conventionalized	Partly conventionalized	Fully conventionalized

Continuum 8.4 Character of the Semiosis

Gesticulation ☐	Pantomime ☐	Emblems ☐	Sign Language ☐
Global and synthetic	Global and analytic	Segmented and synthetic	Segmented and analytic

Types of Co-speech Gestures

Many gesture researchers have decided to focus on the study of co-speech gestures also called "gesticulation" in Kendon's Continuum. They are movements of the hands and arms produced by people when they talk. They do not belong to a fixed repertoire as gestures of sign language, for instance; on the contrary, they are unique, personal and spontaneous. As mentioned before, there are several classifications of gestures; most of them descend from Efron's (1972 [1941]), such as Ekman and Friesen's (1969). Although these are relevant and fine classifications, they are extremely detailed and not always easy to use. That is why David McNeill and his team (1992) have worked on a simplified, easy-to-use scheme made of four categories: iconic, metaphoric, deictic and beats.

Iconic gestures bear a close formal relationship to the semantic content of speech (McNeill, 1992). For instance, someone may say, "I was driving when I heard the news on the radio," and mime holding a steering wheel while saying "drive," or someone may say, "It was as big as that," while showing a width with both hands open and facing. "Most of the time, iconics represent body movements, movements of objects or people in space, and shapes of objects or people. They do so concretely and relatively transparently" (Goldin-Meadow, 2003, p. 7).

Metaphoric gestures are very similar to iconics except that they depict abstract concepts rather that concrete objects. If one cups their hands when saying the word "concept," for instance, it is a metaphoric gesture because the cup acts as a symbolic image for the idea of a concept.

Deictic gestures refer to things by pointing with the hand, the finger, the chin, etc. They can be either concrete, pointing to someone, something or somewhere, as when one says, "Your glasses are here on the table," while pointing towards the table and the glasses. But they can also be abstract, pointing when referring to something/someone absent, or a place, or even a moment in time, as for instance when one points to the right to mean China or behind them to refer to the past. Abstract deictics can be shaped by cultural characteristics as geographical and time references differ between languages and cultures.

Finally, beats are rhythmic movements that have no semantic connection to the speech they accompany. They rather stress important words or phrases. A typical beat would be a flick of the hand or of the finger. McNeill (1992) explains that the critical thing distinguishing beats from other gestures is that it has two movement phases—in/out, up/down, etc.

What We Know about Gesture Production

The Relationship between Gesture and Speech

Gesture and speech are considered by most gesture researchers as being part of one single system (McNeill, 1992); this is why they should not be analyzed separately.

There are two arguments to support the theory of the speech–gesture unified system. The first argument is that there is strong semantic coherence between the two modalities in an utterance. According to McNeill (1992), gesture and speech form a unified communication system; the coherence is possible because gesture and speech share a common cognitive representation: they are part of a single idea. When a speaker produces a message, most of the information s/he wants to share is conveyed in speech while part of the information may be channeled through gesture. However, gesture and speech convey information from different perspectives. In short, speech conforms to a codified, restricted and recognizable system of words and grammatical devices, whereas gesture is free from the standards of form language imposes and conveys meaning on a rather global and visual basis (Goldin-Meadow, 2003). With gestures, one can describe shape, motions or size far more easily than with words. Most of the time, information conveyed through gestures is visual imagery.

Because they are so different, gesture and speech when both implied in the same message do not always bring the same information. Church and Goldin-Meadow (1986) talk about gesture–speech matches when gesture is elaborated on a topic already introduced in speech, and gesture–speech mismatches when gesture introduces new information not conveyed in speech. It is thus not rare in a message that gesture brings information that completes speech. For instance, a woman says, "She chases him out again" (talking about an old lady running after a cat) and moves her hand back and forth revealing that she uses her umbrella as a weapon (McNeill, 1992). In this example, the gesture provides us with information not conveyed in speech and shows us how much gestures can describe things speech cannot. Gesture is not restricted to a fixed form and can vary on several dimensions such as time, form, motion, trajectory, use of space, shape, rhythm, etc., which make it complex.

The second evidence that gesture and speech form a unified system is that they are always synchronous. McNeill (1992) found that 90% of gestures are produced while the gesturer is speaking. It has also been found that gesture and speech are co-temporal in a single utterance: the stroke of the gesture lines up with the linguistic equivalent.

Why Do We Produce Gestures?

A first answer to this question could be: to help our listeners to understand what we say. Indeed, Alibali, Heath, and Myers (2001) have found that people gesture more when talking to a visible interlocutor, and that when they talk to someone hidden behind a screen they tend to use fewer illustrative gestures. Several other studies have come to similar findings (for a review, see Alibali et al., 2001, and Özyürek, 2002).

Özyürek (2000, 2002) explored the communicative function of gesture by analyzing how speakers design their gestures according to the location of their addressees. She found that speakers oriented their gestures depending on where their interlocutors were sitting, so that gestures could be seen.

In order to find out whether gestures were taken into account by the listeners, Kelly and colleagues (Kelly, Barr, Church, & Lynch, 1999) analyzed the role of deictic gestures on the understanding of indirect questions, like saying, "It's hot in here," while pointing to the window, inferring that the listener should go and open it. Results show that deictic gestures help listeners to understand better the hidden intention in the speaker's message. Beattie and Shovelton (1999) showed that subjects listening to someone telling a story understand significantly more details when they see the speaker (and their gestures) than when they do not. Listeners also take into account information conveyed in gesture when it completes or contradicts speech (Cassell, McNeill, & McCullough, 1999).

However, even if gesture helps listeners to better understand a conversation, it seems that this is not the main function. Indeed, in the study of Alibali et al. (2001) already mentioned, even if speakers produced fewer gestures when they did not see their interlocutors, they did still gesture. Moreover, Iverson and Goldin-Meadow (1998) have laid evidence that congenitally blind speakers spontaneously gesture even when they speak to blind listeners. Thus, we can assume that gesture does not solely convey information for the listener but also plays a role for the speaker. This can also explain why we gesture when we talk on the telephone, for instance.

So if we produce gestures for ourselves, what is the function of gesture in speech production? There are several theories on this topic.

The Lexical Retrieval Hypothesis (LRH) holds that gesture plays an active role in lexical access, particularly for words with spatial content (Rauscher, Krauss, & Chen, 1996). Thus gesture plays a role in generating the surface forms of utterances it infers directly in the process of speaking. Alternatively, the Information Packaging Hypothesis (IPH) (Alibali, Kita, & Young, 2000; Kita, 2000) is drawn from McNeill's (1992) and McNeill and Duncan's (2000) theory of gesture and speech as an integrated system (Growth Point). It argues that gesture and speech help to constitute thought and that gestures reflect the imagistic mental representation that is activated at the moment of speaking. In order to find out which theory (LRH or IPH) is likely to be true, Alibali et al. (2000) gave 5-year-olds two oral tasks: one was a description task (the children had to describe different objects) and one was an explanation task (a Piagetian conservation task like, for instance, judging whether two different receptacles contain the same amount of sand). Both tasks required similar lexical use (the same objects to talk about) but inferred different cognitive conceptualizations (one being description and the other explanation). According to the LRH, subjects should use the same gestures in both tasks since they need roughly the same lexical items. Conversely, according to the IPH, as conceptual planning is different in both tasks, gestures should be different. The hypothesis is that if children use different gestures in both tasks while using similar words, then gestures help not only to retrieve words but also to organize thought and conceptualize the message to be verbalized. Results show that, indeed, in the explanation task (more demanding cognitively), children used more gestures conveying perceptual dimensions of the objects and more gestures conveying information that differed from the accompanying speech. Thus, gesture helps cognitive activity. Alibali et al. (2000) conclude that "The action of gesturing helps speakers to organise spatial information for verbalisation, and in this way, gesture plays a role in conceptualising the message to be verbalised" (Alibali et al., 2000, p. 610). However, even if data tends to favor the IPH theory, the authors do not reject the LRH and admit that gesture helps both lexical retrieval and organization of spatial information for verbalization.

One last noticeable element on gesture and production is that it has been found that preventing subjects from gesturing has an effect on speech: for instance, in a description task, gesture-restriction has an effect on the amount of time needed to describe an object (Cohen & Borsoi, 1996) and it also generally decreases speech rate (Morsella & Krauss, 2004).

Gesture Development in Childhood

The first communicative gestures appear at a very early age. Many researchers have analyzed them and their occurrence with speech. It seems that gesture plays a crucial role in transitional knowledge.

What We Know about Gesture Development in Childhood

From the age of 10 months, babies begin to produce some kind of gestures like pointing, giving, showing (Bates, Benigni, Bretherton, Camaioni, and Volterra, 1979; van der Straten, 1991). They repeat behaviors that they know will catch adults' attention. Deictic gestures or pointing, which rapidly increase at the end of the first year of age, are considered by psycholinguists as prelinguistic gestures, for they constitute an important stage in the development of speech. Pointing, accompanied by eye contact with an adult, aims at seeking information or approval and acts as a precursor to spoken and sign naming. Indeed, the sequence of deictic gesture development reveals the gradual distancing of self from object that underlies symbolic development (Capone & McGregor, 2004). The child points to an object not to request it but to refer to it; this reveals that the child can isolate an object from the rest of his/her environment as s/he will soon do with words that will be isolated from the flow of speech the child is exposed to. The ability to decontextualize is crucial as it is related to the ability to use a word in the absence of the referent or to use it with other exemplars of the same referent. In the period between 9 and 13 months, ritualized requests appear, like open–closed grasping motions or pulling an open hand to obtain something (Bates et al., 1979).

Representational gestures begin to emerge around the age of 12 months before the onset of the 25-word milestone. These are not instrumental gestures, for the infant does not manipulate objects but rather represents referents symbolically. For instance, the child represents the action of holding a glass and drinking or flaps his/her arms to represent a bird. Goodwyn and Acredolo (1993) consider that these representational gestures are real examples of language symbols and can be analyzed with the same criteria used to define spoken words. They argue that a gesture or a word is symbolic if it refers to multiple exemplars including pictures and absence of the referent, if it is produced spontaneously (without following the model of an adult), and if it is not part of a well-rehearsed routine (Goodwyn & Acredolo, 1993).

Between 12 and 18 months, the child gestures in an isolated way, which means that s/he either gestures or speaks, but hardly both in the same time. The child thus chooses between the two systems s/he knows (McNeill, 1992). Iverson, Capirci, and Caselli (1994) found that 16-month-old children have a preference for either words or gestures, but by 20 months there is a significant increase in types and tokens of spoken words.

As we have already stated, gesture and speech in adults seem to belong to a single system (McNeill, 1992). This hypothesis is supported by two characteristics: the integration of gesture and speech in a semantic coherent unit (the fact that gesture is combined with speech in a meaningful way) and the temporal synchrony between speech and gestures in a single utterance. But is that also true for young children? Is gesture–speech integration characteristic of the earliest communications of young children? Or does integration of the two modalities emerge at a consistent point in the young child's linguistic development? To answer these questions, Butcher and Goldin-Meadow (2000) have longitudinally observed three boys and three girls during the transition from one- to two-word speech. They started to videotape their subjects during play sessions when they were beginning their one-word period of language development (age range 12 to 21 months, mean 15.5 months) and until the stage of two-word combination (range from 18 to 26.5 months). During the one-word period, for five of the six children, 20% of the total number of their communications (speech and/or gesture) included a gesture (for the sixth child, it was approximately 40%). During the first session, data uncovered that most of the subjects (five out of six) produced the majority of their gestures without speech (to compare, McNeill, 1992, has found that only 10% of adults' gestures are produced without speech). Then, during the following sessions, a general decline in the proportion of gestures produced without speech was observed. Thus, children began the one-word period producing gestures without speech, and by the end of this period they mainly used gesture–speech combinations.

The two characteristics of adults' productions of speech and gestures are the synchrony of both modalities and the semantic coherence. Consequently, Butcher and Goldin-Meadow (2000) observed whether children's productions of speech and gestures bear these same characteristics. As far as synchrony is concerned, during the first session, five of the six children produced gesture–speech combinations that were not synchronous with speech (the sixth child produced synchronously timed combinations throughout the observation period). During the next sessions, combinations became more and more harmonious. The authors thus suggest that "gesture and speech do not form a completely integrated system from the start but may require some time to become aligned with one another" (Butcher & Goldin-Meadow, 2000, p. 246). As far as semantic content is concerned, McNeill (1992) discovered that gesture and speech "cover the same idea unit" (1992, p. 27) even if gesture and speech do not convey precisely the same information. When analyzing the gestures combined with meaningful words produced by their children, Butcher and Goldin-Meadow (2000) found that the number of gesture–speech combinations increased during the observation period. The children produced both occurrences of gesture conveying the same information as speech (point to the box and say "box") and occurrences of gestures conveying different but related information (point to the box and say "open"). In this later case, the child can express two different elements in a single utterance (one in gesture and one in speech), something s/he is not yet able to do in speech only. "Thus the ability to combine gesture and meaningful speech in a single utterance greatly expands the child's communicative range" (Butcher & Goldin-Meadow, 2000, p. 248).

By putting together all these findings, the authors highlighted the striking fact that the three events converge in time: gesture-alone communications began to decline and "synchronous gesture–speech combinations began to increase at just the moment when gesture was first combined in the same utterance with a meaningful word" (Butcher & Goldin-Meadow, 2000, p. 248). To sum up the observed developmental sequence: the child begins to produce communicative symbolic gestures mostly without speech; when gesture is combined with words, speech is meaningless and gesture is not synchronized with it. Then, gesture and speech become more fully integrated and the child begins to produce synchronized combinations of gestures and meaningful words. This is the beginning of gesture–speech integration as we find it in adult expression. Butcher and Goldin-Meadow (2000) explain that the emergence of combinations in which gesture and speech are semantically related but do not convey the same information represents a communicative, even conceptual, breakthrough for the child and announces the onset of two-word speech. Indeed, in the six children observed, the correlation between the onset of this type of gesture–speech combinations and the onset of two-word utterances is high and significant.

During toddlerhood, children come to prefer verbal to gestural expression as they are learning more and more words. However, children still use gestures and there is a certain increase in the use of deictics, particularly accompanying expressions such as "this" and "that" (Iverson et al., 1994). In the second and third years of life, pointing becomes increasingly integrated with spoken language, particularly to supplement spoken messages (Iverson et al., 1994). From 16 to 20 months, there is a significant increase in pointing gestures co-occurring with representational words. As speech develops, gestures become more and more elaborated, especially in their relation to speech. Iconics tend to appear more and more with verbs and adjectives, rather with nouns, and the relationship between gesture and language extends to the domain of morphosyntax as the children advance in these areas (Capone & McGregor, 2004).

Between the third and the fifth years of age, iconic gestures increase significantly. Iconics and speech become more and more synchronized. Nevertheless, children's co-speech gestures do not yet refer to abstract contents; metaphorics are hardly found in young children's gesture productions. From the age of 5, the rest of the gestural system develops and beats, metaphorics and abstract deictics become more and more numerous (McNeill, 1992).

Colletta (2004) has conducted a vast quantitative study on the development of verbal and non-verbal activity of children from 6 up to 11. He confirms McNeill's findings as far as the emergence of metaphorics and beats is concerned (after the age of 5/6). He also found that multimodal story-telling skills (linguistic, prosodic and gestural) develop together and simultaneously. Colletta also showed that the study of co-speech gestures enables researchers to gather clues and relevant information on the development of concept and mental imagery of children. As children grow older and develop, gestures develop too and appear in cognitive tasks very often, allowing researchers to better understand how the child acquires concepts.

Studying the matches and mismatches in speech and gestures produced by children proves to be very relevant when one tries to understand their cognitive development (Goldin-Meadow, 2003). It appears that when some children explain something they have not yet understood (a math concept, for instance), they tend to convey the same incorrect information both in gesture and in speech, in a single procedure, so to speak. They then enter a discordant state in which they produce different procedures: one in speech and another in gesture. This means that the child is in a zone of proximal development. The information expressed in gesture is different from that expressed in speech. Most of the time, accurate information tends to be that conveyed in gesture. Then, when the concept is acquired by the child, gesture and speech again match in the child's production (Alibali & Goldin-Meadow, 1993). This transitional state is thus characterized by the concurrent activation of more than one procedure, and provides further evidence that gesture can be a powerful source of insight into the processes involved in cognitive development. This phenomenon has been noticed for math and science concepts but is probably applicable to other general concepts. Therefore, gesture has a direct effect on the learning process and scaffolds the child's cognitive development by structuring the various stages of the acquisition of a concept or a skill.

As we have seen, the analyses of the gestures produced by a child can reveal stages of transitional knowledge. The first deictic gestures announce the emergence of the first words. Then the combinations of gesture and speech conveying different but related information precede the first two-word utterances. And finally, as the child develops, it seems that complex concepts emerge in gesture before they appear in speech (or in speech combined with gesture). Globally, gesture–speech mismatches occur in a wide variety of situations and at different ages, from childhood to adulthood (for a review, see Goldin-Meadow, 2003). The study of gesture–speech matches and mismatches offer a window to the mind of the developing child and of the teenager. Goldin-Meadow (2000, p. 237) suggests looking "beyond children's words to the secrets that, until now, have been locked in their hands" to discover more about children's learning.

For Further Research

As far as development of the gestural system is concerned, most of the studies concern very young children who are acquiring their first language. Consequently, less attention has been devoted to older children and how they develop their way of gesturing while acquiring new discursive skills. Colletta's study (2004) is thought worth mentioning, since it concerns gesture development between 6 and 11 years old. Gestures of children after 11 and of teenagers have not been much studied. This is perhaps due to the fact that most of the first language is acquired and that significant changes are very slow to occur. However, it seems relevant to study how a teenager develops his/her own style of gesturing at this particular period of self-constructing. The way somebody gestures depends on many factors (detailed in the next section), among them personality. Teenagers may also be influenced by fashion in their way of gesturing. Gestures used by rap signers, for instance, seem to influence young individuals, especially boys. Gender is a factor which seems worth studying as well. Whether boys and girls gesture the same way is something left to discover.

Research on gestures and children is, as we have seen, relevant to understanding how a child acquires a first language and how gestures participate in cognitive development. These researches have implications in the field of education. For instance, it seems relevant to work on gestures children look at when they learn, and in the field of education this means teachers' gestures. Singer and Goldin-Meadow (2005) have laid evidence that teachers' gestures do not always convey the same information as their speech.

This mismatch thus offers learners a second message (one conveyed by gesture and the other by speech). To determine whether learners take advantage of this information, Singer and Goldin-Meadow gave 160 children in the third and fourth grades instruction in mathematical equivalence (for example: "6 + 4 + 3 = _ + 3"). Children were taught either one or two problem-solving strategies in speech accompanied by no gesture, gesture conveying the same strategy, or gesture conveying a different strategy. The chosen strategies are commonly used by teachers when teaching mathematical equivalence: "(a) equalizer, a strategy highlighting the principle underlying the problem, and (b) add subtract, a strategy highlighting a procedure for solving the problem" (2005, p. 86). Results show that the children were likely to profit from instruction with gesture, but only when it conveyed a different strategy than speech did. Moreover, two strategies were effective in promoting learning only when the second strategy was taught in gesture, not speech. Singer and Goldin-Meadow (2005) conclude that gesture has an active hand in learning.

In the field of second language teaching to young children, it has also been found that teachers' gestures help children to better understand the second language without translation. They also help the child to remember L2 lexical items better when s/he visualizes an illustrative gesture while listening to the matching word. Data has also shown that children who reproduce their teacher's gestures while repeating new L2 words remembered significantly more items than those who just looked at them (Tellier, 2006).

However, one may wonder whether a child always understands adults' gestures, since gestures reflect mental imagery and adults' and children's mental imagery differs because of their different cognitive states and experiences of life. Adults tend to use a lot of metaphoric gestures that may not be understood by young children, since they do not use such gestures and do not represent the world in a abstract and symbolic way. Misunderstandings of adults' gestures by 5-year-old children have been found (Tellier, 2006), but more data is definitely needed on this topic, extending to various age ranges to help teachers think about how they can improve their teaching gestures.

Gesture Development in Adulthood

While many researchers work on the development of gestures during childhood, there seem to be very few studies on this development during adulthood. Studies on development focus essentially on acquisition and decline, for example loss of language and language-related gestures. However, we can also notice some temporary changes due to change of jobs or related to belonging to/integrating into a specific community. One explanation for this lack of studies may be that development in adulthood is much slower than in childhood, and therefore it would take longitudinal studies of several years to notice changes in the development of a single subject, while children change so quickly that studying a child during a period of a few months is enough to notice and analyze the changes in both his/her speech and gesture skills. This is probably why most studies concerning adults are comparative studies in which subjects of different age groups are given the same task so that results can be compared according to the age variable. Another explanation for the rarity of studies on adults is that interest is rather focused on childhood, when most of the development takes place. However, we cannot assume that gesture production does not change across the lifespan once an individual has reached the stage of adulthood. In this section, we will review the studies on adults and the evolution of their gestures across the lifespan, and we will expose what research needs to focus on in the years to come.

Discussion Questions

1. How does the importance of gestures reading support the fad of baby sign language?
2. What are the criticisms of using gestures during early stages of language learning?
3. Would you use baby sign language or support the use for someone you know having a baby? What evidence would you give them for why they should or shouldn't use it?

Assignment

Assess baby sign language websites, products, and information. Do these popular materials go along with what you read in the article? Are some of them supported by information outside of the research you read? Are some of the products or websites better than others? How do you determine this?

Promoting Emotional Competence in the Preschool Classroom

By Hannah Nissen and Carol J. Hawkins

Beginning in the preschool years and continuing through the elementary years, successful and positive interactions with peers have been shown to be a central predictor of ongoing mental health and school success (Denham, 2001, 2006). As children become more skilled in interacting with others and managing emotions during interactions, they are better able to negotiate their ever-expanding social worlds. In recent years, the development of emotional competence also has received extensive attention in the literature on early childhood development and school readiness (Bracken & Fischel, 2007; Hyson, 2002; Knitzer & Lefkowitz, 2005; Raver & Knitzer, 2002).

Components of Emotional Competence

Emotional competence has been defined as having three specific components: emotional expressiveness, emotional knowledge, and emotion regulation (Denham et al., 2003). Each plays a key role in determining young children's ability to interact and form relationships with others (Denham, 2006).

Emotional expressiveness is central to emotional competence. Patterns of positive expression of emotion, such as happiness, aid in friendship development, while negative expressions of emotion, such as anger, interfere with peer relationships (Denham et al., 2003). Children often develop characteristic emotional responses, and these patterns of expressiveness either lead to positive interactions with age-mates or serve as barriers to successful interactions.

Emotional knowledge involves identifying emotional expressions in others and responding to the emotional displays of others in acceptable ways. Children who comprehend the expressions of others or the emotions typically associated with social situations are more likely to respond in prosocial ways, and are regarded as more likeable by peers and teachers (Denham et al, 2003).

Emotional regulation, also a critical element of emotional competence, involves the ability to manage arousal and behavior during social interaction (Denham, 2006). Young children have limited resources for emotional regulation; both negative and positive emotions can overwhelm the child, often leading to disorganized thinking and problematic behavior (Ashiabi, 2000). For children who demonstrate difficulty in regulating emotion, their expression of emotion often seems aggressive or intense. This has the potential to interfere with these children's ability to interact with others in socially acceptable ways. Peers and adults are likely to have negative perceptions to such emotional responses.

The Importance of Emotional Competence

Research suggests that a child's state of emotional development impacts development in all domains. According to the National Association for the Education of Young Children (2004), development in physical, social, cognitive, and emotional domains all contribute to a young child's ability to adapt to school life. Emotional competence, especially, has been shown to link to social competence in profound ways (Denham et al., 2003).

Social, emotional, and cognitive learning are interconnected to a greater extent in younger children. Studies indicate that many young children struggle to develop the emotional and behavioral strategies necessary to succeed in school (Knitzer & Lefkowitz, 2005). Consequently, building emotional competence helps children form positive social relationships and positive self-esteem, and is critical for school readiness and ongoing academic success.

Children's ongoing emotional health is influenced by their growing ability to express, understand, and regulate various emotions (Denham et al., 2003). Researchers found that children who enter kindergarten lacking curiosity, persistence in learning situations, and an eagerness to learn are less successful, academically, at the end of the 1st grade (Hemmeter & Ostrosky, 2006). Thus, children's relationships with teachers and peers, their interest and motivation to participate in learning experiences, and their ability to learn can be influenced, negatively or positively, by their emotional development (Peth-Pierce, 2001; Raver & Knitzer, 2002).

Beyond children's home environments and interactions with parents and caregivers, the classroom context provides endless opportunities to foster emotional health and competence. Every encounter with a child provides an opportunity to support the development of emotional skills that will allow children to experience success within the classroom and other contexts. Throughout the day, children are involved in a variety of routine, planned, and spontaneous contexts. As they participate in classroom life, they both experience and express a variety of emotions—some in ways that suggest a positive course of development and others that may indicate deleterious effects on a child over time. Teachers play an important role in fostering healthy development through identification of behaviors that may interfere with emotionally healthy response patterns (Ashiabi, 2000). However, teachers are rarely trained in the assessment and promotion of emotional competence. This lack of educational preparation often causes teachers to overlook or minimize the implications of emotional competence.

Promoting Emotional Competence

Nurturing and individualized teacher-child relationships provide important contexts for the promotion of children's emotional health (Bagdi & Vacca, 2005). As they interact with children, teachers have opportunities to coach children regarding appropriate responses during peer interactions and classroom activities, and serve as role models of appropriate expression of emotions (Hyson, 2004). When teachers organize child-centered classroom environments, they are preparing an emotional climate that is positive and conducive to learning. Finally, as educators create learning communities in which children are valued, children experience psychological safety and security (Keogh, 2003) (see Figure 1).

The Teacher as Relationship Builder

According to theory rooted in principles of attachment, teacher-child relationships contribute in significant ways to a child's growing emotional competence (Howes, Hamilton, & Matheson, 1994). Nurturing relationships with teachers who are responsive to children's unique needs are necessary to foster healthy development in many areas, including empathy, self-regulation, and peer relationships (Shonkoff & Phillips, 2001). Children who are able to form secure relationships with their teachers are often able to use that relationship as a secure base from which to explore the classroom and participate in activities with others (Howes, Hamilton, & Matheson, 1994). Dependent and conflicting teacher-child relationships, however, may interfere with children's ability to participate positively in the school experience and negatively influence their learning and academic achievement (Coplan & Prakash, 2003).

Individualized relationships with children create an arena in which teachers model healthy emotional expression, as well as informally assess a child's emotional well-being. In the context of a trusting relationship, teachers begin to recognize children's characteristic emotional responses and ability to regulate these responses in various classroom scenarios. Teachers can ascertain children's knowledge about emotions, and plan for support as necessary.

Children's individual differences necessitate that the relationships teachers form with each child be specific and unique. Tailoring one's style of interaction to the characteristics, interests, and needs of each child will provide the context in which a relationship supportive of development can evolve. A child who is characteristically cautious, for example, may be best suited to a style of interaction that provides time for adapting and developing a level of comfort before engaging in interaction or activity. Such a child may enter the classroom each day standing in the doorway, cautiously observing the activity in the classroom. To match the child's style, the teacher could calmly approach the child and quietly greet him. Quiet conversation with the child might ensue, and the child could explore the arrival activities when he is ready. Pressuring the child to enter the classroom and participate may cause this child to experience discomfort and thus withdraw, as the child may feel psychologically threatened. Careful observations of children during arrival time, as they interact with peers and adults, and as they participate in classroom activities and routines, provide useful information to help teachers tailor their interactions to be respectful of children's individual behavioral styles.

As a child encounters new experiences or changes, the teacher should observe the child's responses and determine the extent to which the experiences cause stress. These observations allow the teacher to determine the level and forms of support the child may require to feel secure. A change in schedule, for instance, may be a source of stress for some children, as the element of predictability has been removed. Such a child may exhibit signs of distress, withdraw, or even display aggression. The trusted teacher can offer support as the child tries to adapt to the change, possibly by remaining near and providing a simple, age-appropriate explanation of the change. Helping the child reestablish a sense of predictability by describing what will happen next also may be stabilizing. Furthermore, with this knowledge about the child in mind, the teacher can now plan for supports that may benefit this child in coping with future changes and unfamiliar experiences. Acknowledging the child's feelings, making advance preparation for change, encountering a new experience alongside the child, or modeling means for adapting to or approaching a new experience are effective strategies for bolstering children's emotional health. Anticipating children's needs and being responsive to those needs demonstrates that the child is valued, promotes a sense of psychological safety, and ultimately fosters children's emotional competence and well-being.

Teacher as Coach and Role Model

Much of emotional competence promotion is something that cannot be planned for; opportunities simply present themselves throughout the day (Hemmeter & Ostrosky, 2006). During daily routines and activities, one of the teacher's important roles is to carefully observe and reflect upon children's specific behaviors and responses. These observations help the teacher create an emotional profile of the child and serve to guide the practitioner in coaching children's behavior and responses, applying supportive strategies, and role-modeling.

When a child faces an upsetting or perplexing situation (e.g., a block structure that keeps falling) and gets angry (e.g., by kicking the blocks), the teacher has the opportunity to coach the child in problem-solving skills. By helping the child identify the problem, guiding the child in generating possible solutions, and co-playing with the child in trying out the new idea, a teacher serves as both a coach and a role model of appropriate behavior and emotional expression and regulation.

Promoting Emotional Competence

Teacher As Relationship Builder
Observe children's abilities to regulate emotional responses
Establish nurturing, individualized relationships with children
Respond in ways that demonstrate the child is valued
Tailor interactions to the characteristics and needs of each child

Teacher As Coach and Role Model
Coach children in problem solving during activities and peer interactions
Help children verbalize their frustrations and use language in solving problems

Coach children in recognizing and naming their feelings
Model appropriate expression of emotions

Teacher As Creator of Healthy Environments
Establish a "good fit" between children's needs and characteristics and the expectations of the learning
   environment
Provide appropriate choices and challenges
Create soft spaces to serve as a retreat from stress
Establish predictable routines
Organize an environment that encourages autonomy and responsibility
Provide blocks of time for free play
Build understanding of emotions through intentional teaching
Establish a climate of respect
Believe that each child can succeed

Other developmental challenges might present themselves throughout the day. Challenges can be small, like a stuck zipper that frustrates a child trying to fix it. In this situation, the teacher can work with the child to fix the zipper. At the end of the episode, the two can celebrate overcoming the challenge.

The challenge could be more complex, such as two children wanting to use the same item at the water table. A lack of communication skills often creates challenges for young children when they are in social encounters with peers. Children struggle to find the words to communicate their ideas and feelings in ways that are clearly understood.

Working through potential negative social situations requires expression of emotions in an acceptable manner. When children get into conflict, the helpful teacher assists them in becoming constructive problem solvers (Hyson, 2004). Ahn (2005a) states that teachers need to verbally guide children to express their feelings clearly and constructively. When the child approaches a peer, such statements as "use your words" are of limited value. Often, it is clear that children do not know what words to use. Coaching is necessary so that children will have confidence to use language to solve problems, and appropriately assert their rights. Children then will begin to realize that conflicts can be resolved verbally, rather than through aggression.

Teacher as Creator of Healthy Environments

The creation of emotionally healthy, nurturing classrooms requires careful organization of the physical environment, predictable routines, appropriate play activities, and a positive emotional climate (Hemmeter & Ostrosky, 2006). Thomas and Chess (1977) suggest that to support emotional competence, environmental expectations and demands should reflect the unique nature of the children in the classroom and establish a "good fit" with each child. The characteristics and behavioral style of each child must be respected and should be considered in planning both the physical and social environment within the classroom (Keogh, 2003). Attention to creating a "match" between the child's style and the environment ensures that children can interact with the environment in a positive and growth-promoting manner. For example, the choices that are available to the children affect the development of emotional regulation. By providing choices that match the needs of the children within the group, the teacher supports their emotional regulation. Environments that are either too stimulating or not stimulating enough can provide too much stress for a child. The child may respond to excessive stress by withdrawing, or, on the opposite end of the spectrum, by displaying aggression. In such a scenario, the mismatch between the child and the environment creates an obstacle to healthy peer interaction and learning-focused exploration.

In addition to appropriate choices, comfortable and soft spaces within classrooms also support children's emotional health. Such a place serves as a safe zone or a quiet area to which children can retreat from stress. This space is not to be associated with punishment, but rather should be considered a place to go when children seek some privacy, quiet, and comfort. It might be a quiet spot away from classroom traffic, furnished with pillows, a rug, and other soft surfaces.

Children often require a teacher's help to recognize when they need to go to this quiet place. Acknowledging and reflecting to the child a sense of what the child is experiencing and feeling bolsters knowledge about emotions and emotional expression. With practice, children learn to tune into their inner self-control and thus regain internal equilibrium and balance. The sensitive teacher remains nearby to observe and guide the process of emotional regulation as needed. When appropriate, the children return to the group and explore constructively once again.

Effective teachers establish routines throughout the classroom day (LaParo, Pianta, & Stuhlman, 2004). During carefully planned routines, and through organization of a child-centered environment, children learn what to expect, as well as what is expected of them. The predictability that results is psychologically stabilizing and preventive of difficult behavior (Hemmeter & Ostrosky, 2006). For example, a child learns through practice as he enters the classroom that he needs to store his belongings in his personalized cubby. If select activities have been organized in advance, the child comes to know that after he finishes hanging his coat, he may choose an available activity until the time for clean-up is signaled. Through thoughtfully constructed routines, children build a sense of responsibility and participate autonomously and positively in the classroom community.

The nature of the curriculum also has a significant impact on children's emotional competence. Children should have ample time for free play in which to experiment with appropriate releases of frustration and stress. During these times, children participate in activities that support emotional regulation and understanding. Lindsey and Colwell (2003) found that high levels of pretend play were associated with high emotional understanding in girls and boys, and with high emotional regulation and emotional competence in girls. Physical play was associated with boys' emotional competence with peers.

Classrooms that support healthy emotional development are characterized by a positive emotional climate and genuine respect for children's developmental characteristics, interests, and needs. Teachers hold developmentally appropriate expectations that guide the organization of the environment, the curriculum, and interactions with children. Effective teachers believe that children can succeed, provide opportunities for children to experience success, and recognize both their efforts and successes. In caring, child-centered classrooms such as these, children gain a sense of belonging, and learn about emotions. Teachers influence children's knowledge of emotion by discussing emotions during everyday interactions (Blair, Denham, Kochanoff, & Whipple, 2004). Building understanding of emotion-related words occurs through intentionally teaching children to label both negative and positive emotions, as well as understand the causes of emotion. Books are useful tools as teachers strive to help children identify emotion-related words, understand the causes of emotion, and manage emotions positively (Ahn, 2005b).

Conclusion

Early emotional competence—encompassing emotional regulation, expression, and knowledge—is strongly linked to children's mental health, influences children's social interactions and relationships, and affects school success. Teachers have critical roles in promoting emotional competence through forming nurturing and specific relationships with individual children, coaching children's emotional responses during social interactions and during activities and routines, modeling healthy emotional expression, building an understanding of emotions, and creating environments in which children feel valued and can thrive. Careful observation of children in classroom contexts allows educators to analyze current levels of emotional competence and plan for promotion of mental health. Such efforts are key to ensuring that children have the skills necessary to function effectively in a range of social and school contexts.

References

Ahn, H. (2005a). Child care teachers' strategies in children's socialization of emotion. *Early Childhood Development and Care, 175,* 49–61.

Ahn, H. (2005b). Teachers' discussions of emotion in child care centers. *Early Childhood Education Journal, 32,* 237–242.

Ashiabi, G. (2000). Promoting the emotional development of preschoolers. *Early Childhood Education journal, 28,* 79–84.

Bagdi, A., & Vacca, J. (2005). Supporting early childhood social-emotional well being: The building blocks for early learning and school success. *Early Childhood Education Journal, 33,* 145–150.

Blair, K. A., Denham, S. A., Kochanoff, A., & Whipple, B. (2004). Playing it cool: Temperament, emotional regulation, and social behavior in preschoolers. *Journal of School Psychology, 42,* 419–443.

Bracken, St. S., & Fischel, J. E. (2007). Relationships between social skills, behavioral problems, and school readiness for Head Start children. *NHSA Dialog, 10,* 109–126.

Coplan, R. J., & Prakash, K. (2003). Spending time with teacher: Characteristics of preschoolers who frequently elicit versus initiate interactions with teachers. *Early Childhood Research Quarterly, 18,* 143–158.

Denham, S. A. (2001). Dealing with feelings: Foundations and consequences of young children's emotional competence. *Early Education and Development, 12,* 5–10.

Denham, S. A. (2006). Social-emotional competence as support for school readiness: What is it and how do we assess it? *Early Education and Development, 17,* 57–89.

Denham, S. A., Blair, K. A., DeMulder, E., Levitas, J., Sawyer, K., Auerbach-Major, S., & Queenan, P. (2003). Preschool emotional competence: Pathway to social competence? *Child Development. 74,* 238–256.

Hemmeter, M. L., & Ostrosky, M. (2006). Social and emotional foundations for early learning: A conceptual model for intervention. *School Psychology Review, 35,* 583–601.

Howes, C, Hamilton, C.E., & Matheson, C.C. (1994). Children's relationships with peers: Differential associations with aspects of the teacher-child relationship. *Child Development, 65,* 253–263.

Hyson, M. (2002). Emotional development and school readiness. *Young Children, 57,* 76–78.

Hyson, M. (2004). *The emotional development of young children.* New York: Teachers College Press.

Keogh, B. K. (2003). *Temperament in the classroom.* Baltimore: Brookes Publishing.

Knitzer, J., & Lefkowitz, J. (2005). *Resources to promote social and emotional health and school readiness in young children and families.* New York: National Center for Children in Poverty.

LaParo, K., Pianta, R., & Stuhlman, M. (2004). The classroom assessment scoring system: Findings from the prekindergarten year. *The Elementary School Journal, 104,* 409–426.

Lindsey, E., & Colwell, M. (2003). Preschoolers' emotional competence: Links to pretend and physical play. *Child Study Journal, 33,* 39–52.

National Association for the Education of Young Children. (2004). *Where we stand on school readiness.* Washington, DC: Author.

Peth-Pierce, R. (2001). *A good beginning: Sending America's children to school with the social and emotional competence they need to succeed.* Chapel Hill, NC: University of North Carolina.

Raver, C. C., & Knitzer, J. (2002). *Ready to enter: What research tells policymakers about strategies to promote social and emotional school readiness among three- and four-year-olds.* New York: National Center for Children in Poverty.

Shonkoff, J. P., & Phillips, D. (Eds.). (2001). *From neurons to neighborhoods: The science of early child development.* Washington, DC: National Academy Press.

Thomas, A., & Chess, S. (1977). *Temperament and development.* New York: Brunner/Mazel.

Discussion Questions

1. When you think of your own school experiences, do you think any of your teachers helped foster your emotional competence? If yes, how? Provide examples.
2. Teachers today are often overworked and underappreciated. Do you think that it should be part of the teacher's responsibility to support the development of emotional competence in children?
3. How could we test this article's assertion that if teachers promote emotional competence in their classrooms, it will have larger impact on emotional competence in children vs. classrooms that don't use these methods?

Assignment

Pretend you are a preschool or early elementary teacher and use the article's suggestions to come up with a classroom environment that supports emotional competence. Give five specific examples of situations that might arise during your class and how you would act to promote the student's emotional competence.

Come out and Play

Shyness in Childhood and the Benefits of Organized
Sports Participation

By Leanne C. Findlay and Robert J. Coplan

Positive peer relations in childhood are consistently associated with positive social and psychological adjustment (Rubin, Bukowski, & Parker, 2006). Although the literature on children's peer relations is quite extensive, much of the research has focused on peer interactions and relationships in the school context. However, this focus "provides a narrow view of childhood social relations, and reflects neither the breadth nor the dynamic nature of children's peer interactions" (Hymel, Vaillencourt, McDougall, & Renshaw, 2002, p. 273). Other social milieus, such as the sport context, provide opportunities for peer interaction and also provide an environment that fosters social support, security, and self-esteem. Sport is clearly tied to developing peer relations because children who have increased opportunities for social interaction are expected to be more socially skilled and have higher functioning.

Sport has previously been associated with such positive benefits as improved peer relations, increased self-esteem, and decreased anxiety (Kirkcaldy, Shephard, & Siefen, 2002; Marsh, 1998; Smith, 2003). However, relatively little is known about the potentially unique influence of sport participation for different "types" of children, such as shy children. It was the objective of this research to investigate the interplay between sport and social behaviour in the prediction of adjustment outcomes. In particular, we explored the role of sport as a potential protective factor in the socioemotional adjustment of shy children by examining sports participation as a moderator (see Baron & Kenny, 1986) between shyness and psychosocial outcomes.

Benefits of Sport Participation

Fostering and developing relationships with peers are key reasons cited by children for participating in sports; however, the impact of sport peer relations on child adjustment is highly understudied (Ebbeck & Weiss, 1998; Smith, 2003). Although there is little empirical literature addressing children's social behaviour characteristics (e.g., shyness) and sport, there is evidence to suggest that sport has a positive effect on children's social well-being overall, with respect to both peer relations (Smith, 1999) and psychological functioning (Kirkcaldy et al., 2002; Marsh, 1998). Sport involvement has been associated with increased social status, particularly for boys (Chase & Dummer, 1992), and children's perceived as well as actual physical competence (Weiss & Duncan, 1992). Furthermore, Page, Frey, Talbert, and Falk (1992) found that children aged 6 to 11 years with higher physical activity scores reported lower scores on loneliness. They suggested that children who withdraw from their peer group are less likely to participate in social activities, including sport.

Aggressive behaviour has been suggested to be a potentially negative social consequence of sport involvement. Gender is particularly relevant; boys not only participate in a greater number of contact sports, but have also been shown to be more adversely affected by participation (Bredemeier, 1988). More recent research suggests that aggressiveness is not necessarily related to sports involvement, even if that involvement is in contact team sports. McHale, Vinden, Bush, Richer, Shaw, and Smith (2005) found that middle-school-age children who had engaged in sport over the previous year were not more likely to be rated as aggressive by their physical education teachers. However, a sport-by-gender interaction revealed that sport-involved girls were more likely to be rated to be aggressive than were non-sport-involved girls, and sport-involved boys were rated to be less aggressive.

Sports participation has also been studied in terms of the potential effects on self-esteem and anxiety. Marsh and colleagues (Marsh, 1998; Marsh, Perry, Horsely, & Roche, 1995) have repeatedly demonstrated that adolescent and adult athletes have higher self-esteem than do nonathletes. Marsh et al. (1995) found that elite athletes had significantly higher physical ability self-esteem, social self-esteem, and global self-esteem. Finally, Kirkcaldy and colleagues (2002) found that German adolescents who frequently participated in endurance sports displayed significantly lower anxiety than did adolescents who never participated or seldom participated. To date, however, there is no literature to address the impact of sport on younger children's social anxiety in particular whether or not sport can have differential effects based on personal characteristics. It was therefore of particular interest to examine the benefits of sport participation for particular "sub-groups" of middle-school-age children, namely those with peer relations difficulties.

Shyness in Childhood

Shyness is often conceptualized as social accompanied by behavioural responses, such as inhibition and withdrawal, in response to social and novel situations (Henderson & Zimbardo, 2001). Asendorpf (1990) characterised shy children as being trapped in an approach-avoidance conflict; they are motivated to play with others (i.e., have a desire to approach) but are apprehensive or wary due to anxiety. Hence, many shy children may have limited social experience. It is this latter point that leads to the investigation of participation in sport, a venue for social interaction, as a protective factor for shy children.

Shyness has been associated with peer relation difficulties, including peer rejection (Coplan, Arbeau, & Armer, in press; Fordham & Stevenson-Hinde, 1999) and internalizing difficulties such as anxiety and loneliness (Coplan, Closson, & Arbeau, 2007; Crozier, 1995; Eisenberg, Shepard, Fabes, Murphy, & Guthrie, 1998). Hymel, Woody, and Bowker (1993) found that children in Grades 4 to 6 who were identified as withdrawn by their peers had more negative overall self-esteem, lower athletic competence, and reported greater dissatisfaction within the peer group. The research therefore suggests that shy children have lower self-perceptions, especially in the area of peer relations and athletic competence.

Links between shyness and sport. Very little research is available on the social outcomes of sport participation in terms of children's individual characteristics. It might be expected that children would respond to the sport environment differently based on their social preferences and/or characteristics. In terms of rates of participation, Page and Zarco (2001) reported that shy adolescent boys and girls participated in fewer vigorous activities than did average or low-shy children, in particular team sports. They argued that shy individuals may have less self-confidence and avoid participating in sport out of fear. McHale and colleagues (2005) also found that middle-school-age children who participated in sport were reported by their physical activity teacher to be less shy-withdrawn and to have higher social competence than their nonparticipating peers. These results were maintained even after controlling for teacher perceptions of athletic ability.

Other research has pointed to a link between sport anxiety and social anxiety. In a sample of Hispanic fifth and sixth graders. Storch, Bartlas, Dent, and Masia (2002) found that social anxiety was significantly related to sport anxiety and that girls experienced greater sport anxiety than did boys. Anxiety in sport could be linked to decreased participation, which would result in fewer social opportunities. Storch and colleagues suggested that sport anxiety be further investigated as one manifestation of more general social anxiety and that psychosocial interventions to address social anxiety should include sport as a domain of treatment.

The Current Study

The goal of the current study was to examine the protective role of sport participation in the psychosocial outcomes of shy children. To address this goal, a short-term longitudinal study was undertaken, tracking children's sport participation, social behaviour (shy and aggressive tendencies) and socioemotional adjustment over a 1-year period. Previous research in this area has relied primarily on cross-sectional data (e.g., Ebbeck & Weiss, 1998). It was hypothesized that sport participation would have unique benefits for shy children in terms of their peer relationships, socioemotional functioning, and general well-being. That is, shy children who participate in sport were expected to report higher psychosocial functioning than did shy children who did not participate in sport. It is also possible that the positive outcomes associated with sport participation might be beneficial to children with peer relations difficulties in general (and not shy children in particular). In order to investigate this possibility, a group of physically aggressive children were also included.

Method

Participants

The participants in this study were 355 children in Grades 4 and 5 (181 boys, 174 girls), recruited from public elementary schools in and around Ottawa, Canada. At the beginning of the study (Time 1), children ranged from 8.9 to 11.8 years of age (M_{age} = 10.1 years, SD = 0.6). At Time 2 (approximately 1 year later). 96 boys and 105 girls (n = 201) remained in the study, which represented a retention rate of approximately 56% from Time 1 to Time 2. No significant Time 1 differences were found between children who did/did not participate in the study at Time 2 on measures of shyness, aggression, sports participation, or parental education.

Measures

Social skills. Parents completed the *Social Skills Rating Scale* (SSRS; Gresham & Elliot, 1990), which has previously been shown to have adequate internal consistency (α's ranging from .65 to .87), good test-retest reliability, and good criterion validity. Of particular interest for the present study were the externalizing problem behaviours subscale (6 items, Time 1 α = .79, Time 2 α = .81) and the four social skills subscales (10 items each): cooperation (Time 1 α = .80, Time 2 α =.79, assertion (Time 1 α = .66, Time 2 α = .75), responsibility (Time 1 α = .51, Time 2 α = .71) and self-control (Time 1 α = .83, Time 2 α = .84).

Shyness. Crozier's (1995) 27-item *Children's Shyness Questionnaire* (CSQ) was administered to the children to assess shyness in middle childhood. As suggested by Crozier (1995), one item ("I enjoy singing aloud when others can hear me") was eliminated. Previous research has found the measure to have god reliability (α = .82, Crozier, 1995). Scores were summed to create a value for total shyness, and internal consistency was found to be adequate (α = .77 at Time 1, α = .80 at Time 2).

Aggression. Children's physical aggression was measured with a self-report scale based on the *Conflict Tactics Scale* (CTS; Strauss, 1979) and modified for the current research to reflect physically aggressive behaviour engaged in by the child over the last six months. The CTS has previously been shown to have adequate reliability (α's ranging from .56 to .82) and shows construct validity with similar scales of aggression. In the modified version used for the current study, children were asked to respond along a 5-point Likert scale (1 = *never*, 5 = *always*) with reference to 9 behaviours. Items were summed to create a mean score for physically aggressive behaviour (ranging from 9 to 45). Internal consistency in the current study was found to be good (Time 1 α = .83, Time 2 α = .86).

Sport participation. Information on children's sport participation was collected using the *Sport Participation Information Sheet* (Bowker, Gadbios, & Cornock, 2003). At time 1, children were asked to list all of the sport that they had ever participated in, including information on the number of years they had participated and the level of participation ("*just for fun*", "*at school*", "*recreationally*" or "*competitively*"). At Time 2, children were only asked to indicate the sports that they had participated in over the past year, the purpose being to report any additional sport participation. Total years in sports were then summed to create a summary score of children's participation. For instance, if the child had participated in organised soccer for 3 years and hockey for 2 years, his or her total sports score was 5. In this way, sports were represented along a continuum with more sports representing a greater number of sport (i.e., peer) experiences. As a further step, coding allowed for the creation of groups of nonparticipants (list no sports or sports just for fun) versus participants (participated in some organised sport at the recreational or competitive level).

General well-being. Children were asked to complete a 10-item well-being questionnaire designed by Allison and Furstenberg (1989; see also Coplan, Wilson, Frohilick, & Zelenski, 2006). Children rated their social dissatisfaction and distress; items were summed to create an overall well-being score (Time 1 α = .76; Time 2 α = .79).

Self-system. Based on the Shavelson, Hubner, and Stanton (1976) hierarchical model of the self-system, the *Self-Description Questionnaire* (SDQ) is one of the most commonly employed measures of the self (e.g., Hymel, Bowker, & Woody, 1993; Marsh, 1984). Children were asked to respond along a 5-point scale (1 = *false* to 5 = *true*). Four subscales were of interest for the current study, including those pertaining to physical ability (α = .83 and .84 at Times 1 and 2, respectively), physical appearance (α = .89 and (α = .91), peer relationships (α = .86 and (α = .88), and general self ((α = .78 and (α = .84).

Social anxiety. Children's social anxiety was measured using the Social Anxiety *Scale for Children Revised* (SASC-R; La Greca and Stone, 1993). The measure consists of 22 items and reflects three subscales: fear of negative evaluation (FNE; 8 items, e.g., "I worry about what other kids think of me"), social avoidance and distress a new situations (SAD-New; 6 items, e.g., "I get nervous when I meet new kids"), and social avoidance and distress in general (SAD-General; 4 items, e.g., "I feel shy even with kids I know well"). Each item was rated in terms of how much the items was "true of you" on a 5-point Likert-type scale (1 = *not at all*, 5 = *all the time*). Social anxiety was summed across the three subscales, and internal consistency was found to be good (Time 1 α = .90, Time 2 α = .91).

Loneliness. Asher, Hymel, and Renshaw's (1984) *Loneliness and Social Dissatisfaction* measure was employed to assess children's loneliness and social dissatisfaction. The measure consists of 16 items (plus 8 filler items), and children respond on a 5-point scale indicating how much each statement is true. Items were summed to create a total loneliness and social dissatisfaction score ranging from 16 to 80. All 16 items have been found to load onto one principal factor (Asher et al., 1984). In the current study, internal consistency was adequate (α = .74 at Time 1, α = .73 at Time 2).

Positive and negative affect. Finally, children's affect was measured using the *Positive and Negative Affect Schedule for Children* (PANAS-C). The PANAS-C, designed for use with preadolescent children, is the child version of the PANAS (Watson, Clark, & Tellegen, 1988), a common tool used to assess adult symptoms of poor adjustment, such as anxiety and depression. Characteristics of positive affect include interest, engagement, and energy, whereas negative affect reflects moods such as fear, sadness, and guilt (Laurent et al., 1999).

The PANAS-C consists of 30 items, half representing each of the two factors (positive and negative affect). Children were asked to retrospectively indicate the extent that they had felt certain feelings or emotions over a 2-week period on a scale of 1 to 5 (1 = *very slightly*, 5 = *extremely*). Items were summed for each subscale (Positive Affect: Time 1 α = .83, Time 2: α = .83; Negative Affect: Time 1 α = .88; Time 2 α = .90).

Procedure

Upon obtaining University Ethics, School Board, and individual school approval, parental consent was obtained via permission letters sent home through the child's classroom teacher. Children were given the opportunity to deny participation if they so desired. Parent-provided demographic information (child age, gender, parental education) was collected at Time 1 only. Information regarding parental income could not be collected; therefore, parental education was used as a proxy for socioeconomic status. Written parental consent and all other measures were collected at both Time 1 and Time 2. For those children with positive consent, group testing was employed. Task instructions were read aloud by the researcher and children independently read and responded to the questionnaires unless assistance was requested.

Results

Preliminary Analyses

An aggregate index of parental education was calculated by summing maternal and paternal education scores. Parental education was not significantly correlated with sport participation. However, parental education was significantly correlated with many of the dependent variables, as well as shyness ($r = -.15, p < .01$). Thus, parental education was included as a covariate in subsequent analyses.

To explore gender differences in shyness and aggression over time, a 2 × 2 Repeated Measures MANOVA was conducted for shyness and aggression with Time as a within-subjects variable and Gender as a between-subjects variable. Results indicated a significant main effect of Gender, $F(2, 197) = 15.79, p < .001$, and of Time, $F(2, 197) = 4.85, p < .01$. Follow-up univariate analyses revealed a significant effect of Gender for both shyness. $F(1, 198) = 20.57, p < .001$, and aggression, $F(1, 198) = 11.48, p < .001$. An examination of means indicated that boys reported being less shy ($M = 15.60, SD = 7.82$) and more aggressive ($M = 14.38, SD = 5.47$) than girls ($M_{shy} = 19.85, SD = 8.13, M_{agg} = 11.80, SD = 4.02$). Univariate analyses also revealed a significant effect of Time for shyness, $F(1, 198) = 9.71, p < .01$, with shyness decreasing from Time 1 ($M = 17.38, SD = 8.24$) to Time 2 ($M = 15.83, SD = 8.28$). Finally, shyness ($r = .68, p < .001$) and aggression ($r = .60, p < .001$) were relatively stable from Time 1 to Time 2. Shyness and aggression were not significantly correlated at either Time 1 or Time 2.

Shy and aggressive groups. Following pervious research (Hymel et al., 1993; Page & Zarco, 2001), a categorical approach to the assessment of shyness and aggression was taken by creating extreme groups of shy and aggressive children. Given the gender differences found for both shyness and aggression and following the procedures of Rubin, Chen, & Hymel (1993) and Prakash and Coplan (2007), percentile scores were calculated within gender. An 85th percentile was selected to indicate extreme groups of children (see Kagan, 1989). Children who reported shyness scores in the top 15% within gender and below the mean on aggression were classified as shy ($n = 48$ at Time 1); children who scored in the top 15% within gender on aggression and below the mean for shyness were classified as aggressive ($n = 48$). Finally, children who scored below the mean on both shyness and aggression comprised the comparison group ($n = 110$). One hundred and fifty-five children were therefore excluded from the analyses at Time 1.

Sport participation. Children had previously participated in M = 2.45 (SD = 2.87, range = 0 to 15) sports at Time 1, and an additional $M = 1.00$ ($SD = 1.03$) sports at Time 2. Overall, boys ($M = 3.97, SD = 3.35$) had participated in significantly more sports than had girls ($M = 3.08, SD = 3.15$), $t(193) = 1.51, p = .05$. Result from partial correlations (controlling for parental education) indicated that participation in organised sport at Time 1 was significantly and negatively associated with shyness ($r = -.22, p < .001$) but not aggression ($r = .02, ns$).

Sport participation, Shyness, Aggression, and Outcomes at Time 1

Overview. The first set of analyses concerned Time 1 data only. Following this, a repeated measures design was employed to investigate the longitudinal effects of sport participation over a 1-year period. Outcomes related to sport, shyness, and aggression were assessed with a series of Multivariate and Univariate Analyses of Covariance. Dependent variables were grouped conceptually for multivariate analyses and their associations were checked empirically using factor analyses. Each grouping loaded onto a single principle factor with loadings above .60 (ranging from .69 to .86). Parental education and gender were included as covariates for all analyses. The main effects of Sport Participation (no organised sport, some organised sport) and Behaviour Group (shy, aggressive, comparison) were examined, as well as interaction effects. Although power is limited by the relatively small sample size of the extreme groups, three-way interactions were interpreted with some caution given that they were of particular theoretical interest in the current study. Only significant results are presented (accepted at the $p < .05$ level) and effect sizes are reported for significant univariate results. Trends at the $p \leq .07$ level are also noted due to the small sample size of the groups.

Social skills. Significant multivariate effects were found for Behaviour, $F(8, 356) = 3.79, p < .001$, and Sport, $F(4, 178) = 5.82, p < .001$. Univariate analyses for Sport revealed a significant main effect for assertion, $F(1, 181) = 12.18, p < .001, \eta = .06$, and for self-control, $F(1, 181) = 7.38, p < .01, \eta = .04$. An examination of means indicated that children who had participated in organised sport were reported to be more assertive and had more self-control than did children who had not participated in sport (see Table 1 for a comparison of means).

In terms of the main effect of Behaviour group, follow up univariate tests revealed a significant effect for assertion, $F(1, 181) = 5.46, p < .05, \eta = .03$; self-control, $F(1, 181) = 5.58, p < .01, \eta = .06$; and cooperation, $F(1, 181) = 4.51, p < .05, \eta = .04$. As shown in Table 2, results from Tukey's post hoc testing indicated that aggressive children were reported to display less cooperation and self-control than were comparison children (whereas shy children did not differ from either group). Shy children were reported to be significantly less assertive than were aggressive or comparison children (who did not differ).

Table 1. Mean (SD) outcomes for sport and non-sport participants

	Sports M (SD)	No sports M (SD)
Social skills		
Assertion	16.20[a] (2.34)	14.80[b] (2.72)
Self-control	14.13[a] (3.60)	12.23[b] (3.63)
Cooperation	12.88 (3.41)	12.13 (3.45)
Responsibility	13.44 (2.86)	13.25 (2.28)
Self-esteem		
Physical ability	38.25[a] (5.39)	32.86[b] (8.17)
Physical appearance	32.39[a] (8.41)	29.30[b] (8.46)
Peer	34.31[a] (7.06)	29.75[b] (9.05)
Internalizing		
Anxiety	43.21 (15.60)	49.01 (18.52)
Loneliness	29.88 (10.34)	34.83 (13.25)
Negative affect	28.24 (10.05)	31.03 (11.70)
Positive adjustment		
Well-being	43.43[a](5.60)	40.77[b] (6.43)
Positive affect	56.75[a] (9.07)	50.49[b] (11.30)
Externalizing behaviours	2.62[a] (2.20)	4.02[b] (2.68)

Note: Differences in subscripts indicate a significant difference at $p < .05$ level.

Table 2. Mean (SD) outcomes for shy, aggressive, and comparison children

	Shy M (SD)	Aggressive M (SD)	Comparison M(SD)
Social skills			
Assertion	14.39[a] (2.96)	16.10[b] (2.06)	15.95[b] (2.47)
Self-control	12.63[ab] (4.02)	11.78[a] (3.12)	14.23[b] (3.57)
Cooperation	11.96[ab] (3.87)	11.30[a] (3.13)	13.27[b] (3.21)
Responsibility	13.30 (2.52)	12.94 (2.85)	13.54 (2.58)
Self-esteem			
Physical ability	33.47[a] (7.44)	35.34[at] (6.38)	37.30[b] (7.14)
Physical appearance	28.35[a] (8.28)	29.82[at] (9.85)	32.74[b] (7.79)
Peer	28.33[a] (8.09)	30.91[a] (8.48)	34.69[b] (7.47)
Internalizing			
Anxiety	62.67[a] (14.16)	44.95[b] (13.61)	38.63c (14.19)
Loneliness	40.22[a] (10.46)	34.57[b] (11.15)	27.43c (10.52)
Negative affect	33.54[a] (10.22)	33.52[a] (9.95)	26.08[b] (10.34)
Positive adjustment			
Well-being	39.36[a](6.87)	40.31[b] (6.53)	44.33[b] (4.81)
Positive affect	48.91[a] (9.43)	53.55[b] (12.35)	56.56[b] (9.38)
Externalizing behaviours	3.65[a] (2.39)	4.29[b] (2.45)	2.68[a] (2.47)

Note: Differences in subscripts indicate a significant difference at $p < .05$ level ($\dagger p < .07$).

Self-esteem. Turning to self-esteem outcomes, significant multivariate effects were found for Sport, $F(4, 178) = 7.30, p < .001$, and Behaviour, $F(8, 356) = 3.35, p < .001$. In addition, a significant multivariate interaction was seen between Behaviour and Sport, $F(8, 356) = 2.01, p < .05$. To examine the highest order effect (i.e., the interaction between Behaviour and Sport), results were examined at the univariate level; only general self-esteem demonstrated a significant interaction effect, $F(1, 181) = 9.76, p < .01, \eta = .05$. To examine the interaction for general self-esteem further, analyses were performed for each Behaviour group (shy, aggressive, comparison) separately, collapsed across gender. For shy children, a univariate effect of Sport was found for general self-esteem, $F(2, 43) = 5.96, p < .02, \eta = .12$. For aggressive children, a significant trend was also shown, $F(2, 43) = 3.57, p < .07, \eta = .09$; however, a significant effect of Sport for general self-esteem was not found for comparison children, $F(2,43) = 1.52, ns$. As shown in Figure 1, shy and aggressive children who had participated in sport had higher general self-esteem than children who had not participated in sport. For comparison children, the effect of sport on self-esteem was not significant.

Given the nonsignificant Behaviour by Sport interactions for physical ability, physical appearance, and peer self-esteem, main effects of Behaviour and Sport were examined. All three types of self-esteem displayed a significant effect of Sport: physical ability, $F(1, 181) = 25.46, p < .001, \eta = .12$; physical appearance, $F(1, 181) = 5.86, p < .05, \eta = .03$; and peer self-esteem, $F(1, 181) = 7.36, p < .01, \eta = .04$. An examine of means revealed that children who participated in sport had higher physical ability self-esteem, physical appearance self-esteem, and peer self-esteem than did children who had not participated in organised sport (see Table 1).

Turning to the main effect of Behaviour on self-esteem, again all three remaining types of self-esteem displayed significant effects of Behaviour: physical ability, $F(2, 181) = 4.90, p < .01, \eta = .05$; physical appearance, $F(2, 181) = 3.80, p < .05, \eta = .04$; and peer self-esteem, $F(2, 181) = 8.55, p < .001, \eta = .09$. As shown in

Table 2, shy and aggressive children reported significantly lower physical ability, physical appearance, and peer self-esteem than did comparison children (with no differences between shy and aggressive children).

Internalizing problems. For Internalizing Problems, Significant Multivariate Effects Were found for Behaviour only, $F(6, 358) = 16.30$, $p < .001$. Univariate analyses indicated significant effects for social anxiety $F(2, 181) = 45.20$, $p < .001$, $\eta = .33$; loneliness, $F(2, 181) = 20.42$, $p < .001$, $\eta = .18$; and negative affect, $F(2, 181) = 9.86$, $p < .001$, $\eta = .10$. As shown in Table 2, shy children were significantly more anxious and lonely than were aggressive

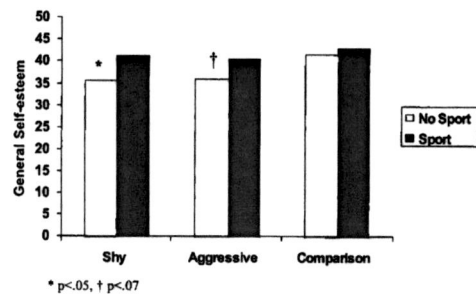

Figure 1. General self-esteem for shy, aggressive, and comparison sport and nonsport participants.

children, who were in turn more anxious and lonely than comparison children. Finally, shy and aggressive children reported greater negative affect than did comparison children.

Positive adjustment. The final MANCOVA for positive adjustment revealed significant effects for Sport, $F(2, 180) = 6.71$, $p < .01$, and for Behaviour, $F(4, 180) = 7.65$, $p < .001$. For the multivariate main effect of Sport, univariate analyses indicated a significant effect for both positive affect, $F(1, 181) = 12.69$, $p < .001$, $\eta = .07$, and well-being. $F(1, 181) = 6.92$, $p < .01$, $\eta = .04$. As shown in Table 1, children who had participated in organised sport experienced greater positive affect and well-being than did children who had not participated in sport.

In addition, the main effect of Behaviour was further examined for both well-being and positive affect. A significant main effect of Behaviour was found for positive affect $F(1, 181) = 7.76$, $p < .001$, $\eta = .08$, and well-being, $F(2, 181) = 13.73$, $p < .001$, $\eta = .13$. Follow-up Tukey's tests revealed that shy children had significantly lower positive affect than did aggressive or comparison children (with no differences between aggressive and comparison children). Shy and aggressive children were found to have significantly lower well-being than comparison children (see Table 2).

Externalizing problem behaviours. The final analysis at Time 1 was a 3 × 2 ANCOVA, with Behaviour (shy, aggressive, comparison) and Sport (none, some) as independent variables and externalizing problems as the dependent variable. A significant effect was found for both Sport, $F(1, 181) = 12.98$, $p < .001$, $\eta = .07$, and for Behaviour, $F(2, 181) = 5.56$, $p < .01$, $\eta = .06$. A comparison of means indicated that children who had participated in organised sport were reported to have significantly fewer externalizing problems than did nonsport participants (see Table 1). With respect to Behaviour, Turkey's post hoc testing revealed that aggressive children displayed more externalizing behaviour than did comparison or shy children (see Table 2).

Longitudinal Analyses

Overview. The next set of analyses sought to answer whether participation in sport over a 1-year period impacts child outcomes. Four Repeated Measures MANCOVAs and one RM-ANCOVA were conducted to examine the effects on social skills, self-esteem, internalizing problems, positive adjustment, and externalizing problems. Given that the interest of the analyses were only in the specific effects of Sport participation over Time, only significant main effects of Time and interactions that involved both Time and Sport Participation are reported. No significant effects were found for social skills, self-esteem, positive adjustment, or externalizing problem behaviours; therefore, these outcomes are not reported herein. Also to note is that Sport reflects only the organised sports that the child had participated in over the 1-year period

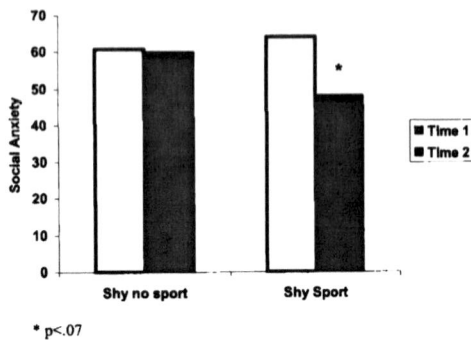

* p<.07

Figure 2. Shy sport and nonsport participants' social anxiety over time.

(none: $n = 52$; some: $n = 143$). In addition, due to attrition sample sizes at Time 2 were reduced (shy children: $n = 25$, aggressive: $n = 24$, comparison: $n = 69$).

Internalizing problems. In examining the internalizing outcomes of social anxiety, loneliness and negative affect, a significant multivariate Time by Behaviour by Sport interaction was revealed, $F(6, 188) = 2.57, p < .05$. In order to interpret the interaction, univariate results were examined. A three-way interaction was found for anxiety, $F(2, 96) = 6.27, p < .01, \eta = .12$; however, loneliness, $F(2, 96) = 1.83, ns$, and negative affect, $F(2, 96) = 1.56, ns$, were not found to be significant. Thus, analyses were conducted separately by Behaviour (collapsed across gender), looking at the effects on social anxiety only. Beginning with shy children, a trend was shown for the Time by Sport interaction, $F(1, 19) = 3.80, p < .07, \eta = .17$. For aggressive, $F(1, 19) < 1, ns$, and comparison, $F(1, 62) = 1.31, ns$, children, no significant univariate interactions for anxiety were shown. As shown in Figure 2, Tukey's post hoc testing revealed that shy children who participated in sport over a 1-year period demonstrated a decrease in anxiety over time.

Discussion

The aim of the current study was to explore the protective role of sport participation in the psychosocial outcomes of shy children. Overall, our results indicated that shyness was negatively associated with sport participation. Sport participation was associated with positive psychosocial outcomes, including higher positive affect and well-being and greater social skills. Shy children were found to have greater internalizing problems, whereas aggressive children displayed more externalizing and internalizing difficulties than comparison peers. It is most interesting to note that shy and aggressive children who participated in sport were found to report higher self-esteem (unlike their nonsport participating peers). In addition, shy children who participated in sport demonstrated a trend whereby social anxiety decreased over time.

Benefits of Sport Participation

Participation in organised sports was related to various positive psychosocial outcomes. For example, children who participated in sport were found to be more assertive and expert more self-control than did children who did not participate in sport and to report more positive affect and well-being than did nonparticipants. Children who had participated in sport were also found to have higher physical ability self-esteem, physical appearance self-esteem, and peer self-esteem than did children who had not participated in organised sport. These findings coincide with previous research linking sport participation with positive self-esteem (Marsh, 1998; Marsh et al., 1995) and well-being (Kirkcaldy et. al., 2002). It can be suggested that sport provides children with opportunities for mastery, which in turn leads to greater well-being. Alternatively, children who participate in sport may have a greater number of peer contacts or peer experiences.

Children who participate in sport may feel more competent and more physically fit (and perhaps attractive) and thus report higher physical ability and physical appearance self-esteem. It is also possible that children who are already higher in self-esteem are more likely to participate in sport. Children may previously possess certain attributes or characteristics that drive them to participate in sport or that may influence their choice of activities rather than sport itself fostering such characteristics (Page & Hammermeister, 1995). Sport may attract certain types of children; sport may also provide an opportunity to demonstrate these attributes. Longer term longitudinal studies would better be able to address the issue of directionality in future research.

Correlated of Shyness

Shy children were found to be more anxious and more lonely than were aggressive or comparison children; reported higher negative affect and less positive affect than did comparison children; and were found to have lower physical appearance, physical ability, and peer self-esteem than did comparison children. Finally, shy children were found to be less assertive than their aggressive or comparison counterparts. This is not surprising given that shy children are by definition wary in social situations and are thus less likely to act in a sociable or outgoing way. These findings are in accordance with previous research suggesting that shy children are more likely to report greater internalizing problems, such as loneliness, anxiety, and lowered self-esteem (Coplan et al., 2007; Eisenberg et al., 1998; Hymel et al., 1993).

Shyness and sport. Given the positive impact of sport for all children, it was particularly of interest to investigate the value of sport for specific subgroups of children based on their social behaviour. Indeed, our findings suggest that sport participation may be particularly advantageous for shy children as a buffer for some of the negative correlates of shyness.

As expected, shyness was negatively associated with participation in sport. Previous research has focused on the relation between sport and shyness in an adolescent or adult population (Page & Hammermeister, 1995; Page & Zarco, 2001). However, the current results support the notion that shy children are less likely to engage in sport in middle childhood.

Two interesting interaction effects were found with respect to sport participation and shyness. Shy children who participated in sport were found to have higher general self-esteem than did shy children who did not participate in sport. By contrast, this effect was not seen for comparison children; that is, whether the comparison child did or did not participate in sport did not appear to impact general self-esteem. This would suggest that by participating in sport, shy children in particular do not report the negative effects on self-esteem typically seen for shy children (Coplan, Findlay, & Nelson, 2004; Eisenberg et al., 1998). Perhaps this benefit to self-esteem is a reflection of the importance of sport participation as a social status determinant for children. That is, shy children who participate in sport may feel valuable or competent in their social network, thus increasing their self-esteem.

Moreover, shy children who participated in sport over a 1-year period demonstrated a significant decrease in social anxiety. That is, shy children had higher social anxiety than did their aggressive and comparison peers, but for those who participated in sport, their anxiety decreased over this one year period to the point that it did not differ from comparison children.

Children who participate in organised sport have greater opportunities for peer interaction, be that only for a couple of hours every week. In the sport context, children have specific experiences: they are given a role within the team or group; they must communicate with other members of the social group;

they learn similar skills/tasks; and they work toward common goals. This experience could provide a social context to practise interacting with their peers and for peer-mediated learning of both physical and social skills. Participation in a sport provides children with a common ground, a context that is shared with a select group of other children. Not only can this provide children with a sense of belonging (that may be particularly relevant for shy children), but it may also give them a subject matter to discuss with peers.

It is also possible that shy children who participate in sport are merely exposed to an additional source of social anxiety to which they become conditioned, thus extinguishing the fear response. Norton, Burns, Hope, and Bauer (2000) found that adults who experience a higher degree of social evaluative fear in general also experience such fear in sport situations. It is possible that children who experience both social and sport-related anxiety develop mechanisms to deal with this anxiety, which translates into decreased anxiety over time.

Finally, sport participation may also provide the shy child with mastery experiences that contribute to self-esteem. Although all children benefit from triumphs, for shy children this may be particularly important considering their high degree of anxiety in social situations. Nonshy children may not need as many experiences to feel good about themselves, whereas shy children are particularly fearful or self-conscious. Thus, shy children benefit from repeated success in various domains in order to buffer the typically negative effect of shyness on self-esteem.

Aggression and Sport

Although aggression was not a primary focus of this investigation, we comment briefly on our results related to aggression. Aggressive children were found to be less cooperative and have less self-control than did comparison children, and they were found to utilise more externalizing strategies than shy or comparison children. Moreover, they reported greater anxiety, loneliness, and negative affect than did comparison children (but less anxiety and loneliness than shy children) and lower physical ability, physical appearance, and peer self-esteem than did comparison children. These findings coincide with previous research linking aggression with heightened "acting out" behaviour and maladaptive social problem solving skills (see Dodge, Coie, & Lynam, 2006, for a recent review), and reaffirm that there are both internalizing and externalizing ramifications of aggressive behaviour.

In terms of psychosocial functioning, the only significant (trend) interaction between aggression and sport occurred for self-esteem; aggressive children who participated in sport reported higher general self-esteem than did aggressive children who did not participate in sport. These findings coincide with those for shy children. What this again suggests is that for socially "deviant" groups, sport participation seems to have a positive impact on self-esteem, perhaps because of the pervasiveness of sport as a positive social status determinant.

Caveats and Directions for Future Research

The current findings have important implications in terms of the benefits of sport participation, in particular for shy children; however, certain limitations should be considered. For example, data collection for the present study relied primarily on child self-reports. This may have heightened inter associations amongst variables because of shared-method variance. Future research might consider multisource assessments of both social behaviours and outcomes. In addition, some of the subscale internal reliability values were low (e.g., α = .51 for the Time 1 *SSRS* responsibility subscale), although overall internal consistencies of the scales were adequate and thus accepted for the current study.

The assessment of sport participation may have also had some limitation. For example, children may have had difficulty recalling all of the sports they had participated in or may have been influenced by the seasonal nature of participation. However, other researchers have also employed self-report measures, including 7-day recall of physical activity (e. g., Sallis, Prochaska, Taylor, Hill, & Geraci, 1999) and self-report questionnaires of activity (e. g., Smith, 1999).

Future researchers might also consider exploring other outcome variables of conceptual interest. For example, it could be argued that a measure of competence would allow researchers to determine the role of aptitude in children's sport experience. Sport competence might be particularly important for shy children who are already lower in feelings of competence (Hymel et al., 1993).

Finally, a cautionary note should be made regarding attrition. Whilst the children who selectively chose to participate at Time 2 were not different on any of the independent variables than the participants who were lost, the children who ceased to participate were found to be less cooperative, less assertive, and more socially anxious at Time 1. Some variability in these outcomes may have been lost at Time 2, which may have limited statistical power to detect differences across time.

The results from the current study provide evidence of the benefits of sport participation for children including higher positive affect and well-being as well as social skills. In addition, shy children were found to be at risk for internalizing difficulties; in particular they were more anxious and lonely than their peers, experienced more negative affect and were less assertive. These findings reaffirm the notion that middle childhood aged children who are deviant from the peer group seem to be vulnerable to psychosocial health risk factors. Unique to the current study is that sport participation was found to play a protective role against some of the negative outcomes associated with shyness. In particular, it was revealed that shy children who participated in sport reported greater general self-esteem than did shy nonparticipants. In addition, shy children who participated in sport were found to experience a decrease in social anxiety not evidenced by their nonsport-participating shy peers. The results have both theoretical and practical implications in the fields of developmental psychology and physical education, as sport can be suggested not only as a protective factor, but a potential intervention strategy for shy children. In essence, one could suggest that for shy children, the psychosocial benefits of sport are particularly evident, and as such shy children should be encouraged to come out and play.

References

Allison, P. D., & Furstenberg, F. F. (1989). How marital dissolution affects children: Variations by age and sex. *Developmental Psychology, 25,* 540–549.

Asendorpf, J. B. (1990). Beyond social withdrawal: Shyness, unsociability and peer avoidance. *Human Development, 33,* 250–259.

Asher, S. R., Hymel, S., & Renshaw, P. D. (1984). Loneliness in children. *Child Development, 55,* 1456–1464.

Beron, R. M., & Kenny, D. A. (1986). The moderator-mediator variable distinction in social psychological research: Conceptual, strategic, and statistical considerations. *Journal of Personality and Social Psychology, 51,* 1173–1182.

Bowker, A., Gadbois, S., & Cornock, B. (2003). Sports participation and self-esteem: Variations as a function of gender and gender role orientation. *Sex Roles, 49,* 47–58.

Bredemeier, B. J. (1988). The moral of the youth sport story. In E. W. Brown & C. F. Branta (Eds.), *Competitive sports for children and youth: An overview of research and issues* (pp. 285–296). Champaign, IL: Human Kinetics.

Chase, M. A., & Dummer, G. M. (1992). The role of sports as a social status determinant for children. *Research Quarterly for Exercise and Sport, 63,* 418–424.

Coplan, R. J., Arbeau, K. A., & Armer, M. (in press). Don't fret, be supportive! Maternal characteristics linking child shyness to psychosocial and school adjustment in kindergarten. *Journal of Abnormal Child Psychology.*

Coplan, R. J., Closson, L., & Arbeau, K. A. (2007). Gender differences in the behavioral associates of loneliness and social dissatisfaction in kindergarten. *Journal of Child Psychology and Psychiatry (Special Issue on Preschool Mental Health), 48,* 988–995.

Coplan, R. J., Findlay, L. C., & Nelson, L. J. (2004). Characteristics of preschoolers with lower perceived competence. *Journal of abnormal Child Psychology, 32,* 399–408.

Coplan, R. J., Wilson, J., Frohlick, S. L., & Zelenski, J. (2006). A person-oriented analysis of behavioural inhibition and behavioural activation in childhood. *Personality and Individual Differences, 41,* 917–927.

Crozier, W. R. (1995). Shyness and self-esteem in middle childhood. *British Journal of Educational Psychology, 65,* 85–95.

Dodge, K. A., Coie, J. D., & Lynam, D. (2006). Aggression and antisocial behavior in youth. In W. Damon & R. M. Lerner (Eds. in Chief) & N. Eisenberg, (Vol. ed.), *Handbook of child psychology: Vol. 3. Social, emotional and personality development* (6th ed., pp. 719–788). New York: Wiley and Sons.

Ebbeck, V., & Weiss, M. R. (1998). Determinants of children's self-esteem: An examination of perceived competence and affect in sport. *Pediatric Exercise Science, 10,* 285–298.

Eisenberg, N., Shepard, S. A., Fabes, R. A., Murphy, B. C., & Guthrie, I. K. (1998). Shyness and children's emotionality, regulation, and coping: Contemporaneous, longitudinal, and across-context relations. *Child Development, 69,* 767–790.

Fordham, K., & Stevenson-Hinde, J. (1999). Shyness, friendship quality, and adjustment during middle childhood. *Journal of Child Psychology and Psychiatry, 40,* 757–768.

Gresham, F. M., & Elliot, S. N. (1990). *Social Skills Rating System Manual.* Circle Pines, MN: American Guidance Service.

Henderson, L., & Zimbardo, P. (2001). Shyness, social anxiety, and social phobia. In S. G. Hormann & P. M. DiBartolo (Eds.), *From social anxiety to social phobia: Multiple perspectives* (pp. 46–64). Needham Heights, MA: Allyn & Bacon.

Hymel, S., Bowker, A., & Woody, E. (1993). Aggressive versus withdrawn unpopular children: Variations in peer and self-perceptions in multiple domains. *Child Development, 64,* 879–896.

Hymel, S., Vaillencourt, T., McDougall, P., & Renshaw, P. D. (2002). Peer acceptance and rejection in childhood. In P. K. Smith & C. H. Hart (Eds.), *Blackwell handbook of childhood social development.* (pp. 268–284). Great Britain: Blackwell Publishers.

Hymel, S., Woody, E., & Bowker, A. (1993). Social withdrawal in childhood: Considering the child's perspective. In K. H. Rubin & J. B. Asendorpf (Eds.), *Social withdrawal, inhibition, and shyness in childhood* (pp. 237–262). Hillsdale, NJ: Erlbaum, Inc.

Kagan, J. (1989). Temperamental contributions to social behaviour. *American Psychologist, 44,* 668–674.

Kirkcaldy, B. D., Shephard, R. J., & Siefen, R. G. (2002). The relationship between physical activity and self-image and problem behaviour among adolescents. *Social Psychiatry and Psychiatric Epidemiology, 37,* 544–550.

La Greca, A. M., & Stone, W. L. (1993). Social Anxiety Scale for Children—Revised: Factor structure and concurrent validity. *Journal of Clinical Child Psychology, 22,* 17–27.

Laurent, J., Catanzaro, S. J., Joiner, T. E. Jr., Rudolph, K. D., Potter, K. I., Lambert, S., et al. (1999). A measure of positive and negative affect for children: Scale development and preliminary validation. *Psychological Assessment, 11,* 326–338.

Marsh, H. W. (1984). *Self-Description Questionnaire (SDQ): An instrument for measuring multiple dimensions of preadolescent self-concept.* Sydney, Australia: University of Sydney.

Marsh, H. W. (1998). Age and gender effects in physical self-concepts for adolescent elite athletes and non-athletes: A multicohort-multioccasion design. *Journal of Sport and Exercise Psychology, 20,* 237–259.

Marsh, H. W., Perry, C., Horsely, C., & Roche, L. (1995). Multidimensional self-concepts of elite athletes: How do they differ from the general population? *Journal of Sport and Exercise Psychology, 17,* 70–83.

McHale, J. P., Vinden, P. G., Bush, L., Richer, D., Shaw, D., & Smith, B. (2005). Patterns of personal and social adjustment among sport-involved and non-involved middle-school children. *Sociology of Sport Journal, 22,* 119–136.

Norton, P. J., Burns, J. A., Hope, D. A., & Bauer, B. K. (2000). Generalization of social anxiety to athletic situations: Gender, sports involvement, and parental pressure. *Depression and Anxiety, 12,* 193–202.

Page, R. M., Frey, J., Talbert, R., & Falk, C. (1992). Children's feelings of loneliness and social dissatisfaction: Relationship to measures of physical fitness and activity. *Journal of Teaching and Physical Education, 11,* 211–219.

Page, R. M., & Hammermeister, J. (1995). Shyness and loneliness: Relationship to the exercise frequently of college students. *Psychological Reports, 76,* 395–398.

Page, R. M., & Zarco, E. P. (2001). Shyness, physical activity and sports team participation among Philippine high school students. *Child Study Journal, 31,* 193–203.

Prakash, K., & Coplan, R. J. (2007). Socio-emotional characteristics and school adjustment of socially-withdrawn children in India. International *Journal of Behavioural Development, 31,* 1–10.

Rubin, K. H., Bukowski, W., & Parker, J. G. (2006). Peer interactions, relationships, and groups. In W. Damon & R. M. Lerner (Eds. In Chief) & N. Eisenberg. (Vol. Ed.), *Handbook of child psychology: Vol.3 Social, emotional and personality development* (6th ed., pp. 571–645). New York: Wiley and Sons.

Rubin, K. H., Chen, X., & Hymel, S. (1993). Socioemotional characteristics of withdrawn and aggressive children. *Merrill-Palmer Quarterly, 39,* 518–534.

Sallis, J. F., Prochaska, J. J., Taylor, W. C., Hill, J. O., & Geraci, J. C. (1999). Correlates of physical activity in a national sample of girls and boys in grades 4 through 12. *Health Psychology, 18,* 410–415.

Shavelson, R. J., Hubner, J. J., & Stanton, G. C. (1976). Self-concept: Validation of construct interpretations. *Review of Educational Research, 46,* 407–441.

Smith, A. L. (1999). Perceptions of peer relationships and physical activity participation in early adolescence. *Journal of Sport and Exercise Psychology, 21,* 329–350.

Smith, A. L. (2003). Peer relationship in physical activity contexts: A road less travelled in youth sport and exercise research. *Psychology of Sport and Exercise, 4,* 25–39.

Storch, E. A., Bartlas, M. E., Dent, H. E., & Masia, C. L. (2002). Generalization of social anxiety to sport: An investigation of elementary Hispanic children. *Child Study Journal, 32,* 81–87.

Straus, M. A. (1979). Measuring intrafamily conflict and violence: The Conflict Tactics (CT) Scales. *Journal of Marriage and the Family, 41,* 75–88.

Watson, D., Clark, L. A., & Tellegen, A. (1988). Development and validation of brief measures of Positive and Negative Affect: The PANAS scales. *Journal of Personality and Social Psychology, 54,* 1063–1070.

Weiss, M. R., & Duncan, S. C. (1992). The relationship between physical competence and peer acceptance in the context of children's sports participation. *Journal of Sport and Exercise Psychology, 14,* 177–191.

Discussion Questions

1. Do you agree or disagree that sports can be a protective factor for children who are shy?
2. Do you have any personal examples that could support the results of the study?
3. What are your criticisms of this study? What were their limitations?

Assignment

Design an experimental methodology to support or refute the results from the current correlational study. Focus solely on making an experimental study with manipulations related to sports involvement.

Suicidal Behaviour in Adolescence

By Alan Apter

Adolescent suicide and suicidal behaviours have become major public health issues in recent years. Suicide is widely recognized as a major cause of mortality in young people, and nonfatal suicidal behaviours in young people are associated with considerable morbidity. Suicidal behaviour in adolescence covers a wide spectrum of phenomena for which an exact definition and an understanding of the interrelations remain controversial.[1]

The epidemiology of youth suicide is a fascinating story. The 20th century produced a steady rise in the incidence of suicide in young males punctuated by decreases during the World Wars; however, since the 1990s, rates of suicide in young men have steadily declined. This was partly due to an increased number of cars with catalytic converters and to declines in rates of unemployment and divorce.[2] Some researchers, especially in the United States, have strongly supported the important role of selective serotonin reuptake inhibitors use in explaining the reduction of adolescent suicide,[3,4] a claim refuted by Biddle et al.[2] Following the introduction of the black box warning, there was a new rise in adolescent suicide, which some authors attributed to reduced prescriptions of these agents, although Wheeler et al[5] have vigorously disputed this interpretation.

One other major epidemiologic finding in recent years has been the finding that, in China, southern India, and Singapore, the accepted sex differences for suicide are reversed, and that young females are more at risk for suicide than males.[6] In these young females, mental illness seems to be less of a factor in their suicides than has been reported in the West[7] and most fatalities are due to pesticide ingestion. Undoubtedly, the restriction of the use of pesticides is a very important preventative measure in these countries.[8]

It has become increasingly clear that family genetic studies play an important role in understanding suicide and that, especially in youth, suicide is inherited distinctively from any concurrent psychiatric illness.[9] It has also become increasingly apparent that genetic transmission is more characteristic of suicide in youth than that of suicide in older people. The biological mechanism that may be involved is probably related to serotonin metabolism and low turnover of 5-hydroxyindoleacetic acid as measured in the cerebral spinal fluid, which in turn is related to aggression and impulsivity.[10] This, combined with a genetic predisposition for a heightened stress reaction via genetic mechanisms in the hypothalamo–pituitary–adrenal axis,[11] provides a plausible basis for beginning to understanding suicide in youth.

Psychological risk factors that have been the focus of recent attention include overgeneralized autobiographical memory associated with interpersonal relationships,[12] deficits in problem solving,[13] as well as high levels of impulsive-aggressiveness. [14] Additional potential precursors of suicidal behaviour in depressed adolescents are other early development traits, such as temperament and emotional regulation.[15]

Adolescent suicidal behaviour also seems to be related to just about all types of serious psychiatric disorder, including: eating disorders,[16] schizophrenia,[17] and, of course, all forms of depression, especially bipolar disorder.

Social risk factors for adolescent suicide include parental separation, divorce, and family discord, as well as child abuse and imitation.[18] Media reporting and, naturally, alcohol and drug abuse are also important facilitators of suicide among young people. Bullying and peer victimization are extremely dangerous precipitators[19,20] and, together with the understudied effects of immigration, are reviewed more extensively in this issue's In Review.[21,22]

A new social force impinging on youth suicide is the Internet.[2] As an increasingly popular source of information, concerns have been raised about the existence of websites that promote suicide[23] as well as suicide websites that have been claimed to have facilitated suicide pacts among strangers.[24]

Hardly any research exists on treatment for suicidal adolescents. However, there has been tremendous advancement in the treatment of depression, and many studies have assessed the use of cognitive-behavioural therapy (CBT) and interpersonal therapy and medications for depression in youth.

Dialectical behaviour therapy is treatment adapted for suicidal behaviour in adolescents, specifically,[25] although its use still requires a firmer evidence base. A particularly interesting recent report[26] has described the use of CBT with a specific protocol for suicidal adolescents. This report was based on a very large and sophisticated study; however, its relevance for everyday clinical practice remains to be seen. There have been many studies on the use of antidepressants, either alone or in combination with psychotherapy, for depression, but none have addressed suicidal behaviour as the main object of therapy, although there has been much discussion about the potentiating effects of these drugs on suicide. Only one medication has been shown to have a potential antisuicide effect; that is, lithium.[27] Apart from one report,[28] there have been no studies on the effects of lithium on adolescent suicidal behaviour.

Although there are self-report instruments assessing the presence of suicidality as well as risk factors, there are still major problems in objective assessment of suicidal adolescents. Although the principles of clinical assessment are well known and used by clinicians all over the world, an objective orthogonal assessment scale is still problematic. This reflects the difficulties regarding definitions. For instance, are suicidal gestures more serious than suicidal ideation? Is a low-lethal suicide attempt more serious than a suicidal gesture? The only recent publication to deal with this problem is a study by Posner et al[29] describing the Columbia Classification Algorithm of Suicide Assessment; this is a standardized suicidal rating system providing data for the pediatric suicidal risk analysis of antidepressants conducted by the Food and Drug Administration. The lack of such a scale has, in our opinion, severely impeded the progress of research in suicide in adolescents because most of the scales in use do not take these factors into consideration.

Suicide prevention and national prevention programs have become increasingly in vogue.[30] The most important programs use public campaigns to promote the detection and treatment of depression, such as the European Alliance against Depression. Unfortunately, these programs have not been directed distinctively to adolescents. More specific adolescent prevention programs have been well described by Gould et al.[31] Although there are many prevention programs used in various settings (for example, community resources, schools, and emergency departments), the overall empirical evidence about effective ways to prevent or treat suicidality in youth is quite low.[32] Current efforts to establish more solid empirical evidence for suicide prevention include the Evidence-Based Practices Project, a national initiative to develop a national registry of effective prevention programs in the United States.[32] Prevention efforts usually include interventions such as screening for depression and suicide risk in schools and clinical settings gatekeepers training for school staff, means restriction, and, as described above, pharmacological treatment and CBT and (or) skills training. As stated many times before, these strategies and specific programs need further systematic evaluation.[33]

In conclusion, it is probably fair to state that the field of adolescent suicide has advanced considerably, although major areas of study still remain, including:

1. Improving the definitions of different subtypes and phenotypes of suicidal behaviour.
2. Understanding the dramatic time sequence, geographic, and sex differences that effect suicidal behaviour.
3. The continued investigation of biological and genetic factors that interact with environmental factors and put people at high risk of suicide.
4. Understanding some of the social and psychological variables underlying suicidal behaviour.
5. Assessing existing suicide prevention programs for youth in different settings.

The identification of more specific risk factors for suicide will help improve prediction of suicidality and hence create better assessment processes, better treatment, and more targeted prevention programs.

References

1. Apter A, King RA, Bleich A, et al. Fatal and non-fatal suicidal behavior in Israeli adolescent males. Arch Suicide Res. 2008;12(l):20–29.
2. Biddle L, Brock A, Brookes ST, et al. Suicide rates in young men in England and Wales in the 21st century: time trend study. BMJ. 2008;336(7643):539–542.

3. Gibbons RD, Brown CH, Hur K, et al. Early evidence on the effects of regulators' suicidality warnings on SSRI prescriptions and suicide in children and adolescents. Am J Psychiatry. 2007;164:1356–1363.

4. Brent DA. Antidepressants and suicidal behavior: cause or cure? Am J Psychiatry. 2007;164:989–991.

5. Wheeler BW, Gunnell D, Metcalfe C, et al. The population impact on incidence of suicide and non-fatal self harm of regulatory action against the use of selective serotonin reuptake inhibitors in under 18s in the United Kingdom: ecological study. BMJ. 2008;336(7643):542–545.

6. Conner KR, Phillips MR, Meldrum S. Predictors of low-intent and high-intent suicide attempts in rural China. Am J Public Health. 2007;97(10):1842–1846.

7. Li XY, Phillips MR, Zhang YP, et al. Risk factors for suicide in China's youth: a case-control study. Psychol Med. 2008;38:397–406.

8. Gunnell D, Fernando R, Hewagama, et al. The impact of pesticide regulations on suicide in Sri Lanka. Int J Epidemiol. 2007;36:1235–1242.

9. Brent DA, Melhem N. Familial transmission of suicidal behavior. Psychiatr Clin N Am. 2008;31:157–177.

10. Mann JJ, Currier D. A review of prospective studies of biologic predictors of suicidal behavior in mood disorders. Arch Suicide Res. 2007;11:3–16.

11. Wasserman D, Wasserman J, Rozanov V, et al. Depression in suicidal males: genetic risk variants in the CRHR1 gene. Genes Brain Behav. 2009;8(l):72–79.

12. Arie M, Apter A, Orbach I, et al. Autobiographical memory, interpersonal problem solving, and suicidal behavior in adolescent inpatients. Compr Psychiatry. 2008;49(l):22–29.

13. Oldershaw A, Grima E, Jollant F. Decision making and problem solving in adolescents who deliberately self-harm. Psychol Med. 2008;23:1–10.

14. McGirr A, Renaud J, Bureau A, et al. Impulsive-aggressive behaviours and completed suicide across the life cycle: a predisposition for younger age of suicide. Psychol Med. 2008;38(3):407–417.

15. Tamás Z, Kovacs M, Gentzler AL, et al. The relations of temperament and emotion self-regulation with suicidal behaviors in a clinical sample of depressed children in Hungary. J Abnorm Child Psychol. 2007;35(4):640–652.

16. Pompili M, Mancinelli I, Girardi P, et al. Suicide in anorexia nervosa: a meta-analysis. Int J Eat Disord. 2004;36:99–103.

17. Schwartz-Stav O, Apter A, Zalsman G. Depression, suicidal behavior and insight in adolescents with schizophrenia. Eur Child Adolesc Psychiatry. 2006;15(6):352–359.

18. Brodsky BS, Mann JJ, Stanley B, et al. Familial transmission of suicidal behavior: factors mediating the relationship between childhood abuse and offspring suicide attempts. J Clin Psychiatry. 2008;69:584–596.

19. Brunstein Klomek A, Marrocco F, Kleinman M, et al. Bullying, depression and suicidality in adolescents. J Am Acad Child Adolesc Psychiatry. 2007;46(l):40–49.

20. Klomek AB, Marrocco F, Kleinman M, et al. Peer victimization, depression, and suicidiality in adolescents. Suicide Life Threat Behav. 2008;38(2):166–180.

21. Bursztein Lipsicas C, Mäkinen IH. Immigration and suicidality in the young. Can J Psychiatry. 2010;55(5):274–281.

22. Klomek AB, Sourander A, Gould M. The association of suicide and bullying in childhood to young adulthood: a review of cross-sectional and longitudinal research findings. Can J Psychiatry. 2010;55(5):282–288.

23. Recupero PR, Harms SE, Noble JM. Googling suicide: surfing for suicide information on the Internet. J Clin Psychiatry. 2008;69:878–888.

24. Naito A. Internet suicide in Japan: implications for child and adolescent mental health. Clin Child Psychol Psychiatry. 2007;12(4):583–597.

25. Miller AL, Ramus JH, Linehan MM. Dialectical behavior therapy with suicidal adolescents. New York (NY): Guilford Press; 2006.

26. Stanley B, Brown G, Brent D, et al. Cognitive-Behavioral Therapy for Suicide Prevention (CBT-SP): treatment model, feasibility, and acceptability. J Am Acad Child Adolesc Psychiatry. 2009 Aug 26. [Epub ahead of print].

27. Cipriani A, Pretty H, Hawton K, et al. Lithium in the prevention of suicidal behavior and all-cause mortality in patients with mood disorders: a systematic review of randomized trials. Am J Psychiatry. 2005;162:1805–1819.

28. Masters KJ. Anti-suicidal and self-harm properties of lithium carbonate. CNS Spectr. 2008;13(2):109–110.

29. Posner K, Oquendo MA, Gould M, el al. Columbia Classification Algorithm of Suicide Assessment (C-CASA): classification of suicidal events in the FDA's pediatric suicidal risk analysis of antidepressants. Am J Psychiatry. 2007;164(7):1035–1043.

30. Mann JJ, Apter A, Bertolote J, et al. Suicide prevention strategies: a systemic review. JAMA. 2005;294(16):2064–2074.

31. Gould MS; Greenberg T, Velting DM, et al Youth suicide risk and preventive interventions: a review of the past 10 years. J Am Acad Child Adolesc Psychiatry. 2003;42(4):386–405.

32. Rodgers PL, Sudak HS, Silverman MM, et al. Evidence-based practices project for suicide prevention. Suicide Life Threat Behav. 2007;37(2): 154–164.

33. Bursztein C, Apter A. Adolescent suicide. Curr Opin Psychiatry. 2009;22(1):1–6.

Discussion Questions

1. What do you think about the internet's role in suicidal behavior in adolescence? Do you think action should be taken against sites that encourage people to kills themselves (either with tips or who push them to do it with comments)? Is it freedom of speech?
2. Why is operationalizing suicidal behavior in adolescence so important?
3. There isn't a lot of evidence that supports suicide prevention programs. Do you think we should use our time and money to continue these programs if they aren't working? Does it give society false hope?

Assignment

Learn about the evidence-based practices project for suicide prevention. Describe what you have learned and what factors make an effective suicide prevention program.

Death in Disney Films

Implications for Children's Understanding of Death (Excerpt)

With an introduction and conclusion by Carrie Lane

By Meredith Cox, Erin Garrett, and James A. Graham

Editor's Introduction

Most adults find the topic of death difficult and scary. It shouldn't be a surprise, then, that these same adults would struggle to discuss the topic of death with their children. Parents want to protect their children from all the unpleasant aspects of life. In an attempt to protect their children, parents often end up confusing them—or worse, increasing their fear of death. Parents use phrases like "Grandma went to heaven," "Grandma went on a vacation," "Grandma passed away," and "Grandma is sleeping for a long time." For most young children, they are still thinking too concretely to comprehend terms like "heaven" or "passed away." They often want to go to heaven or on vacation so they can see their loved one again. The sleeping example is typically the most confusing and can lead to children fearing sleep. Are there any tools that could help parents discuss this difficult topic without confusing or scaring their children? Grief counselors and therapists have suggested that stories are helpful in dealing with the topic of death. We have also seen children's books used to cover a variety of tough topics like sexism and racism (Malcolm, 2010). This essay examines two different types of media that could be used as a tool to help parents navigate the difficult explanation of death.

The first step in explaining death to children requires an understanding of when they are capable of comprehending death and which factors play a role in their comprehension. There are three age categories of comprehension. Below age 5, children don't understand that death is final and inevitable. Between ages 5 and 9, children understand the finality of death, but believe it only happens to people much older than themselves (Cox et al., 2004). More specifically in this age group, between ages 4 and 8, children are the most active in their search for understanding death (Malcolm, 2010). This search leads to a complete understanding of death at age 10, when children fully understand all aspects of death—that it is final, inevitable, and permanent. These age findings correspond directly to the role biology plays in a child's comprehension abilities. A more developed brain is required to fully process the complex and abstract ideas of death. However, research does show that experience with death can influence a child's comprehension of death. For example, if a parent were to die, a child's understanding of death would occur earlier than typically expected for a child of that age (Cox et al., 2004).

Researchers have examined children's books to determine what messages about death they might be communicating to children. Quite a few children's books communicate messages about heaven. Heaven in these books has similar characteristics: up above earth, lots of clouds, bright lights, and angels. Researchers believed that these regular images of heaven would lead to children seeing that death isn't the end of their existence. The children would also feel as though they could continue to communicate with their deceased loved one (Malcolm, 2010). Besides reading books, children spend quite a bit of time watching television and movies. More specifically, a majority of children in the United States will have some experience with Disney films. The popularity of Disney films spans a large time frame. Many of the early movies are still very popular. Researchers wanted to have a better understanding of what messages these films might contribute to children's understanding of death. They examined ten popular Disney films: *Snow White* (1937), *Bambi* (1942), *Sleeping Beauty* (1959), *The Little Mermaid* (1989), *Beauty and the Beast* (1991), *The Lion King* (1994), *The Hunchback of Notre Dame* (1996), *Hercules* (1997), *Mulan* (1998), and *Tarzan* (1999). Researchers were most interested in how many good guys and bad guys died, if they died on- or off-screen, the reactions of the other characters to their death, was their death final or could they come back, and if their death was intentional, accidental, and/or justified.

Method

Film Selection

The analyzed content consists of 10 Disney Classic animated full-length feature films. The movies were selected only if a death occurred or was a theme in the plotline. The movies were chosen from various decades in order to sample the portrayal of death across time in Disney films. The first animated Disney full-length feature film was released approximately 60 years ago; thus, films were selected from both the first 30 years of production (pre-1970s) and from the last 30 years (post-1970s). Due to a lack of full-length films with death scenes released before the 1970s, only three movies were selected from that period, whereas seven were selected from more recent decades. This limited selection could also be attributed to the fact that full-length animated Disney movies were released on an average of three per decade in the past, whereas 14 were released in the 1980s and 1990s. The films were not chosen haphazardly; rather, the researchers went through the plot outlines of all animated Disney Classic films and chose from that list, being careful to select both older classics and more modern films that children are familiar with today.

The movies examined for this study were: *Snow White and the Seven Dwarfs* (1937), *Bambi* (1942), *Sleeping Beauty,* (1959), *The Little Mermaid* (1989), *Beauty and the Beast* (1991), *The Lion King* (1994), *The Hunchback of Notre Dame* (1996), *Hercules* (1997), *Mulan* (1998), and *Tarzan* (1999).

Coding Categories

Two coders watched the movies together and coded the data individually. Each character's death was analyzed by the following five coding criteria.

Character Status

This category refers to the role the character that died played in the plot. We coded for two different types of characters. First, a *protagonist* is a character that is seen as the "good guy," hero/heroine of the movie, or the main character whom the story revolves around. An *antagonist* is a character who is seen as the "bad guy," villain, nemesis, or enemy of the protagonist.

Depiction of Death

Refers to how the character's death was shown in the film. In an *explicit death* the audience sees that the character is definitely dead because the body is shown being physically damaged/killed and/or the dead, motionless body is shown on screen. An *implicit death* refers to one in which the audience can only assume that the character is dead based on the fact that they do not appear again in the film and/or that they have encountered something that would presumably result in death. Examples include seeing a shadow of a dead body or a character falling off a cliff. *Sleep death* refers to an instance in which a character falls into a state of prolonged sleep. Generally, this is the result of a spell due to an original intent to kill.

Death Status

This category refers to if a death was a true end of life or if it was shown as something negotiable that does not necessarily represent the absolute end of life. A *permanent/final* death is one in which the character does not return in any form. A *reversible* death is one where a character returns in one of two ways. A *reversible-same form* death is one in which the character seemingly comes back from a dead or seemingly dead state in his or her original body. In a *reversible-altered form* death, the character returns either in a physically transformed state or in the form of a spirit.

Emotional Reaction

Refers to how the other characters in the movie responded to or dealt with death. *Positive emotion* refers to a character or characters being visibly happy (e.g., smiling, cheering) or showing signs of relief. *Negative emotion* refers to a character or characters reacting with frustration, remorse, anger, or with general signs of sadness (e.g., crying). *Lacking emotion* refers to characters reacting to death as if it is inconsequential or the death is not dealt with or acknowledged by all characters.

Causality

Causality refers to what led to or caused the death and whether the death was portrayed as being justified or unjustified. In a *purposeful* death, a character dies as the result of another character's intent to harm or kill him or her. An *accidental* death refers to one where the death was unintentional and was the result of an unplanned event. In addition to being either purposeful or accidental, death events were also coded as being either *justified* or *unjustified*. *Justified* deaths were ones in which the character who died had done something that warranted punishment; the general message conveyed was that they "deserved" to die. *Unjustified* deaths were ones in which the character did not do anything wrong; there was a sense that they did not deserve to die.

Table 1. Depiction of death by character type

Depiction of death	Protagonist	%	Antagonist	%	Total
Explicit death	7	63.64	4	36.36	11
Implicit death	3	30.0	7	70.0	10
Sleep death	2	100.0	0	0	2
Total	12	52.17	11	47.83	23

Note: Percentages are row percentages.

Table 2. Death status by character types

Death status	Protagonist	%	Antagonist	%	Total
Reversible/Same	4	100	0	0	4
Reversible/Altered	2	100	0	0	2
Permanent/Final	7	41.18	10	58.82	17
Total	13	56.52	10	43.48	23

Note: Percentages are row percentages.

Table 3. Emotional reactions by character type

Emotional reaction	Protagonist	%	Antagonist	%	Total
Positive emotion	0	0	3	100	3
Negative emotion	10	90.9	1	9.1	11
Lacking emotion	2	22.22	7	77.78	9
Total	12	52.17	11	47.83	23

Note: Percentages are row percentages.

Intercoder Reliability

Two coders rated the selected films. Intercoder reliability was judged as acceptable if the raters achieved more than 70% agreement on all categories, using Cohen's Kappa. The reliability between coders was tested on a randomly selected subsample of four films (40% of the sample). Intercoder reliability was computed for each of the five categories of interest: character status ($K = 1.00$), depiction of death ($K = 0.92$), death status ($K = 1.00$), emotional reaction ($K = 1.00$), and causality ($K = 0.87$).

Results

Our study examined the portrayal of death and grieving in Disney films geared toward children, and focused on five factors.

Character Status

A total of 23 death scenes occurred in the 10 Disney films analyzed. Protagonists and antagonists were portrayed nearly equally in those scenes. Out of the 23 characters who died, 52% were protagonists ($n = 12$) and 48% ($n = 11$) were antagonists (see Table 1).

Depiction of Death

Implicit death accounted for 43% of total deaths ($n = 10$) and explicit death ($n = 11$) accounted for 48%. We found that 64% of explicit deaths occurred among protagonists ($n = 7$) while only 36% of explicit deaths were the deaths of antagonists ($n = 4$). In contrast, implicit deaths occurred more among antagonists: 70% of antagonists died in implicit death scenes ($n = 7$), whereas only 30% of protagonists did ($n = 3$). Sleep death was not nearly as common as "real" death portrayals, occurring in 9% of death instances ($n = 2$). Both sleep deaths occurred among protagonists (see Table 1).

Death Status

A large majority of deaths (74%) were portrayed as permanent, final, and irreversible ($n = 17$). Out of the permanent deaths, 59% were those of antagonists ($n = 10$) and 41% were protagonists ($n = 7$). Reversible death occurred in 26% of death scenes ($n = 6$). Of the six reversible deaths, 67% ($n = 4$) of characters returned in their same form and 33% ($n = 2$) reappeared in altered forms. All of the reversible deaths were among protagonists (see Table 2).

Emotional Reaction

In terms of reactions to a character's death, the most prevalent type of emotion displayed by characters was negative emotion, which occurred in 48% of death scenes ($n = 11$). Negative emotions included typical grieving responses such as fear, crying, and expressing anger or frustration over a loss. Out of the negative emotional responses, 91% ($n = 10$) were for the deaths of protagonists, whereas only 9% ($n = 1$) resulted from the death of an antagonist. Positive emotion, indicated by happiness, relief, or celebration of a loss, occurred in only 13% of deaths ($n = 3$). Positive emotion resulted solely from the deaths of antagonists. Interestingly, neutral or lacking emotion occurred in 39% of death scenes ($n = 9$), which is nearly as frequently as grieving/negative emotion did. The majority of instances of lacking emotion (78%) were associated with the deaths of antagonists ($n = 7$), whereas only 22% of protagonist deaths resulted in neutral or lacking emotion ($n = 2$) (see Table 3).

Editor's Conclusion

The examination of these films concluded that a similar number of good guys and bad guys died in Disney films. The message that this could communicate is that anyone can die. There were also a similar number of deaths occurring on-screen as there were off-screen. Interestingly, coders found that good guys were more likely to die on-screen, and that bad guys were more likely to die off-screen. This could teach children that the death of a bad person isn't that important. It could also have a positive result when a child sees a good guy die on-screen by allowing the child an opportunity to deal with the death of a character they care more about. Researchers found most deaths to be permanent. This is a comprehension issue that children struggle with, and these movies could be a place for parents to reinforce the permanence of death. The reversible deaths only occurred for the good guys, and the message that could be sent to children is that if you want a second chance at life, you have to be good. When good guys died, the emotional reaction was negative. If there was a positive reaction, it was solely for the bad guys. It was also noted that a bad guy's death never occurred intentionally. Their death was always justified.

Several studies have examined different forms of media that could be used to examine children's understanding of death. Most of these studies are exploratory, and to further the investigation into this topic, researchers will need to conduct studies with children. Previous research has also added that the experience with death is powerful enough in impacting understanding that researchers should be sure to use a variety of samples of the population, not just within the United States, but around the world.

Editor's References

Cox, M., Garrett, E., and Graham, J. A. (2004). "Death in Disney Films: Implications for Children's Understanding of Death." Omega, 90(4), 267–280.

Malcolm, N. L. (2010). "Images of Heaven and the Spiritual Afterlife: Qualitative Analysis of Children's Storybooks about Death, Dying, Grief, and Bereavement." Omega, 62(1), 51–76.

Discussion Questions

1. Why do you think someone would be interested in studying the connections between animated Disney movies and children's understanding of death?
2. When is a good time to discuss death with a child? Should you be straightforward or try to soften it for them?
3. After having read how this study was conducted and what the researchers found, what are some different ideas (at least two) you might have for continuing this research? (Think of what might happen next if you were interested in this line of work or what you could change to make it better.)

Assignments

1. How do parents discuss death with their children? Ask two of your peers who aren't in child psychology when they learned about death and how their parents explained it to them. Also describe your first experience with death and how your parents explained death to you.
2. What are other tools that you think parents could use to better explain death to their children? Do you think parents should discuss heaven with children? Is it beneficial or harmful?

Section III: Relational Processes

Gender, Parenting, Play, and Bullying

Assessment & Diagnosis

Childhood Gender Identity ... Disorder? Developmental, Cultural, and Diagnostic Concerns

By Eliza A. Dragowski, María R. Scharrón-del Río, and Amy L. Sandigorsky

A lthough fundamental to the way most of us experience ourselves and others, gender is rarely contemplated. Left unexplored, however, this complex concept often creates misconceptions and stereotypes, such as the belief that gender and sex are synonymous or that gender assigned at birth indicates a specific preference for toys, interests, clothes, and eventual erotic attraction. The aim of this article is to enhance counselor understanding of childhood gender identity development, to aid in assessment and diagnostic processes surrounding this matter. We review childhood gender identity in the context of developmental and cultural factors before considering the diagnosis of childhood gender identity disorder (GIDC), and we explore proposed changes to the diagnosis in the upcoming fifth revision of the *Diagnostic and Statistical Manual of Mental Disorders*.

Terms and Definitions

Misconceptions surrounding gender identity often begin with general confabulation of terms used to communicate about the issue. We thus begin this article with a review of terminology, aiming to define and disentangle biological sex, gender, and sexuality.

Biological Sex

Biological sex relates to one's anatomical and reproductive structures. It is determined by *karyotype* (a specific chromosomal complement, with 46 XY karyotype in typical males and 46 XX karyotype in typical females), *gonads* (testes and ovaries), *external genitalia* (scrotum and penis in typical males; labia and clitoris in typical females), and secondary sex differentiation at puberty (Pasterski, 2008). Most commonly, it follows a binary model assigned at birth based on the presence of external genitalia (Diamond, 2006). This model does not consider persons with disorders of sex development, whose sex chromosomes and genital structure(s) are considered to be incongruent (Pasterski, 2008).

Gender

Jacobs, Thomas, and Lang (1997) used the word gender to refer to "cultural rules, ideologies, and expected behaviors for individuals of diverse phenotypes and psychosocial characteristics" (p. 2). *Gender identity* relates to one's subjective sense of congruence with an attributed gender. *Gender role* is a public display of gender identity conveying societal schemes of how boys and girls should behave (Diamond, 2002; Stryker, 2008).

Transgender is an umbrella term referring to people who move away from the gender assigned to them at birth, thus violating societal conceptualizations of what it means to be a man or a woman (Stryker, 2008). Included in this category are *transsexuals*, people whose gender identity does not correspond to their physical body (Diamond, 2002). Transsexuals sometimes transform their physical body and often assume gender roles that are congruent with their experienced gender identity. According to Diamond (2002), the term *transsexual* best describes adults, not children who may meet criteria for gender identity disorder (GID). In this article, we interchangeably use the terms *gender-variant* and *gender-nonconforming* to describe children whose gender expression, gender role behavior, and/or gender identity do not conform to the traditional norms.

Sexuality/Sexual Orientation

The terms *sexuality* and *sexual orientation* refer to how and with whom people act on their affectionate, intimate, and erotic desires. In classifying sexuality, people tend to depend on the gender identity of the person to whom their desires are directed. Most commonly, to describe sexual orientation, we use the term *heterosexual/straight* to denote a person attracted to a member of another gender, *homosexual/gay/lesbian* to refer to an individual attracted to the member of the same gender, and *bisexual* to refer to a person attracted to a member of any gender (Diamond, 2002; Stryker, 2008).

What Does It All Mean?

Our cultural beliefs dictate that there are only two biological sexes corresponding to two genders. Moreover, males are expected to have masculine gender identifications/roles and to be attracted to women. Females, in turn, are expected to have gender identifications/roles of women and to be attracted to men. These two models are thus considered the norm, and any other combination of biological sex, gender, and sexuality is commonly considered unnatural or pathological (Mintz, & O'Neil, 1990; Newman, 2002; Schilt & Westbrook, 2009).

Other combinations are possible, however. A child whose biological sex is that of a typical female can have a gender identity and role of a boy. As an adult, this person may self-identify as transgender or transsexual and live as a man, who, like any other person, can be of any sexual orientation. On the other hand, a biological male can have a gender identity of a boy/man, be attracted to other men, and identify as gay. Contrary to what our society tends to believe, it is not necessary for people who feel attracted to others of the same gender to express any gender nonconformity. Gay men can be comfortable in their male body and exhibit no gender-variant behaviors, just as lesbian women can be comfortable with their sex and gender roles (Diamond, 2002).

The boundaries expand even further when one considers the variety of human experiences represented outside of Western culture, where "wide variations exist in beliefs about the nature of biology and what constitutes sex, and physical difference per se is not always sufficient to produce gender" (Newman, 2002, p. 354). Driven by the belief that the sex/gender may change later in life, the Zuni Nation does not assign the sex to a child at the time of birth. They interpret biology via rituals designed to discover the gender of the infant and thus determine upbringing (Herdt, 1996, cited in Newman, 2002). Many American Indian/First Nation groups recognize persons of a specific biological sex who take on the role and status of the opposite sex. Collectively denominated as *two-spirit* people, they are at times bestowed high social and spiritual status and regarded as a "third gender" (Jacobs et al., 1997).

In Independent Samoa, part of the population consists of *fa'afafine*, most of whom are biological males who are feminine in behavior and sexually attracted to straight men. In Samoan cultural norms, straight men are those who identify as men and perform masculine gender roles, but whose sexual activity does not have to be limited to women. It is culturally sanctioned for Samoan men to engage in sexual activity with *fa'afafine* or other men, rendering the Western concept of male homosexuality virtually non applicable (Vasey & Bartlett, 2007).

Gender Identity Development

Diversity of experience brings questions about gender identity from the realm of the unexamined to the forefront of our consciousness. How do children know what their gender is and how to behave? Why do some children insist that their gender is not the one assigned to them at birth? Most gender identity theories stand along the nature versus nurture continuum. However, a recent idea gaining prominence is that both innate and acquired aspects of the human experience are inextricably involved in the development of gender identity (Diamond, 2006). We briefly review these paradigms next.

Importance of Nature

Gender development is believed to begin at the time of conception and determined by sex chromosomes. All fetuses begin existence with a set of undifferentiated gonads and two sets of ducts, Mullerian and Wolffian. Determining the fate of gonads between Weeks 6 and 12 of gestation is the sex-determining region (SRY) gene present only on the Y chromosome.

In the course of typical male development, the SRY gene prompts development of testes, which then start production of testosterone and Müllerian-inhibiting substance (MIS). This process halts development of Müllerian ducts. At the same time, testosterone stimulates development of Wolffian ducts into a male genital system. Eventually, part of testosterone is converted into dihydrotestosterone (DHT), which triggers development of typical male genitalia. In a process lasting through late gestation, the brain is also masculinized by a metabolite of testosterone called estradiol (Blakemore, Berenbaum, & Liben, 2009; Bostwick & Martin, 2007).

In the absence of the SRY gene, typical female development begins as the undifferentiated gonads develop into ovaries at approximately 3 months of gestation. The Müllerian structures develop into the uterus, fallopian tubes, and upper segment of vagina, while Wolffian ducts fade away. Absence of DHT results in development of typical female genitalia (Blakemore et al., 2009).

Generally, presence of XX chromosomes indicates phenotypic females who develop into girls/women with culturally accepted characteristics. Similarly, chromosomal makeup XY typically produces phenotypic males who mature into boys/men with masculine characteristics seen as culturally appropriate. Development of a minority of individuals, however, is considered gender-variant with respect to gender identification and expression (Diamond, 2006).

According to biological theories, nonconforming gender identity is a result of "abnormal brain sex differentiation with subsequent gender development occurring along predetermined lines and in conflict with the assigned gender role" (Newman, 2002, p. 353). The Gender Identity Research and Education Society (2006) identified three main pathways to "atypical" gender identity development. The first path involves anomalous prenatal hormonal influences, illustrated by studies showing increased incidence of left-handedness among transsexuals (Green & Young, 2001) and finger ratio measurement of transsexual men resembling that of biological women (Kraemer et al., 2009). The second path points to anatomic brain differences. It is supported by postmortem examinations of brains of male-to-female transsexuals, which show a typically female-sized portion of the central subdivision of the bed nucleus of the stria terminalis, a brain area vital in sexual behavior (Zhou, Hofman, Gooren, & Swaab, 1995). The third path to atypical gender identity development is that of genetic influences. This line of inquiry is supported by studies showing heritability of GID among twins, with the highest concordance rates found among monozygotic twins and lesser but still strong concordance among fraternal twins (Diamond & Hawk, 2004, cited in Diamond, 2006). Additionally, Meyer-Bahlburg's (2010) review of the most recent research indicates presence of various genetic variations that do not cause changes in reproductive anatomical structures but may produce gender-variant identities. It is important to note that most studies validating biological etiology of gender-variant identity are not definitive because they are limited by methodological shortcomings and lack of replication by independent research institutions (Meyer-Bahlburg, 2010).

Importance of Nurture

Environmental influences on the child's gender development often begin before birth. Upon finding the biological sex of the child, parents tend to begin making arrangements—purchasing gender-specific clothes, toys, and nursery items—thus assigning gender identity to a child who has not yet been born. After birth, boys and girls elicit specific parental responses: Boys are seen as stronger, whereas girls tend to be considered finer featured and delicate (Karraker, Vogel, & Lake, 1995). Children are treated differently, especially when engaged in behavior resonating gender stereotypes, with parents encouraging sex-typed activities (Fagot & Hagan, 1991; McHale, Crouter, & Whiteman, 2003). Traditional gender behaviors are reinforced with inclusion and praise, whereas "unacceptable" gender behaviors are stigmatized (Girshick, 2008).

Children learn that, at a fundamental level, men and women are different and have a different set of responsibilities in and out of the home (Diamond, 2000). They understand that gender is connected to a whole set of physical and behavioral characteristics and use this framework to communicate with others. By the age of 2, most children show awareness of their own gender, prefer gender-stereotyped toys, and tend to imitate stereotyped gender behaviors of familiar activities (Campbell, Shirley, & Caygill, 2002; Poulin-Dubois, Serbin, Eichstedt, Sen, & Beissel, 2002; Serbin, Poulin-Dubois, & Eichstedt, 2002). This knowledge is concurrent with preschoolers' admiration of children who engage in sex-stereotyped behavior and rejection of those children who do not (Davies, 2004).

Theories highlighting the importance of socialization on gender development include but are not limited to the following: (a) psychoanalytic theories, which emphasize early childhood experiences and identifications with parents; (b) learning theories, which underscore the role of reinforcement, punishment, imitation, and modeling in gender development; (c) social constructivism, which emphasizes the social construction of gender against the backdrop of time, place, and social experience of people; and (d) cognitive theories, which focus on children's knowledge about gender and gender-related behaviors (Blakemore et al., 2009).

Early theories of gender-nonconforming identification explained it in the context of an intrapsychic conflict stemming from environmental instability. Stoller's (1968, cited in Coates, 1992) blissful symbiosis imprinting theory framed gender-nonconforming identification as resulting from the presence of a bisexual mother, absent father, symbiosis between mother and son, and a special beauty in the boy. Green's (1974, cited in Coates, 1992) reinforcement theory proposed that femininity in boys was reinforced by the family members and associated with peer rejection, which intensified negative self-feelings and further propelled the boy's wish to become a girl.

Some current psychological theories propose that both the child's temperament and a problematic family environment account for childhood gender nonconformity. Zucker and Bradley (2004) hypothesized that gender-nonconforming children are constitutionally anxious and sensitive to parental dynamics, which may include marital discord, conflict about matters of masculinity and femininity, and possible psycho-pathology. These issues are said to render parents preoccupied and inattentive to the child's gender-variant behavior. Meyer-Bahlburg (2002) hypothesized that the developmental pathways to boyhood gender nonconformity are likely to involve temperamental inhibition of the child coupled with a variety of psychosocial risks, including (a) strong familial attachment to women who encourage his participation in feminine activities and discourage rough-and-tumble play; (b) insignificant connection with fathers, who may be avoiding the child because of his effeminate behaviors; and (c) gender-variant boys' avoidance of other boys and their attraction to girl playmates, resulting in rehearsal of typically female behaviors and lack of environment in which to advance male gender roles.

Integration

Because current knowledge does not provide us with an "empirically grounded detailed theory of the mechanisms and processes of gender identity development" (Meyer-Bahlburg, 2010, p. 472), conclusive scientific statements about determinants of gender-nonconforming identity cannot be made. Gender identity formation is seen from an integrative perspective as a complex biological and psychological process, which is unique for each person and which involves a variety of "genetic, hormonal and environmental factors, acting separately or in combination with each other" (Gender Identity Research and Education Society, 2006, p. 38). According to Diamond's (2006) biased interaction theory, infants are born with a certain evolutionary heritage, family genetics, and uterine environment influences that bring about a propensity for certain sexual and gender patterns' expression. However, the patterns eventually expressed depend on the upbringing and societal values. Diamond (2000) noted that transgender children

> have to integrate the gender attributions of society and its constructs with feelings of self. I think all do so and match these feelings with some brain template of "similar or different" which is more crucial than penis or clitoris, more central to their sense of being than is a scrotum or vagina, and more important than their familial rearing. The individual comes to identify as a member of one of those groups (boys or girls, men or women) with whom he or she feels more "similar" and less "different." Fortunately, for most of us, these factors of brain template and the sex-typical biases and inclinations it imparts, are usually in concert with anatomy and cultural construction of gender. When they are not, the mind will usually rule even when in conflict with societal expectations. (p. 51)

Diagnosis and Its Evaluation

Although there are no definitive theories of transgender development, there is a psychiatric diagnosis describing this phenomenon. According to the fourth text revision edition of the *Diagnostic and Statistical Manual of Mental Disorders* (*DSM-IV-TR*; American Psychiatric Association [APA], 2000), GID is a wide diagnostic category, available to diagnose both children and adults. The diagnosis of GIDC is based on four diagnostic features. The first, spelled out in Criterion A, includes "a strong and persistent cross-gender identification" (APA, 2000, p. 581) signifying a desire to be or assertion of being of the other sex. The disturbance is marked by at least four of the following five indicators: (a) repeated insistence or desire to be of the other sex, (b) preference for cross-dressing, (c) strong and continuous affinity for cross-sex roles during play or in fantasy, (d) strong wish to engage in stereotypical play of the other sex, and (e) powerful tendency to play with children of the other sex. The second feature, described in Criterion B, includes "persistent discomfort with his or her sex or sense of inappropriateness in the gender role of that sex" (APA, 2000, p. 581). It is demonstrated by any of the following indicators: in boys, by disgust with or wish not to have a penis and/or refusal to engage in typically male play; and in girls, by refusal to sit for urination, wish to grow a penis, negation of eventual acquiring of typically female secondary sex characteristics, or refusal of typical "normative feminine clothing" (APA, 2000, p. 581). According to Criterion C, no concurrent intersex conditions should be present, and, as spelled out in Criterion D, the cross-gender identification must be accompanied by "clinically significant distress or impairment in social, occupational, or other important areas of functioning" (APA, 2000, p. 581).

GIDC is a controversial diagnosis, seen by many as contributing to gender stereotypes and conflating complex matters of gender identity, emotional suffering, and social nonconformity (Lev, 2005). The following critique focuses on debates involving terminology within diagnostic criteria, psychosexual outcomes of gender-variant youth, and status of GIDC as a mental disorder.

Terminology Within Diagnostic Criteria

The GIDC diagnostic criteria have been criticized not only for their anachronistic language, which over dichotomizes "appropriate" gender roles and behaviors (Hill, Rozanski, Carfagnini, & Willoughby, 2007), but also for the confusing use of terms and concepts. Criterion A, although purporting to scrutinize cross-gender identification, also includes references to cross-sex identifications ("repeatedly stated desire to be or insistence that he or she is, the other sex" [APA, 2000, p. 581]). Similarly, Criterion B appears to confuse sex with gender, as discomfort with one's biological sex and discomfort with gender roles are ascribed to one category. It is unclear why disgust with one's genitals is equated with preference for particular toys or attire (Bartlett, Vasey, & Bukowski, 2000).

Another key concern revolves around failure of criteria to sufficiently differentiate between children who violate societal gender norms in the absence of gender dysphoria and children who are uncomfortable with their biological sex *in addition* to unhappiness with the assigned gender roles. Under current diagnostic criteria, it is not necessary for a child to insist that he or she is or desires to be the other sex or to even be uncomfortable with his or her own biological sex to be diagnosed with GIDC (Bartlett et al., 2000). For example, a boy who is content with his assigned gender and sexual body parts, and who, at the same time, prefers to play with girls, wear more feminine attire, act out feminine fantasy figures, and who refuses to play rough or stereotypically boys' games, can be diagnosed with GIDC, thus increasing the false-positive rate of the diagnosis (Hill et al., 2007).

Studies examining whether a desire to be of the other sex should become a distinct diagnostic criterion are inconclusive, possibly due to frequent co-occurrence but not a complete overlap of cross-sex desires with cross-gender behaviors. According to Bartlett et al. (2000), a child who is uncomfortable with his or her biological sex will likely behave in ways that violate conventional gender norms, but a child engaging in cross-gender behaviors does not automatically wish to be of the other biological sex.

Psychosexual Outcomes

Related debate concerns the psychosexual outcomes of gender-variant children. Although it is commonly believed that children diagnosed with GIDC grow up to be transsexual adults, such is rarely the case. The most common outcome of childhood gender nonconformity is development of gay/lesbian identity in adolescence or adulthood, without persisting GID. About 30% of children diagnosed with GIDC become heterosexual adults, whereas a very small minority will continue to carry the diagnosis of adult GID (Bartlett et al., 2000; Zucker & Spitzer, 2005). According to Hill et al. (2007), these three disparate psychosexual adult outcomes not only highlight the diagnosis's failure to distinguish between these three phenomenologies but also raise questions about its validity and reliability. This issue is magnified by the fact that since the *DSM-IV-TR* publication, there have been no official studies of reliability of GIDC, demonstrating "a serious deficiency in the literature" (Zucker, 2010, p. 486).

Pathologizing children whose most likely psychosexual outcome is homosexuality also troubles many scholars and activists, who perceive the diagnosis as sanctioning the prevention and treatment of homosexuality under the guise of treating GIDC (Schope & Eliason, 2004). Proponents of the diagnosis disagree with such assessment and assert that (a) gender variance and homosexuality are conceptually different and (b) the diagnosis gives access to treatment aimed at eradicating cross-gender behaviors, thus preventing negative emotional consequences resulting from societal stigma. Moreover, those who support this diagnostic category see early successful treatment as preventing adult GID, thus reducing "the need for the long and difficult process of sex reassignment" (Meyer-Bahlburg, 2002, p. 362).

Does GIDC Satisfy *DSM* Criteria for a Disorder?

Controversy also surrounds Criterion D, which states that the disorder causes significant distress or impairment in functioning. The *DSM-IV-TR*'s (APA, 2000) definition of mental disorder requires the dysfunction to be within the individual and not based on conflict between the person and society. Thus, to be diagnosed with GIDC, a child's distress has to be intrinsic and not related to social condemnation and rejection (Vasey & Bartlett, 2007).

Our society is generally intolerant of children who do not fit into "typical" gender categories. Boys, who experience a stronger gender role mandate, are especially vulnerable to society's collective disdain when they are gender nonconforming (Wester, McDonough, White, Vogel, & Taylor, 2010). Emotional difficulties associated with GIDC tend to increase with age, suggesting that these problems are related to the additive effect of constant societal censure and ostracism of gender-nonconforming behaviors (Bartlett et al., 2000). Confirming this hypothesis is Zucker and Cohen-Kettenis's (2008) review of behavioral problems in cross-gender-identified children, showing that childhood gender-nonconforming behavior prominently elicits negative reactions from peers. This issue becomes especially prominent in middle and high schools, where gender-variant youth face harassment and violence even greater than that directed at gender-conforming lesbian, gay, and bisexual youth (Greytak, Kosciw, & Diaz, 2009).

Examining the extent of intrinsic suffering among gender-variant children, Vasey and Bartlett (2007) studied the Samoan *fa'afafine*, who enjoy societal acceptance and tend to see their cross-gender identity and expression as a source of pride rather than distress. The authors concluded that, whereas a small minority of *fa'afafine* were intrinsically distressed about their sexual anatomy, a general lack of such distress rendered the diagnosis with *DSM* in its current form untenable. According to Zucker (2010), although "it remains unclear how distress is to be inferred independently of the clinical indicators" (p. 489) in the diagnostic criteria, "the constructs of distress and impairment require a great deal of further consideration" (p. 490).

The Future of GIDC

In light of the numerous criticisms, several scholars have called for actions ranging from the dismissal of the GIDC diagnosis to the application of the diagnosis only to those who present with demonstrated pathology (Meyer-Bahlburg, 2010). At the same time, proponents maintain that GIDC has its place in the *DSM* and that "the failure to develop a gender identity that is congruent with biological gender is a dysfunction" (Spitzer, 2005, p. 116).

The DSM-5 Development Sexual and Gender Identity Disorders Work Group (APA, 2010) has proposed several revisions to the GIDC diagnosis. The group recommended a new name–*gender incongruence in children*–seen as less stigmatizing and more representative of the symptomatology. The group also proposed that the distress/impairment criterion be removed, acknowledging that most psychiatric problems in the population stem from an "increased experiences of stigma" (APA, 2010, Rationale, End notes, #15). Other suggested changes include (a) the integration of Criteria A and B into one criterion with at least six of eight indicators necessary for diagnosis (six of the proposed indicators relate to gender role transgressions and two concern anatomical dysphoria); (b) demonstration of "a strong desire to be of the other gender or an insistence that he or she is the other gender" (APA, 2010, Gender Incongruence, A.1.) as necessary for diagnosis; (c) replacement of the term *sex* with *perceived gender* to accommodate persons with disorders of sex development; and (d) a 6-month duration requirement to distinguish between transient and more persistent conditions.

The proposed revisions are drawing attention of the GID reform advocates. In official comments submitted to APA, Winters (2010) praised the less stigmatizing name of the condition, the emphasis on "gender incongruence," and the requirement of gender dysphoria for diagnosis. At the same time, Winters recommended that several issues be further revised.

Winters (2010) proposed that the diagnosis be clearly made on the basis of dysphoria caused by incongruence between the experienced gender and current physical characteristics/assigned gender role. According to our review of changes proposed by the DSM-5 Development Group, the diagnosis could still be given to children who reject the assigned gender but who do not experience any anatomical dysphoria. Winters also regarded the proposal for removal of the distress/impairment criterion as possibly leading to over diagnosis of children who do not meet criteria for mental disorder. She proposed that the criterion be kept and that it be based on distress resulting from living in the present gender as opposed to anguish stemming from societal prejudice and discrimination. Furthermore, according to Winters, the term *incongruence* was not effectively defined and was easily confused with social nonconformity. At the same time, Winters assessed the language of diagnostic criteria as anachronistic and pathologizing those who do not conform to "outmoded, sexist, binary gender stereotypes" (Winters, 2010, p. 3). The call to revise the diagnostic language was also previously made by other authors who advocated for this diagnostic category to be written in language reflecting contemporary views of gender rather than views that are based on gender-specific games or clothing (Hill et al., 2007; Martin, 2008).

Conclusion

Meaningful understanding of gender identity in its developmental and cultural context is paramount in the counseling process whenever determinations about diagnosis and treatment of gender-nonconforming children have to be made. Although in our culture "sexed bodies and gender expressions are severely proscribed, assigned, and delineated" (Lev, 2005, p. 42), decisions about what is gender appropriate depend not only on the geographical location of the individual but also on her or his historical context. After all, most professional women of today would have been considered abnormal 60 years ago. This issue is further complicated by the lack of definitive theories of gender development, prohibiting a definitive declaration about whether gender-nonconforming identity represents a pathological phenomenon (Meyer-Bahlburg, 2010, p. 472).

Psychiatry has a long history of pathologizing human diversity, including race, ethnicity, and sexual orientation (Lev, 2005). Therefore, we must not only be well informed but also especially thoughtful when making decisions about the lives of children who do not adhere to gender norms presently accepted by our society. This stance of awareness, thoughtfulness, and nonpathologizing of diversity that we advocate is imperative in adequately assessing and clinically addressing both the distress inflicted by society and the intrapersonal suffering of children whose gender identity does not match their physical body. While it may be challenging to distinguish between culturally induced and intrinsic suffering, the clinical and social ramifications of the GIDC diagnosis bring to the forefront the importance of the conscientious and mindful assessment and diagnosis of gender-variant children.

References

American Psychiatric Association. (2000). *Diagnostic and statistical manual of mental disorders* (4th ed., text rev.). Washington, DC: Author.

American Psychiatric Association. (2010). *DSM-5 development: 302.6. Gender identity disorder in children: Proposed revision*. Retrieved from http://www.dsm5.org/ProposedRevisions/Pages/proposedrevision.aspx?rid=192

Bartlett, N., Vasey, P., & Bukowski, W. (2000). Is gender identity disorder in children a mental disorder? *Sex Roles, 43*, 753–785. doi:10.1023/A:1011004431889

Blakemore, J. E. O., Berenbaum, S. A., & Liben, L. S. (2009). *Gender development*. New York, NY: Psychology Press.

Bostwick, J., & Martin, K. (2007). A man's brain in an ambiguous body: A case of mistaken gender identity. *American Journal of Psychiatry, 164*, 1499–1505. doi:10.1176/appi.ajp.2007.07040587

Campbell, A., Shirley, L., & Caygill, L. (2002). Sex-typed preferences in three domains: Do two-year-olds need cognitive variables? *British Journal of Psychology, 93*, 203–217. doi:10.1348/000712602162544

Coates, S. (1992). The etiology of boyhood gender identity disorder: An integrative model. In D. L. Wolitzky (Ed.), *Interface of psychoanalysis and psychology* (pp. 245–265). Washington, DC: American Psychological Association. doi:10.1037/10118-010

Davies, D. (2004). *Child development: A practitioner's guide* (2nd ed.). New York, NY: Guilford Press.

Diamond, M. (2000). Sex and gender: Same or different? *Feminism & Psychology, 10*, 46–54. doi:10.1177/0959353500010001007

Diamond, M. (2002). Sex and gender are different: Sexual identity and gender identity are different. *Clinical Child Psychology and Psychiatry, 7*, 320–334. doi:10.1177/1359104502007003002

Diamond, M. (2006). Biased-interaction theory of psychosexual development: "How does one know if one is male or female?" *Sex Roles, 55*, 589–600. doi:10.1007/s11199-006-9115-y

Fagot, B., & Hagan, R. (1991). Observations of parent reactions to sex-stereotyped behaviors: Age and sex effects. *Child Development, 62*, 617–628. doi:10.2307/1131135

Gender Identity Research and Education Society. (2006). A typical gender development: A review. *International Journal of Transgenderism, 9*, 22–44. doi:10.1300/J485v09n01_04

Girshick, L. B. (2008). *Transgender voices: Beyond men and women*. Lebanon, NH: University Press of New England.

Green, R., & Young, R. (2001). Hand preference, sexual preference, and trans sexualism. *Archives of Sexual Behavior, 30*, 565–574. doi:10.1023/A:1011908532367

Greytak, E. A., Kosciw, J. G., & Diaz, E. M. (2009). *Harsh realities: The experiences of transgender youth in our nation's schools*. New York, NY: Gay, Lesbian and Straight Education Network.

Hill, D. B., Rozanski, C, Carfagnini, J., & Willoughby, B. (2007). Gender identity disorders in childhood and adolescence: A critical inquiry. *International Journal of Sexual Health, 19*, 57–75. doi:10.1300/J514vl9n01_07

Jacobs, S. E., Thomas, W., & Lang, S. (1997). *Two-spirit people: Native American gender identity, sexuality, and spirituality*. Urbana and Chicago, IL: University of Illinois Press.

Karraker, K., Vogel, D., & Lake, M. (1995). Parents' gender-stereotyped perceptions of newborns: The eye of the beholder revisited. *Sex Roles, 33*, 687–701. doi:10.1007/BF01547725

Kraemer, B., Noll, T., Delsignore, A., Milos, G., Schnyder, U., & Hepp, U. (2009). Finger length ratio (2D:4D) in adults with gender identity disorder. *Archives of Sexual Behavior, 38,* 359–363. doi:10.1007/sl0508-007-9262-4

Lev, A. I. (2005). Disordering gender identity: Gender identity disorder in the DSM-IV-TR. *Journal of Psychology & Human Sexuality, 17,* 35–69. doi:10.1300/J056vl7n03_03

Martin, J. I. (2008). Nosology, etiology, and course of gender identity disorder in children. *Journal of Gay and Lesbian Mental Health, 12,* 81–94. doi:10.1300/J529vl2n01_06

McHale, S., Crouter, A., & Whiteman, S. (2003). The family contexts of gender development in childhood and adolescence. *Social Development, 12,* 125–148. doi:10.1111/1467-9507.00225

Meyer-Bahlburg, H. F. L. (2002). Gender identity in young boys: A parent- and peer-based treatment protocol. *Clinical Child Psychology and Psychiatry, 7,* 360–375. doi.10.1177/1359104502007003005

Meyer-Bahlburg, H. F. L. (2010). From mental disorder to iatrogenic hypogonadism: Dilemmas in conceptualizing gender identity variants as psychiatric conditions. *Archives of Sexual Behavior, 39,* 461–476. doi:10.1007/sl0508-009-9532-4

Mintz, L. B., & O'Neil, J. M. (1990). Gender roles, sex, and the process of psychotherapy: Many questions and few answers *Journal of Counseling & Development, 68,* 381–387. Retrieved from http://search.ebscohost.com.ezproxy.brooklyn.cuny.edu:2048/login.aspx?direct=true&db=psyh&AN=l990-17846-001&site=ehost-live

Newman, L. K. (2002). Sex, gender and culture: Issues in the definition, assessment and treatment of gender identity disorder. *Clinical Child Psychology and Psychiatry, 7,* 352–359. doi:l0.1177/1359104502007003004

Pasterski, V. (2008). Disorders of sex development and a typical sex differentiation. In D. L. Rowland & L. Incrocci (Eds.), *Handbook of sexual and gender identity disorders* (pp. 354–375). Hoboken, NJ: Wiley.

Poulin-Dubois, D., Serbin, L., Eichstedt, J., Sen, M., & Beissel, C. (2002). Men don't put on make-up: Toddlers' knowledge of the gender stereotyping of household activities. *Social Development, 11,* 166–181. doi:10.1111/1467-9507.00193

Schilt, K., & Westbrook, L. (2009). Doing gender, doing heteronormativity: "Gender normals," transgender people, and the social maintenance of heterosexuality. *Gender & Society, 23,* 440–464. doi:10.1177/0891243209340034

Schope, R., & Eliason, M. (2004). Sissies and tomboys: Gender role behaviors and homophobia. *Journal of Gay & Lesbian Social Services: Issues in Practice, Policy & Research, 16,* 73–97. doi:10.1300/J041vl6n02_05

Serbin, L., Poulin-Dubois, D., & Eichstedt, J. (2002). Infants' response to gender-inconsistent events. *Infancy, 3,* 531–542. doi:10.1207/S15327078IN0304_07

Spitzer, R. L. (2005). Sexual and gender identity disorders: Discussion of questions for *DSM-V. Journal of Psychology & Human Sexuality, 17,* 111–116. doi:10.1300/J056vl7n03_06

Stryker, S. (2008). *Transgender history.* Berkeley, CA: Seal Press.

Vasey, P., & Bartlett, N. (2007). What can the Samoan "fa'afafine" teach us about the Western concept of gender identity disorder in childhood? *Perspectives in Biology and Medicine, 50,* 481–490. doi:10.1353/pbm.2007.0056

Wester, S. R., McDonough, T. A., White, M., Vogel, D. L., & Taylor, L. (2010). Using gender role conflict theory in counseling male-to-female transgender individuals. *Journal of Counseling & Development, 88,* 214–219. Retrieved from http://aca.metapress.com/link.asp?id=97hhlk6351780200

Winters, K. (2010). *Comments on the proposed revision to 302.6 gender identity disorder in children.* Retrieved from http://www.gidreform.org/201004APAGICHILDkwB.pdf

Zhou, J., Hofman, M. A., Gooren, L. J. G., & Swaab, D. F. (1995, November 2). A sex difference in the human brain and its relation to transsexuality. *Nature, 378,* 68–70. doi:10.1038/378068a0

Zucker, K. J. (2010). The *DSM* diagnostic criteria for gender identity disorder in children. *Archives of Sexual Behavior, 39,* 477–498. doi:10.1007/sl0508-009-9540-4

Zucker, K. J., & Bradley, S. J. (2004). Gender identity and psychosexual disorders. In M. K. Dulcan (Ed.), *The American Psychiatric Publishing textbook of child and adolescent psychiatry* (3rd ed., pp. 813–835). Arlington, VA: American Psychiatric Publishing, Inc.

Zucker, K., & Cohen-Kettenis, P. (2008). Gender identity disorder in children and adolescents. In D. L. Rowland & L. Incrocci (Eds.), *Handbook of sexual and gender identity disorders* (pp. 376–422). Hoboken, NJ: Wiley.

Zucker, K., & Spitzer, R. (2005). Was the gender identity disorder of childhood diagnosis introduced into DSM-III as a backdoor maneuver to replace homosexuality? A historical note. *Journal of Sex & Marital Therapy, 31,* 31–42. doi:10.1080/00926230590475251

Discussion Questions

1. How do children know what gender is and how to behave?
2. Why would a child insist that he or she is not the gender "assigned" to him or her?
3. Do you think, based on this reading, gender identity that doesn't match physical body should be classified as a disorder?

Assignment

Write an essay about the issue of gender identity. Use evidence from this article and one other journal article to support your perspective on whether this is a disorder in children.

Parent—Child Aggression

Association With Child Abuse Potential and Parenting Styles

By Christina M. Rodriguez

I n 2006, over 900,000 children were substantiated victims of child abuse and neglect in the United States, and physical abuse constituted 16% of those reports (U.S. Department of Health & Human Services [DHHS], 2008). Others estimate that physical abuse may actually range from over 23% (King, Trocme, & Thatte, 2003) up to nearly 30% of all cases of child maltreatment (Jones & McCurdy, 1992). More troubling are estimates based on anonymous parent report that severe physical assault toward children is in fact 5–11 times greater than official reports (Straus, Hamby, Finkelhor, Moore, & Runyan, 1998). Thus, physical abuse remains a critical concern even considering only those cases that rise to the exacting substantiation standards of child protective services, an agency that received an estimated 3.3 million referrals in 2006 (DHHS, 2008) while simultaneously witnessing steady declines in rates of substantiation (see King et al., 2003 , for discussion).

Physical child abuse is typically defined as non-accidental injury to a child (Child Abuse Prevention, Adoption and Family Services Act of 1988), implying the resultant harm was intentional. However, physical abuse often arises when- parents unintentionally escalate their administration of physical discipline (Herrenkohl, Herrenkohl, & Egolf, 1983 ; Whipple & Richey, 1997). Physical discipline has been defined as "the use of physical force with the intention of causing a child to experience pain, but not injury, for the purpose of correction or control of the child's behavior" (Straus, 2000 , p. 1110). Physical discipline toward children is virtually universal in this country, with nearly 94% of American parents indicating they had employed physical discipline by the time their child was 3 or 4 (Straus & Stewart, 1999). From Violence and Victims, pp. 728-741. Copyright © Springer Publishing Company 2010. Provided by ProQuest, LLC. All rights reserved. Reprinted with permission.

Distinguishing between physical abuse and physical discipline is both challenging and controversial. In a review of 8,000 substantiated cases of physical abuse, injurious and non-injurious child maltreatment were comparable with regard to child, parent, and socioeconomic characteristics (Gonzalez, Durrant, Chabot, Trocme, & Brown, 2008). Parents who are physically abusive also apply excessive, unreasonable physical discipline toward their children (Veltkamp & Miller, 1994 ; Whipple & Webster-Stratton, 1991). Parent–child aggression has been linked to negative behaviors in the recipients, whether the parental behavior is expressed as child abuse (e.g., Edwards, Holden, Felitti, & Anda, 2003 ; Runyon, Deblinger, Ryan, & Thakkar-Kolar, 2004) or corporal punishment (e.g., see Gershoff, 2002 , for review). Consequently, a number of researchers recommend any form of physical parent–child aggression be conceptualized on a physical discipline–child abuse continuum (Graziano, 1994 ; Greenwald, Bank, Reid, & Knutson, 1997 ; Rodriguez & Richardson, 2007 ; Salzinger, Feldman, Hammer, & Rosario, 1991 ; Straus, 2001a , 2001b ; Whipple & Richey, 1997), with mild physical discipline at one endpoint and extreme physical abuse at the other; harsh physical discipline could thus escalate to abuse somewhere along the continuum.

Given such a conceptualization, research relying on confirmed perpetrators of physical abuse would provide insight to a valuable endpoint of the continuum but a potentially restricted component of parent–child aggression. Maltreatment may be undetected by or unreported to protective services (Sedlak & Broadhurst, 1996), and the complex process of substantiation (King et al., 2003) typically yields high false negative rates (see DeGarmo, Reid, & Knutson, 2006 , for discussion). Parents identified by protective services likely represent a selective, potentially atypical, fraction of those engaging in abusive parent–child aggression. Moreover, conclusions founded solely on substantiated perpetrators are not optimal when considering approaches intended to prevent abuse. Many abused children never encounter the social services system, and in order to better prevent child abuse, studying those not identified by the system (either low risk or at-risk) can provide a glimpse into how sub-abusive discipline can escalate to child abuse further along the continuum.

One popular line of research concentrates on pinpointing those beliefs and characteristics predictive of a parent's risk to physically maltreat a child (Milner, 1986 , 1994), estimating the likelihood a parent will become abusive. This likelihood, termed child abuse potential, is estimated by such measures as the Child Abuse Potential Inventory (CAPI) which incorporates interpersonal and intrapersonal difficulties as well as inflexible attitudes regarding children observed in parents who physically abuse their children (Milner, 1986). Scores on the CAPI distinguish substantiated child abusers from comparison groups (Milner, Gold, & Wimberley, 1986) and predict which parents are likely to become abusive (Milner, Gold, Ayoub, & Jacewitz, 1984). CAPI scores also demonstrate an association with observed coercive parenting styles (Haskett, Scott, & Fann, 1995 ; Margolin, Gordis, Medina, & Oliver, 2003).

Although the CAPI (Milner, 1986) is widely regarded as a leading instrument to assess child abuse risk, the measure does not explicitly elicit any information regarding actual discipline practices in general or maltreatment behaviors in particular. Indeed, as noted above, the CAPI taps a range of personal issues and attitudes toward children that are characteristics of abusive parents. In contrast, epidemiological surveys have utilized such instruments as the Parent–Child Conflict Tactics Scale (CTSPC; Straus et al., 1998) to determine the frequency of actual behaviors implemented toward children during parent–child conflict. Remarkably little research has yet evaluated the association between child abuse potential and reports of actual parent–child physical aggression, either increased use of physical discipline or physically abusive behaviors. One study utilizing a modified earlier version of the Conflict Tactics Scale (Straus, 1979) determined if child abuse potential was related to a parent's personal history of maltreatment (Caliso & Milner, 1992), but one's own aggressive behavior toward a child was still not assessed. Although measures of child abuse potential should relate to parent–child physical aggression, their actual association has not been studied empirically.

Furthermore, relatively little research has evaluated the connections between parenting styles and child abuse potential or parent–child aggression. Baumrind's (1966) classic conceptualization of parenting style characterizes parental control as generally manifest in three broad styles: permissive (in which the parent exerts minimal control over the child with few demands); authoritarian (in which the parent enforces control of the child by ensuring unquestioned adherence to absolute standards); and authoritative (in which adherence to rules is a cooperative endeavor between parent and child but the parent remains firm in setting standards). Although authoritarian parenting style appears potentially beneficial in some ethnic minority groups (e.g., African American and Chinese American families; Baumrind, 1972 ; Chao, 1994), authoritative parenting is typically considered optimal whereas permissive and authoritarian parenting are generally construed as dysfunctional approaches (Baumrind, 1966 , 1996).

Conceptually, authoritarian parenting would be expected to relate to child abuse risk, supported by empirical research that observational indices of authoritarian parenting are associated with child abuse potential scores (Haskett et al., 1995). Likewise, although parenting style was not measured specifically, child abuse potential was positively associated with coercive parenting approaches and negatively associated with sensitive and consistent parenting in a community sample of parents (Margolin et al., 2003). Overall, however, the pattern of associations between actual physically abusive behavior and physical discipline, child abuse potential, and different disciplinary styles has not yet been adequately clarified. Indeed, although researchers in this field are more apt to concentrate on authoritarian styles, permissive parenting styles are also considered problematic (Arnold, O'Leary, Wolff, & Acker, 1993 ; Baumrind, 1996) but the literature has not yet explored how permissive styles may relate to child abuse potential. Permissive parenting which results in minimal oversight could conceptually be consistent with neglectful parenting. Given that neglect is often identified in families who engage in physical abuse (DHHS, 2008), it is possible abuse risk relates to permissive parenting styles as well, particularly because the personal issues and attitudes captured by the CAPI may not be unique to physical abuse.

Presumably, parent–child aggression, in the form of both frequent physical discipline and physical maltreatment, would be expected to relate to increased physical child abuse potential and dysfunctional parenting styles. Therefore, the purpose of the present investigation was to evaluate whether child abuse potential, parent–child discipline and abuse, and dysfunctional parenting styles (particularly more authoritarian approaches) would be intercorrelated. Furthermore, parents engaging in parent–child aggression indicative of child maltreatment specifically were expected to demonstrate greater child abuse potential and more maladaptive disciplinary styles. Such associations would provide additional construct validity for the leading measure of abuse risk, the CAPI, as well as lending some insight into how abuse risk and parent–child aggression relate to differing parenting styles. To evaluate these hypotheses, three independent studies were examined, two with low-risk community samples of parents and a third with a clinical at-risk sample of parents of children with externalizing behavior disorders (given that children with behavior problems exhibit behaviors resulting in more frequent discipline incidents that exacerbate abuse risk; Wolfe, 1999).

Methods

Instruments across All Studies

The *Child Abuse Potential Inventory* (CAPI; Milner 1986) includes 160 statements to which respondents agree or disagree. Designed to screen for physical child abuse, the CAPI assesses rigidity and intrapersonal and interpersonal difficulties characteristic of identified physically abusive parents. Only 77 items comprise the Abuse Scale score and its six underlying factors, with the remaining statements serving as items for experimental scales or as measures of distortion biases. The factors within the Abuse Scale include: Distress, Rigidity, Unhappiness, Problems with Child and Self, Problems with Family, and Problems with Others.

With regard to internal consistency of the Abuse Scale score, the CAPI manual reports split-half reliability ranging from .96 (for control groups) to .98 (for abuse groups) and Kuder-Richardson reliability coefficients ranging from .92 (for control groups) to .95 (for abuse groups), suggesting high internal consistency for community, at-risk, and abusive samples (Milner, 1986). Retest reliabilities range from .91 after one day to .75 after 3 months (Milner, 1986). In terms of predictive validity, studies have indicated a correct classification rate of 81.4% of confirmed child abusers and 99% of comparison parents, with an overall pattern indicating that a lower cut-off score leads to classification rates in the low-90s% range and that a higher cut-off score leads to greater false-negatives of child abusers (Milner, 1994).

The *Parent-Child Conflict Tactics Scale* (CTSPC; Straus et al., 1998) is a revision of an epidemiological survey of family violence, the Conflict Tactics Scale (Straus, 1979). The CTSPC contains 22 items in which a parent reports on the frequency with which they have engaged in a series of behaviors arising from parent–child conflicts (response categories as follows: 0 = this has never happened; 1 = once in the past year; 2 = twice in the past year; 3 = 3–5 times in the past year; 4 = 6–10 times in the past year; 5 = 11–20 times in the past year; 6 = more than 20 times in the past year; 7 = not in the past year, but it happened before). Responses are scored based on the frequency range reported by the parent: responses of 0, 1, and 2 correspond to scores of 0, 1, and 2, respectively; a score of 4 (the midpoint) is assigned for a parent selecting the 3–5 times category; a score of 8 is assigned to the 6–10 times category; a score of 15 is assigned for the 11–20 times category; and a score of 25 is given for the final category, 20 or more times in the past year.

Thirteen of the CTSPC items directly address varying levels of physical tactics applied toward children, comprising a subscale entitled Physical Assault (with subcategories of minor assault/corporal punishment, severe assault/physical maltreatment, and very severe assault/severe physical maltreatment). Given the subcategories, actions tapped by the Physical Assault subscale range from spanking, slapping, or pinching up to beating or burning. In addition to the Physical Assault subscale, four items of the CTSPC comprise the Non-Violent Discipline subscale (including such actions as removal of privileges and "time-out") and five items contribute to the Psychological Aggression subscale (involving such behaviors as verbal threats and yelling). Although the CTSPC Physical Assault scale was of most interest, some intriguing results emerged regarding the Psychological Aggression scales and will be reported and discussed. In addition to analyses using the three subscales, physical maltreatment in particular was isolated by computing a classification score based on parents' report of ever using any of severe assault/physical maltreatment (three items) or very severe assault/severe physical maltreatment (four items) behaviors; respondents indicating that they had engaged in any of the seven maltreatment items were categorized in a CTS Maltreatment group whereas those reporting none of these behaviors were categorized in a CTS No Maltreatment group.

Straus and colleagues (1998) report moderate internal consistency at .55 for the Physical Assault scale, .60 for the Psychological Aggression scale, and .70 for the Nonviolent Discipline scale. These moderate reliability coefficients likely reflect the diverse behaviors included in the measure as well as the very low reported frequency of many of the items (Straus et al., 1998). The authors provide supportive evidence of construct and discriminant validity, and some indication of modest correlations among subscales (Straus et al., 1998).

The *Parenting Scale* (Arnold et al., 1993) was utilized to identify parents' dysfunctional parenting styles. Thirty items present parents with a typical parent–child conflict situation and asks them to indicate their response to the situation along a 7-point scale, with two opposing reactions at endpoints of each scale. The Parenting Scale yields a Total score intended to indicate overall dysfunctional parenting style. Based on the original factor analysis (Arnold et al., 1993), this general dysfunctional parenting style subsumes three separate response styles: Overreactivity (representing a harsh, angry discipline style, consistent with an authoritarian parenting style), Laxness (reflecting a permissive style of parenting), and Verbosity (in which parents rely on verbal persuasion even when ineffective). However, a subsequent normative sample with 785 parents of 2- to 12-year-old children (Collett, Gimpel, Greenson, & Gunderson, 2001) indicated that a new factor analysis did not support a separate Verbosity factor. Consequently, for the purposes of the present study, the Overreactivity and Laxness subscales were targeted as the most potentially meaningful parenting styles to test the hypotheses. Scores are computed by summing across items for the scale and dividing by the number of items, with higher scores indicative of more dysfunctional parenting styles. An example of an Overreactivity item would offer a prompt, such as "When my child misbehaves" and then asks the parent to select between, "I handle it without getting upset," versus, "I get so frustrated and angry that my child can see I'm upset." An example of a Laxness item would prompt, "When I say my child can't do something" followed by the two choices, "I let my child do it anyway," versus, "I stick to what I said."

Internal consistency reported by the test authors for the Total score is moderately high at .84, with Laxness and Overreactivity at .83 and .82, respectively (Arnold et al., 1993), which are comparable to those reported in the more recent normative study (Collett et al., 2001). Over a 2-week period, test–retest reliability was relatively high for the Total, Laxness, and Overreactivity scores, at .84, .83, and .82, respectively (Arnold et al., 1993). In addition, scores were significantly related to clinical observations of parent–child interactions (Arnold et al., 1993).

Study 1

Participants. In the first study, 327 parents of children younger than 12 responded to an online parenting study. The mean age of these parents was 30.48 years (standard deviation [SD] = 6.22 years), with the majority of respondents female (84%), married (91%), with an average of 1.89 children (SD = 1.1). Respondents identified themselves as Caucasian (84.7%), African American (5.2%), Hispanic (4.0%), Asian (3.7%), American Indian/ Alaskan Native (1.2%), or Other (1.2%). The mean annual family income was $54,299, with a median of $45,000 that likely more accurately represents the sample because of some outliers. Participants reported on their highest educational attainment: 1.5% not high school graduates,

18.7% high school graduates, nearly 30% with some college or vocational degree, 37% college degree, and 12.8% graduate school.

Procedures. Study procedures were approved by the university institutional review board. Selected World Wide Websites devoted to parenting (e.g., www.ibaby.com, www. parentsoup.com, www.parenting.com) were targeted for an online parenting study. Links to a webpage for the parenting study were advertised on bulletin boards at these sites. Interested parents linked to the study website, which first presented them with an online consent form. Participants were then presented with a series of measures, including the CAPI, Parenting Scale, and CTSPC, which they could complete anonymously. Upon completion of this 60-minute study, respondents received a gift certificate code for $5 redeemable toward the purchase of an item sold online. Each participant's data was independently screened for accuracy and consistency in responding, with any questionable or incomplete files purged from the data set. For example, any respondent who obtained an elevated score on any of the three CAPI response bias indices was purged from the dataset ($n = 38$). Any files judged remotely questionable (uniform responding on any measure; $n = 24$) or largely incomplete ($n = 8$) were also removed from the data set, yielding 327 verified participants eligible for analyses with complete data on these three measures.

Study 2

Participants. Participants in this second community sample were 115 parents of children between ages 7 and 12; mothers ($n = 86$) and fathers ($n = 29$) were recruited for a larger parenting study conducted in a session in their home. The mean age of parents was 37.62 years ($SD = 7.91$ years), and the majority of parents in this sample (83.5%) reported they were living with a partner, with an average of three children. Based on self-identification, 92.2% described themselves as Caucasian, 6.1% as Hispanic, approximately 1% as Native American, and about 1% as "Other." The mean annual family income was $50,067 per year, with a median of $45,000. Nearly all participants (93.9%) reported graduating from high school, with 7.8% no education past high school; 46.1% reported they attended voca tional school or some college, 28.6% obtained a college degree, and 11.3% reported a graduate school degree.

Procedures. The study protocol was approved by the university institutional review board and the local school district. Parents in this second study were recruited from their child's school from notices/consent forms sent home about a study on factors affecting parenting and discipline. Interested parents returned a contact information sheet from which a 90-minute session was scheduled in their home for them to complete the larger study on a laptop computer. By using a computer, the participants were able to enter their responses to the questions anonymously and efficiently. Part of this study included the CAPI, the Parenting Scale, and the CTSPC, which were extracted for the present analyses. Parents received $10 as compensation for their time involved participating in this larger study.

Study 3

Participants. A clinical sample of parents constituted the third sample, with participants from a parenting study focusing on mothers of 7- to 12-year-old children with diagnosed externalizing behavior problems. In this study, 74 mothers participated, with a mean age of 40.65 years ($SD = 10.53$ years). Of these parents, 71.6% reported they were currently living with a partner, and they had an average of three children in the home. Based on self-report, the majority of the sample was Caucasian (82.4%), with 12.2% of Hispanic origin, 2.7% American Indian/ Alaskan Native, 1.4% African American, and 1.4% Asian. The mean annual family income was $41,016, with a median of $35,000. Most of the sample had graduated from high school

(83.6%); 22% had no education beyond high school, 43.2% obtained vocational training or some college, 12.2% attained a college degree, and 5.4% attained a graduate degree.

Procedures. Study procedures were approved by the university institutional review board. Mothers were recruited from flyers distributed to mental health agencies and school psychologists working with children with behavior problems. Participants for this parenting study had to be a mother of a child age 5–12 who was receiving mental health services for a diagnosed externalizing behavior problem. Interested parents meeting these criteria were scheduled for a 2-hour session in their home for a larger parenting and discipline study of at-risk children. Parent responses were entered anonymously onto a laptop computer, with the series of questionnaires including the CAPI, the Parenting Scale, and the CTSPC. Mothers received $20 for participating in this larger study.

Results

Preliminary Analyses: Comparison to Previous Norms and Correlations

All statistical analyses were conducted using the SPSS for Windows 15.0 statistical package. Means and standard deviations for the three measures for all three studies appear in Table 1 . The obtained sample CAPI Abuse Scale means in Studies 1 and 2 were comparable to the normative sample mean of 91.0 reported in the manual (Milner, 1986), with 14.5% of sample 1 and 15.2% of sample 2 obtaining scores above the clinical cut-off. In contrast, the sample of parents raising children with behavior problems in Study 3, considered an at-risk sample, obtained scores on the CAPI Abuse Scale significantly higher than the normative mean (t (73) = 5.16, $p \leq .001$). Although definitive normative means are not reported by the test authors for the Parenting Scale scores (Arnold et al., 1993), the obtained scores for the community samples in Studies 1 and 2 are comparable to those reported in the normative study (individual means per school grade are reported, ranging from 2.77 to 2.94; Collett et al., 2001). In contrast, Parenting Scale scores for Study 3 were comparable to those reported by the test authors for a clinical sample of mothers raising behavior problem children ($M = 3.1$; Arnold et al., 1993). For the CTSPC, the epidemiological results present mean scores on the Physical Assault, Psychological Aggression, and Non-Violent Discipline scales only for those who had engaged in at least one of the behaviors in the past month (Straus et al., 1998). Consequently, those means would be considerably higher than those obtained in the present investigation's three studies. For comparison purposes, however, the epidemiological means were 46.0 for Non-Violent Discipline, 21.7 for Psychological Aggression, and 13.4 for Physical Assault (Straus et al., 1998).

Although not part of the research questions for this paper, the correlations between the Parenting Scale Overreactivity and Laxness Scales ranged from $r = .33$ and .38 (both $p < .001$) for the two community samples of Studies 1 and 2, consistent with other community samples ($r = .36$; Prinzie, Onghena, & Hellinckx, 2007); for the Study 3 at-risk sample, the association between the two Parenting Scale scores was $r = .62$ ($p < .001$); although generally not reported, one study that included parents raising hard to manage toddlers reported a correlation of $r = .58$ (Slep & O'Leary, 1997). With regard to correlations within the CTSPC, Physical Assault scores correlated with the Non-Violent Discipline scores ranging from $r = .08$ to .26 and with the Psychological Aggression scores from $r = .27$ ($p < .05$; Study 3) to .62 ($p < .001$; Study 2); the Non-Violent Discipline scores were correlated with the Psychological Aggression scores ranging from $r = .21$ ($p = .07$) to .37 ($p < .001$). Correlations between the scales of CTSPC have not been traditionally reported and are greatly impacted by sampling characteristics.

Table 1. Means, standard deviations, and correlations

	M	SD	CAPI Abuse Scale (r)	Parenting Overreactivity (r)	Parenting Laxness (r)
CAPI Abuse Scale					
Study 1	92.58	73.31			
Study 2	94.74	83.38			
Study 3	146.28	92.18			
Parenting Scale Overreactivity					
Study 1	2.54	.86	.54**		
Study 2	2.86	.89	.51**		
Study 3	3.06	.93	.50**		
Parenting Scale Laxness					
Study 1	2.32	.84	.16*		
Study 2	2.59	.71	.25*		
Study 3	2.83	1.01	.49**		
CTSPC Physical Assault					
Study 1	9.84	17.36	.39**	.37**	.13a
Study 2	7.48	11.23	.32**	.43**	.08
Study 3	10.49	16.07	.33*	.37**	.24a
CTSPC Nonviolent Discipline					
Study 1	49.65	26.44	–.01	.10	–.08
Study 2	51.18	25.51	.08	.10	–.03
Study 3	59.76	24.64	–.14	–.15	–.27a
CTSPC Psychological Aggression					
Study 1	13.08	14.53	.43**	.56**	.14a
Study 2	18.56	16.96	.33**	.58**	.18
Study 3	27.46	21.41	.29*	.48**	.16

Note: CAPI = Child Abuse Potential Inventory; CTSPC = Parent–Child Conflict Tactics Scale.
[a]Because the significance level was reduced to $\alpha = .01$, these correlations were observed only at $p \leq .05$.
*$p \leq .01$. **$p \leq .001$.

Correlational Analyses

Correlations among the measures were examined (see Table 1). Given the number of correlations of interest, a more conservative significance level of .01 per study was adopted for these analyses.

CAPI and Parenting Scale Correlations. An examination of the pattern of these relationships indicates that across the three samples, CAPI Abuse Scale scores were significantly positively correlated with Parenting Scale scores (Overreactivity and Laxness). However, the CAPI Abuse Scale scores appear to be more strongly correlated with Overreactivity than with Laxness scores, with the exception of the third study sample. Indeed, for Study 1, the CAPI Abuse Scale correlation with Overreactivity was significantly stronger ($T2 = 6.62, p < .001$) than the CAPI correlation with Laxness (based on Steiger's [1980] recommendations regarding Williams' formula for comparing dependent correlations). Similarly, for Study 2, the difference between the CAPI Abuse Scale-Overreactivity and CAPI Abuse Scale-Laxness correlations were also significantly different ($T2 = 2.74, p < .01$). Only the third sample of at-risk parents demonstrated an association between CAPI Abuse Scale and Laxness ($r = .49$) virtually equivalent to the CAPI Abuse Scale association with Overreactivity ($r = .50$).

CAPI and CTSPC Correlations. With respect to the association between the CAPI and the CTSPC scales, across all three studies, abuse potential was not significantly correlated with reported CTSPC Non-Violent Discipline tactics. Interestingly, the overall pattern of associations suggests the CAPI Abuse Scale scores were related to reported use of Psychological Aggression virtually comparable to the use of Physical Assault actions.

CTSPC and Parenting Scale Correlations. Turning to the associations between the Parenting Scale and the CTSPC, Parenting Scale scores were not significantly related to the CTSPC Non-Violent Discipline items. However, for the at-risk sample of Study 3, more use of permissive parenting approaches was marginally associated with lower use of CTSPC Non-Violent discipline tactics (marginal given the reduced significance level). Across all three studies, Parenting Scale Overreactivity scores were significantly associated with the general parent—child aggression assessed by the CTSPC Physical Assault scale. Furthermore, across studies the Parenting Scale Overreactivity scores were also significantly associated with the CTSPC Psychological Aggression, in all cases of higher magnitude than with the Physical Assault scale. The Parenting Scale Laxness scores were not significantly correlated with either the CTSPC Physical Assault or Psychological Aggression scales across all three studies (although for the at-risk sample of Study 3, Laxness was marginally associated with greater frequency of physical assault behaviors).

Maltreatment Classification Group Differences

Parents were classified into maltreatment groups based on their responses to only the maltreatment items on the CTSPC. Differences between these two groups for each study appear in Table 2 . For Study 1, 6.1% of the sample endorsed at least one item of maltreatment. Those parents classified into the Maltreatment Group obtained significantly higher CAPI Abuse Scale scores and Parenting Scale scores than those who reported no instances of administering physical maltreatment toward their children. For Study 2, 20% of the parents in this community sample were classified into the Maltreatment Group. Those parents indicating they had engaged in any physical maltreatment obtained higher CAPI Abuse Scale scores and higher Parenting Scale Overreactivity scores than those who did not report such tactics. The obtained difference between the two groups was in the expected direction for the Parenting Scale Laxness scores, but was only marginally significant ($p = .067$). In Study 3, 17.6% of parents were classified into the Maltreatment Group. Again, the Maltreatment group differed from the No Maltreatment Group on the CAPI Abuse Scale and the Parenting Scale Overreactivity scores but not on the Laxness scores.

Table 2. Means, standard deviations, and group comparisons between CTSPC maltreatment versus no maltreatment groups

	Study 1			Study 2			Study 3		
	M	SD	t^a	M	SD	t	M	SD	t
CAPI Abuse Scale									
No Maltreatment Group	88.41	70.02	4.13***	83.90	71.72	2.87**	138.36	95.55	2.84--
Maltreatment Group	156.60	93.08		138.09	110.89		221.92	100.81	
Parenting Over-reactivity									
No Maltreatment Group	2.48	.84	4.51***	2.71	.85	3.76***	2.94	.91	2.45*
Maltreatment Group	3.36	.87		3.46	.87		3.62	.89	
Parenting Laxness									
No Maltreatment Group	2.28	.81	3.62***	2.53	.66	1.91	2.77	.94	1.07
Maltreatment Group	2.97	1.11		2.84	.84		3.10	1.33	

Note: CAPI = Child Abuse Potential Inventory; CTSPC = Parent–Child Conflict Tactics Scale.
[a] t-test statistic for between group differences.
*p ≤ .05. **p ≤ .01. ***p ≤ .001.

Discussion

The current investigation included three independent studies to evaluate the connections among child abuse potential, physical discipline and child abuse, and dysfunctional parenting style. Two studies involved lower risk community samples whereas the third study involved an at-risk group of parents. Overall, the results suggest a pattern of associations whereby parent–child physical aggression in various forms is associated with both dysfunctional parenting style (particularly more authoritarian approaches) and child abuse potential.

Across all studies, reported physically aggressive behavior in general, inclusive of corporal punishment, was significantly associated with increased child abuse potential. Furthermore, parents who reported they had engaged in behavior that would be considered physical maltreatment obtained significantly higher CAPI scores than those who did not report ever using any of those tactics. These findings lend support to the construct validity of the CAPI and are consistent with findings regarding the ability of the CAPI to distinguish physically abusive parents and predict future abuse (Milner, 1994). Consequently, child abuse potential appears associated with the actual reported use of corporal punishment in addition to physical maltreatment behaviors specifically.

Similarly, as hypothesized, results from all three studies suggest that overall parent– child aggression is related to dysfunctional, overreactive, authoritarian parenting. Similar results were obtained in the comparison of those parents who had engaged in some type of physical maltreatment behavior versus those who had not. In contrast, parent–child aggression in general was not significantly correlated with permissive parenting approaches in any of the samples. However, an examination of group differences for those parents who specifically engaged in maltreatment behaviors indicated that lax parenting was indeed more frequently reported in the first community sample but only marginally in the second community sample. Given that permissive parenting is considered problematic (Baumrind, 1966 , 1996), notably with respect to behavior problems (Arnold et al., 1993), it is intriguing to find the marginal correlation of permissive parenting style to general parent–child aggression observed only in the at-risk sample of parents raising children with behavior problems. The reduced power in this last sample may complicate identifying significance. However, it may be this finding reflects that parents raising children with behavior problems are inconsistent, vacillating between permissive and overreactive discipline strategies (as evidenced by their strong correlation in that sample). Overall, this pattern does suggest that greater inquiry into the link between permissive parenting practices and parent–child aggression may be warranted, especially in at-risk samples.

Interestingly, although not the main focus of this investigation, across all three samples, greater child abuse potential was also significantly associated with parents' use of psychological aggression although not with the use of non-violent discipline. This connection of the CAPI (which targets physical abuse risk) to psychological aggression likely underscores the intersection between instances of physical maltreatment and psychological maltreatment (e.g., Claussen & Crittenden, 1991). Yet it is also notable that dysfunctional parenting style scores (namely Overreactivity) were more strongly related to psychological aggression than with parent–child physical aggression. Given that earlier studies have linked parental verbal aggression to psychosocial problems in children (e.g., Vissing, Straus, Gelles, & Harrop, 1991), further study of psychological aggression may prove insightful to understanding the correlates of emotional maltreatment (see Glaser, 2002 , for review of emotional abuse). Potentially, an authoritarian parenting style may involve psychological aggression tactics that precede and escalate into physical discipline encounters. An interesting avenue for future research could pursue investigating such a progression, although the design of such a study would be admittedly challenging.

Additionally, as anticipated, greater child abuse potential was also significantly associated with dysfunctional disciplinary style across the studies. For the two community samples, this association largely reflected the strength of an overreactive, authoritarian discipline style, consistent with prior research (e.g., Haskett et al., 1995 ; Margolin et al., 2003). However, for the third at-risk clinical sample, child abuse potential was also strongly associated with a lax discipline approach. As noted earlier regarding the findings on parent–child aggression, perhaps for at-risk samples both authoritarian and permissive dysfunctional parenting styles are associated with abuse risk. The nature of some of the personal problems and attitudes captured by the CAPI items could readily be associated with more neglectful parenting, which is consistent with the under-involved, permissive approach tapped by the Parenting Scale Laxness scale. Future studies should consider whether other at-risk parents demonstrate a similar pattern of abuse risk relating to harsh as well as permissive discipline styles.

A number of limitations to the present study should be acknowledged. Although the current investigation drew from three separate samples of parents in order to minimize the limitations of a single given study, all three are limited by their reliance on parental self-report. All of the studies obtained information from parents anonymously but parents' responses may still be susceptible to underreporting. Therefore, some of these findings may actually reflect conservative estimates of physical discipline use, maltreatment, and abuse risk. Optimally, a study that involves child abuse potential, discipline style, and parent– child aggression could be supplemented by observations of parent–child behavior (e.g., see Haskett et al., 1995 study of abuse potential and observations), although self-report for such constructs is typical because of the inherent difficulty of observing such behaviors. Furthermore, data were gathered from a single source (the parent), which may amplify observed associations. Nonetheless, meaningful distinctions were detected among different parenting styles and aggression types using three measures with no item overlap.

In addition, the nature of the individuals who participated across studies should also be considered given that, despite compensation for participation, the samples involved parents who were willing to participate in a research study. Again, this issue may have led to more conservative estimates of the variables of interest. Yet a considerable minority of the first two community samples obtained clinically elevated CAPI scores, suggesting that abuse risk is apparent even among populations not identified as at-risk (e.g., as compared to Sample 3). Moreover, greater ethnic diversity in the sample distribution should be a goal in future research, and the online sample of the first study appears relatively better educated than either of the two subsequent studies. Although the third sample included at-risk parents, a more thorough investigation with other potential secondary prevention groups would be useful. Indeed, a research design with at-risk samples, accompanied by a group of parents who have been substantiated for abuse, could provide a comparison of how such issues may differ across different risk groups.

Overall, in order to advance prevention efforts, future research should continue to investigate how different parenting styles may relate to physical abuse risk and parent–child aggression. Progressive approaches to prevention could identify which parenting strategies could be modified that may in turn decrease the incidence of not only abusive parent–child aggression but perhaps aggressive tactics more broadly, including psychological aggression. Identification of the salient parenting attitudes and behaviors linked to varying levels and manifestations of parent–child aggression may help clarify how best to intervene on the continuum of behaviors that emerge during parent–child conflicts.

References

Arnold, D. S., O'Leary, S. G., Wolff, L. S., & Acker, M. M. (1993). The Parenting Scale: A measure of dysfunctional parenting in discipline situations . *Psychological Assessment, 2,* 137–144.

Baumrind, D. (1966). Effects of authoritative parental control on child behavior. *Child Development, 37,* 887–907.

Baumrind, D. (1996). The discipline controversy revisited . *Family Relations, 45,* 405–414.

Baumrind, D. (1972). An exploratory study of socialization effects on black children: Some Black-White comparisons . *Child Development, 43,* 261–267.

Caliso, J. A., & Milner, J. S. (1992). Childhood history of abuse and child abuse screening . *Child Abuse & Neglect, 16,* 647–659.

Chao, R. K. (1994). Beyond parental control and authoritarian parenting style: Understanding Chinese parenting through the cultural notion of training . *Child Development, 65,* 1111–1119.

Claussen, A., & Crittenden, P. (1991). Physical and psychological maltreatment: Relations among types of maltreatment . *Child Abuse & Neglect, 15,* 5 – 18.

Collett, B. R., Gimpel, G. A., Greenson, J. N., & Gunderson, T. L. (2001). Assessment of discipline styles among parents of preschool through school-age children . *Journal of Psychopathology and Behavioral Assessment, 23,* 163–170.

DeGarmo, D. S., Reid, J. B., & Knutson, J. F. (2006). Direct laboratory observations and analog measures in research definitions of child maltreatment . In M. Feerick, J. F. Knutson, P. Trickett, & S. Flanzier (Eds.), *Child abuse and neglect: Definitions, classifications, and a framework for research* (pp. 293 –328). Baltimore: Brooks.

Edwards, V. J., Holden, G. W., Felitti, V. J., & Anda, R. F. (2003). Relationship between multiple forms of childhood maltreatment and adult mental health in community respondents: Results from the adverse childhood experiences study. *American Journal of Psychiatry, 160,* 1453–1460.

Gershoff, E. T. (2002). Corporal punishment by parents and associated child behaviors and experiences: A meta-analytic and theoretical review. *Psychological Bulletin, 128,* 539–579.

Gonzalez, M., Durrant, J. E., Chabot, M., Trocme, N., & Brown, J. (2008). What predicts injury from physical punishment? A test of the typologies of violence hypothesis . *Child Abuse & Neglect, 21,* 752–765.

Glaser, D. (2002). Emotional abuse and neglect (psychological maltreatment): A conceptual framework . *Child Abuse & Neglect, 26,* 697–714.

Graziano, A. M. (1994). Why we should study subabusive violence against children . *Journal of Interpersonal Violence, 9,* 412–419.

Greenwald, R. L., Bank, L., Reid, J. B., & Knutson, J. F. (1997). A discipline-mediated model of excessively punitive parenting . *Aggressive Behavior, 23,* 259–280.

Haskett, M. E., Scott, S. S., & Fann, K. D. (1995). Child abuse potential inventory and parenting behavior: Relationships with high-risk correlates . *Child Abuse & Neglect, 19,* 1483–1495. Herrenkohl, R. C., Herrenkohl, E. C., & Egolf, B. P. (1983). Circumstances surrounding the occurrence of child maltreatment. *Journal of Consulting and Clinical Psychology, 51,* 424–431.

Jones, E. D., & McCurdy, K. (1992). The links between types of maltreatment and demographic characteristics of children. *Child Abuse & Neglect, 16,* 201–215.

King, G., Trocme, N., & Thatte, N. (2003). Substantiation as a multiplier process: The results of a NIS-3 Analysis. *Child Maltreatment, 8,* 173–182.

Margolin, G., Gordis, E. B., Medina, A. M., & Oliver, P. H. (2003). The co-occurrence of husband-towife aggression, family-of-origin aggression, and child abuse potential in a community sample. *Journal of Interpersonal Violence, 18,* 413–440.

Milner, J. S. (1986). *The Child Abuse Potential Inventory: Manual* (2nd ed.). Webster, NC: Psyctec.

Milner, J. S. (1994). Assessing physical child abuse risk: The Child Abuse Potential Inventory. *Clinical Psychology Review, 14,* 547–583.

Milner, J. S., Gold, R. G., Ayoub, C., & Jacewitz, M. M. (1984). Predictive validity of the Child Abuse Potential Inventory. *Journal of Consulting and Clinical Psychology, 52,* 879–884.

Milner, J. S., Gold, R. G., & Wimberley, R. C. (1986). Prediction and explanation of child abuse: Cross-validation of the Child Abuse Potential Inventory. *Journal of Consulting and Clinical Psychology, 54,* 865–866.

Prinzie, P., Onghena, P., & Hellinckx, W. (2007). Reexamining the Parenting Scale: Reliability, factor structure, and concurrent validity of a scale for assessing the discipline practices of mothers and fathers of elementary-school-aged children. *European Journal of Psychological Assessment, 23,* 24–31.

Rodriguez, C. M., & Richardson, M. J. (2007). Stress and anger as contextual factors and pre-existing cognitive schemas: Predicting parental child maltreatment risk. *Child Maltreatment, 12,* 325–337.

Runyon, M. K., Deblinger, E., Ryan, E. E., & Thakkar-Kolar, R. (2004). An overview of child physical abuse: Developing an integrated parent-child cognitive-behavioral treatment approach. *Trauma, Violence, & Abuse, 5,* 65–85.

Salzinger, S., Feldman, R. S., Hammer, M., & Rosario, M. (1991). Risk for physical child abuse and the personal consequence for its victims. *Criminal Justice and Behavior, 18,* 64–81.

Sedlak, A. J., & Broadhurst, D. D. (1996). *Third national incidence study of child abuse and neglect: Final report*. Washington, DC: U.S. Dept of Health and Human Services.

Slep, A. M., & O'Leary, S. G. (1997). *Pre-emptive parenting: Relations with discipline style and child behavior*. Poster presented at the annual conference of the Association for the Advancement of Behavior Therapy, Miami, FL.

Steiger, J. H. (1980). Tests for comparing elements of a correlation matrix. *Psychological Bulletin, 87,* 245–251.

Straus, M. A. (1979). Measuring intrafamily conflict and violence: The Conflict Tactics Scales. *Journal of Marriage and Family, 41,* 75–88.

Straus, M. A. (2000). Corporal punishment and primary prevention of physical abuse. *Child Abuse & Neglect, 24,* 1109–1114.

Straus, M. A. (2001a). *Beating the devil out of them: Corporal punishment in American families and its effects on children*. New Brunswick, NJ: Transaction.

Straus, M. A. (2001b). New evidence for the benefits of never spanking. *Society, 38,* 52–60.

Straus, M. A., Hamby, S. L., Finkelhor, D., Moore, D. W., & Runyan, D. (1998). Identification of child maltreatment with the Parent-Child Conflict Tactics Scales: Development and psychometric data for a national sample of American parents. *Child Abuse & Neglect, 22,* 249–270.

Straus, M. A., & Stewart, J. H. (1999). Corporal punishment by American parents: National data on prevalence, chronicity, severity, and duration, in relation to child and family characteristics. *Clinical Child and Family Psychology Review, 2,* 55–70.

United States Department of Health and Human Services. (2008). *Child Maltreatment 2006*. Washington, DC: Government Printing Office.

Veltkamp, L. J., & Miller, T. J. (1994). *Clinical handbook of child abuse and neglect.* Madison, CT: International Universities Press.

Vissing, Y. M., Straus, M. A., Gelles, R. J., & Harrop, J. W. (1991). Verbal aggression by parents and psychosocial problems of children . *Child Abuse & Neglect, 15,* 223–238.

Whipple, E. E., & Richey, C. A. (1997). Crossing the line from physical discipline to child abuse: How much is too much? *Child Abuse & Neglect, 5,* 431–444.

Whipple, E. E., & Webster-Stratton, C. (1991). The role of parental stress in physically abusive families . *Child Abuse and Neglect, 15,* 279–291.

Wolfe, D. A. (1999). *Child abuse: Implications for child development and psychopathology.* Thousand Oaks, CA: Sage.

Discussion Questions

1. Is it possible to predict who will abuse children?
2. Do you think that psychological abuse is as damaging as physical abuse? Why? Does it receive as much attention in the media as physical abuse?
3. What are the limitations of the study?

Assignment

Taking into consideration the limitations of the study, please explain how you would make changes to the current study to help improve our knowledge and understanding of the topic of parent-child aggression. Also consider topics like socio-economic status, education level, and age of parents.

What Kids Don't Get to Do Anymore and Why

By John A. Sutterby

One of the concerns I have for children's mental, physical, and emotional health is the role that parental anxiety plays in the lives of children today. The way I see it, parental anxiety is leading parents to limit children's opportunities to explore the world as they travel their path to adulthood. As a child growing up in Houston, Texas, in the 1970s, I had a lot of room to roam. My bicycle gave me all the freedom I needed to travel around our suburban neighborhood. I rode my bike to school every day; in fact, so many children rode their bicycles to school that we were often warned by the school principal not to ride more than two abreast. We usually ignored these warnings, and the swarms of bicycles frequently spread all the way across the right lane of the road. Today, the number of children walking or riding their bicycles to school has so declined that less than 10% of children's trips are on bicycle or foot, down from an estimated 60% less than 30 years ago (Corless & Ohland, 1999).

At my own children's school, there are no racks for locking bicycles and only a handful of children walk. A six-foot-tall chain link fence surrounds the school, and parents must be buzzed in to gain entrance. At the end of each school day, a long line of cars, SUVs, and trucks wait for the children to exit the school so they can be ferried to their next activity or to home for more schoolwork (or television viewing). I rarely see children playing in the streets around my suburban home, as they are all locked away "safe" in their homes.

It hasn't always been this way. In *The Archaeology of Childhood*, Baxter (2005) describes how archaeological digs of 19th-century homes uncovered children's artifacts scattered both indoors and out. Many of these childhood artifacts were found in areas close to the home, indicating that some children played under the observation of adults. Yet archaeologists also consistently find groupings of children's artifacts in hidden away areas, which most likely were not under the observation of adults. This suggests that children had opportunities to engage in unsupervised outdoor play.

Literature gives us an idea of what was considered safe parenting in past decades. The character of Ramona Quimby, in *Ramona the Pest* (Cleary, 1968), walked without adult supervision to school while she was still in kindergarten. As Cleary writes, "The time came when Mrs. Quimby and Mrs. Kemp decided the time had come for Ramona and Howie to walk to school by themselves. ... 'Wait for the traffic boy near the school,' said Mrs. Quimby, 'and don't talk to strangers' said Mrs. Kemp" (pp. 81–82). Forty years later, many would consider this practice negligent parenting or perhaps even child abuse. A fear of strangers is conflicting with the desire for children to develop independence and capabilities–skills that I worry our future generations of children will not have.

My own experiences and Ramona's took place during what Wortham (1992) called "the Golden Age of Childhood," roughly from 1950–1975. This time generally corresponds to the baby boom years. Wortham attributes the healthy state of childhood during that era to the increase in government spending for programs to help children's welfare, through President Kennedy's "New Frontier" programs and President Johnson's "Great Society." Wortham also notes the importance of improving economic conditions and improvements in standard of living for most Americans. Children's health improved over these years, as vaccinations and greater access to medical facilities decreased the child mortality rate. Since this golden age of childhood, however, we have become increasingly concerned for children's safety (e.g., regarding child abuse, abductions, etc.) as well as concerned with children's academic success.

Since 1981, the amount of time children spend with each other or alone without adult supervision has declined, especially in the area of outdoor free play. Free time for children has declined 16% between 1981 and 1997. Moreover, the amount of time that children spend in structured adult activities is increasing (Hofferth, 1999), even though, as Furedi, 2002) states,

> There is no evidence that children face greater dangers outdoors today than in the past. Playgrounds are no more dangerous than twenty or forty years ago. What has changed is society's perception of children's resilience. Physical injury to children is no longer accepted as a fact of growing up. (pp. 47–48)

What has happened to so dramatically change the range of children's freedom of movement and adults' concern over children's safety? A number of researchers have examined societal changes over the last century, especially from the mid-1970s to today. According to Stearns (2003), parental anxiety has risen throughout the 20th century, as children are perceived as both more valuable and more vulnerable. With falling mortality rates for children and increases in parental advice came the idea that if anything bad happened to the child, then the parents were somehow responsible. This valuation of children and the responsibility placed on parents has become so great that that it meant those few parents actually confronted with death [of a child bore] an almost unbearable sense of sorrow and guilt. Revealingly, few marriages in the 20th century survived the death of a child, so great was the sense that someone had done something wrong. (p. 31)

As previously mentioned, children today are considered more vulnerable. Prior to the 20th century, children were generally viewed as resilient and, if they were not corrupted, as capable of growing up with good character. Nineteenth-century parents believed that given the right environment, children would grow well if they were left alone. Our current times, however, portray children as having numerous flaws that need to be fixed and that parents need to fret over: for example, ADD, crooked teeth, dyslexia, and emotional disorders (Stearns, 2003). This article explores the increase in parental anxiety, the role of information in creating this anxiety, and the resultant consequences for children.

The Increase in Parental Anxiety

One sunny afternoon as our children played nearby, I asked a neighbor at what age she would allow her son to bicycle around the block by himself.

"I don't think I would ever do that," she replied. "The world is a very different place now than it was when we were growing up." (Williamson, 2007)

Researchers are concerned about parental anxiety, specifically how it limits children's activities. Mary Rivkin (1995) wrote of being alarmed that children were not being allowed outdoors any more: "Children's access to outdoor play has evaporated like water in sunshine" (p. 2). No one single factor can be blamed for children not having opportunities to be on their own; traffic, television, dangerous streets, and fear of crime and predators are just a few of the culprits.

The Gallup Polling Company has been tracking parental fear since 1977 (Jones, 2006). They have found that parents' fears for their children's safety at school generally spikes after a school shooting; 55% of parents, for example, stated that they were afraid for their children's safety at school after the Columbine shootings, up from 45% the year before and the highest level recorded to date. In October 2006, Gallup found that parental fear reached 35% after the Amish schoolhouse shootings, up from historic lows of 25% just two months prior.

There also has been an increased fear of child predators. Despite the statistics showing that child abductions are on the decline and extremely rare, most parents do not let their children out to play unsupervised (Williamson, 2007). Jenkins (1998) suggests that we are in the midst of a "panic" over child abduction and child abuse, using that term to describe how fear of a particular crime rises despite the evidence that the risk of that crime has not changed.

This fear of child predators causes all sorts of over-reactions. One school in my city requires faculty and staff to memorize the photographs of all the registered sex offenders in the neighborhood. This information is secured from a website called the National Alert Registry, which will tell you the number of sex offenders in your zip code; for a $10 fee, the registry will even send you their names, addresses, photographs, and profiles. They also will alert you by e-mail when any change occurs in the sex offender registry in your zip code.

Parents are not only more anxious about their children being a victim of crime or a fatal accident; they are also anxious about bullying and academic struggles. This parental fear has been transmitted to the schools and child care centers. One of the greatest concerns for all educators and child care professionals is the fear of litigation, which is partly to blame for schools banning recess and outdoor play (Brody, 2007). One school has even gone so far as to ban running on the playground (Bennet, 2007).

The Role of Information

Usually, it is better to become more informed about issues, but it appears that parents' increased access to information about child safety is artificially heightening their anxiety, rather than relieving it. Parents have more information than ever about risks to their children. Although this information is helpful in preventing some injuries, the vast amount of information available to parents makes it difficult for them to decide what is a real threat and what is primarily a perceived threat. Despite the limitations on how information is helping parents, government organizations, safety experts, and the media continue to issue many warnings to parents.

Standards and Government Advice. The Consumer Product Safety Commission (CPSC) was created in 1973 to help consumers know more about the risks posed by commercial products. Also, standards committees, such as the American Society for Testing and Materials (ASTM), work to make products safer for children. Manufacturers try to comply with these standards and regulations in order to avoid litigation (Frost, Wortham, & Reifel, 2005). Despite increased standardization and information, parents still are very concerned for their children's health and safety beyond the risks that exist in the everyday world. Government recalls of children's products are media events that increase parental anxiety without providing information about the severity or likelihood of a serious injury, leaving that up to the parent to decide.

Experts. The child study movement that began in the 19th century led to greater knowledge of childhood and child development, but it also gave rise to the "expert." Experts in child development give advice to parents based on what they have learned through their research and observations. These experts have played a part in increasing parental anxiety by making parents uncertain of their own common sense. Thus, parents may believe they cannot make their own decisions about their children, but must follow the advice of these experts or risk damaging their children (Stearns, 2003). Ironically, as trends in expertise have come and gone, from Freud to Skinner to Spock to Ferber and beyond, the experts' advice for parents has swung back and forth, often contradicting the advice given just a few years before.

Media. Media also play a role in creating anxiety in parents. Rather than focus on real hazards for children—for example, the fact that automobile accidents are the number one cause of accidental deaths for children—the media prefer to focus on more sensational but much more rare events, like child kidnappings. This focus on the strange and unusual gives families the impression that such events are more common than they really are.

Perception of risk is often very much at odds with the actual level of risk itself. Unknown risks tend to be perceived as much greater than known risks, and involuntary risks tend to be perceived as much greater than voluntary risks. Finally, parents tend to overestimate the level of risk to their children ("The logic of irrational fear," 2002). In one study, the perception of risk associated with tick-borne Lyme disease was much greater than the actual incidence of Lyme disease in one community. When the participants in the study were informed of the actual incidence of Lyme disease in their community, their perception of risk was reduced (Armstrong, Brunet, Spielman, & Telford, 2001).

Media can have a positive influence on patterns of behavior; for example, it has been shown to change attitudes toward smoking (Wakefield, Flay, Nichter, & Giovino, 2003) and to promote responsible sexual behavior (Keller & Brown, 2002). Yet media frequently enhances a sense of risk by hyping an event through round the clock coverage ("The logic of irrational fear," 2002). In one dramatic case, a media story on a chemical applied to some apples, Alar, led to the perception that "one bite of an apple treated with Alar could strike you dead." The actual risk associated with Alar was extremely small (Ross, 1995, p. 47). Nevertheless, people take information from media sources seriously, even when it differs from their own experiences. The media also tend to focus on exceptional or unusual cases of risks to children rather than typical cases, thus overestimating the risk from these unusual cases (Furedi, 1997).

Consequences for Children

The consequences for children in a world where parents are constantly anxious about their safety, development, and opportunities can be very severe. As parents remain reluctant to allow unsupervised outdoor play, we now see a growing number of children who are overweight and obese. According to the National Center for Health Statistics (2004), only about 4% of 6- to 12-year-old children were overweight in 1971; by 2002, 16% were overweight. Being overweight is a significant indicator for other health issues, such as heart problems and diabetes. Type II diabetes, which is primarily caused by overweight and lack of exercise, used to be called adult onset diabetes before it became so prevalent in children.

Another important consequence of parents' anxiety is that fewer children get the opportunity to try an activity and fail. As Furedi (2002) writes, "The attempt to construct an injury-free childhood can only inhibit children's development. ... [T]he risk of a child injuring herself is worth taking in order to allow her the freedom to explore her environment" (p. 48). Children growing up in this overprotected environment are missing out on many opportunities that can benefit them cognitively, socially, and emotionally.

More recently, such authors as Richard Louv (2005) have expressed concern about children's lack of access to natural environments, which he calls "nature deficit disorder," defined as "the human costs of alienation from nature... diminished use of the senses, attention difficulties, and higher rates of physical and emotional illnesses" (p. 34). According to Wilson (1986), humans have a natural affinity for nature and find exposure to nature and natural elements to be restorative, both mentally and physically. Children who spend all of their time indoors because parents are afraid to let them outside do not get the opportunity to be healed through this exposure to nature.

Clearly, children are suffering consequences as a result of parental fear. They have fewer opportunities to be alone, to take risks, or to explore. Their health is suffering due to lack of exercise and movement. I grew up in a generation of children who roved the suburban landscape. Future generations of children will grow up with even less knowledge than the current one of how to get around, other than the view from a car window.

Conclusions

Of course, I am not advocating that parents desert their children to the streets. At the same time, I think of my own, more independent, experiences as a child, and I know they have made me a more capable adult. I am confident traveling; I can take subways in strange cities and in foreign countries. I know how to get around in unusual places and recognize and avoid dangerous situations, based on my experience.

On the other hand, my own children have generally been ferried everywhere and have little to no sense of direction and easily get lost when I encourage them to explore on their own.

What will our next generation be like? I grew up when Halloween went from a candy fest free-for-all to a time when parents fretted about poisoned candy and razor blades in apples. Homemade Halloween treats quickly disappeared and hospitals began taking x-rays of children's candy, a practice that continues today. How will children today adapt to a world in which *no* place is considered safe and no unknown person is assumed to be kindly? How will this impact them as adults?

In the meantime, the influence of media and expert advice on childrearing will continue and parents will continue to face an influx of messages about dangers for their children. We can hope that the pendulum eventually will swing back to a common-sense parenting approach, and lessen the stranger-danger drumbeat.

References

Armstrong, P., Brunet, L., Spielman, A., & Telford, S., III (2001). *Risk of Lyme disease: Perceptions of residents of a Lone Star tick-infested community. Bulletin of the World Health Organization, 79*(10), 916–925.

Baxter, J. E. (2005). *The archaeology of childhood: Children, gender, and material culture.* Walnut Creek, CA: Altamira Press.

Bennet, D. (2007, April 15). *Back to the playground.* The Boston Globe. Retrieved May 6, 2009, from www.boston.com/news/globe/ideas/articles/2007/04/15/back_to_the_playground/.

Brody, J. (2007, April 3). A playground of monkey bars and slides. *The New York Times.* Retrieved May 6, 2009, from query.nytimes.com/gst/fullpage.html?res=9E02E3DBlF30F930A35757C0A9619C8B63.

Cleary, B. (1968). *Ramona the pest.* New York: William Morrow and Company.

Corless, J., & Ohland, G. (1999). *Caught in the crosswalk: Pedestrian safety in California.* Retrieved October 25, 2007, from www.transact.org/ca/caught99/caught.htm

Frost, J., Wortham, S., & Reifel, S. (2005). *Play and child development* (2nd ed.). Upper Saddle River, NJ: Pearson, Merrill, Prentice Hall.

Furedi, F. (2002). *Paranoid parenting: Why ignoring the experts may be best for your child.* Chicago: Chicago Review Press.

Hofferth, S. (1999). Changes in American children's time, 1981–1997. *Brown University Child and Adolescent Behavior Letter, 15*(3), 1, 5.

Jenkins, P. (1998). *Moral panic: Changing concepts of the child molester in modern America.* New Haven, CT: Yale University Press.

Jones, J. (2006). *Parents' concern about children's safety at school on the rise.* Retrieved October 25, 2007, from www.gallup.com/poll/25021/Parent-Concern-About-Childrens-Safety-School-Rise.aspx#l.

Keller, S., & Brown, J. (2002). Media interventions to promote responsible sexual *behavior. Journal of Sex Research, 39*(1), 67–72.

Logic of irrational fear, The. (2002, October 19). *The Economist, 365,* 29–30.

Louv, R. (2005). *Last child in the woods: Saving our children from nature-deficit disorder.* Chapel Hill, NC: Algonquin Books.

National Center for Health Statistics. (2004). *Prevalence of overweight among children and adolescents: United States* 1999–2002. Retrieved October 27, 2007, from www.cdc.gov/nchs/products/pubs/pubd/hestats/overwght99.htm.

Rivkin, M. (1995). *The great outdoors: Restoring children's right to play outdoors.* Washington, DC: National Association for the Education of Young Children.

Ross, J. (1995). Risk: Where do real dangers lie? *Smithsonian, 26*(8), 42–51.

Stearns, P. (2003). *Anxious parents: A history of modern childrearing in America.* New York: New York University Press.

Wakefield, M., Flay, B., Nichter, M., & Giovino, G. (2003). Role of the media in influencing trajectories of youth smoking. *Addiction, 98*(5), 79–103.

Williamson, L. (2007, March 29). Let kids outdoors: Crime is down, but parents shelter their children as if there's a child predator on every corner. *Los Angeles Times.* Retrieved October 25, 2007, from www.latimes.com/news/opinion/commentary/la-oe-williamson-29mar29,0,6859834.story?coll=la-home-commentary

Wilson, E. (1986). *Biophilia.* Cambridge, MA: Harvard University Press.

Wortham, S. (1992). *Childhood: 1892–1992.* Olney, MD: Association for Childhood Education International.

Discussion Questions

1. What do you think has caused parents to have increased anxiety over their child's safety?
2. What do you think about the banning of recess and running in schools?
3. What role did child development research/experts play in increasing parental anxiety?

Assignment

Based on this article, do you think parents are being overprotective and experiencing unnecessary anxiety? Use evidence from this article and other sources for this assignment. Comment also on your own childhood. Does it match the style of parenting with anxiety or the parenting without as much anxiety? What about your own children? How will you raise them?

Can You Imagine A World Without Recess?

By Michael M. Patte

R ecess has been a staple of the elementary school day for generations. Participating in child-initiated, outdoor play has provided hours of unstructured fun. Such breaks supply the emotional, physical, and social rejuvenation that developing bodies and minds need. But are these experiences now only a faded, nostalgic memory from the past?

While fond memories of recess abound for grown-ups, they are lacking for many children, because many schools across the United States are eliminating recess due to the belief that time is more wisely spent on academics (Patte, 2009). Indeed, over the duration of my teaching career, I have witnessed the increased devaluation of recess. In my current role as a university professor, I have visited many school sites that provide little time for daily recess. These personal experiences conjured up images of a story I read as a child, "All Summer in a Day" (Bradbury, 1959), in which recess is limited and the impact on children is profound. This fictional story offers keen insights into the dangers of eliminating recess from children's lives.

Fiction or Reality

I first read Ray Bradbury's "All Summer in a Day" as a child. Some years ago, I read it to my 5th-grade students; at the time, however, I thought that the content of the text was unimaginable. Now, I see it unfolding at my very own school.

The eerie setting of the story is an underground classroom on the planet Venus. All of the children are 9 years old and all have grown up on Venus, except for Margot, who was born on Earth. While on Earth, Margot experienced the wonders of the sun and playing outdoors. In contrast, life on Venus is one of almost unceasing torrential rain, with the sun appearing for just two hours every seven years. Lacking appropriate exercise and exposure to the sun, the children from Venus bask under heat lamps and consume vitamin supplements.

Because the children from Venus had experienced the sun and joy of playing outdoors for only two hours in their entire lifetimes, the concept of sun left only a vague impression. Each time Margot shared her recollections of the sun, her classmates' disbelief and disdain grew; when the teacher stepped out of class, they locked Margot in a closet. A monumental transformation happens, however, when the rare hours of sun occur and the children experience their first recess in seven years. Just moments earlier, the class had been an angry mob; once able to explore the world outside, they were transformed into a joyful brood.

In reading the story again, I could not help but think about my 5th-grade students, who lacked sufficient time to exercise at recess. Many of them were overweight and received a daily dosage of medication from the school nurse in order to address a variety of "conditions" I believe were exacerbated by restrictions on their urge to play. On days without recess, my students tended to be more edgy, agitated, unfocused, and disruptive. If afforded even a 15-minute outdoor recess break, however, the children tended to reenter the classroom calm, relaxed, focused, and well-behaved.

The most endearing quality of children is their indomitable spirit. It fills up every nook and cranny of the classroom. You can see it in their eyes and hear it in their voices. In my experience, the human spirit in each child is actualized in its purest form throughout the school day during recess—for many, recess is the only time when they are free to explore the world on their own terms. The most tragic element of "All Summer in a Day" is Margot being denied her basic human right to play, a violation that takes place all too often throughout America each day.

Schools Without Recess

Can you imagine a school day without recess? Many children are experiencing just that. In the present landscape of schooling, the notion of recess is disturbingly becoming a thing of the past. According to Marano (2008), some 40,000 schools across the United States now contribute to the suppression of curiosity and imagination by eliminating recess. Current research across multiple disciplines links the absence of recess to the following negative effects for children:

- Underdeveloped social skills—School violence, emotional outbursts, and underdeveloped social skills are all common elements in schools today ("Play Matters," 2009, p. 6).
- Increasing diagnoses of attention deficit hyperactivity disorder (ADHD)—Four and one-half million children between the ages of 3-17 are diagnosed with ADHD (CDC, 2007, p. 5).

- Lack of resiliency—Lacking exposure to challenging experiences impairs the ability to develop coping skills and the inner resources necessary to adapt to a fluid world (Marano, 2008).
- Poor health—More than 23 million youths are overweight or obese (Robert Wood Johnson Foundation, 2009, p. 1).
- Heightened levels of anxiety and depression—Diagnoses of anxiety disorders and depression in children are on the rise, with a corresponding increase in the use of psychoactive drugs to treat them (Marano, 2008).

Implications

What are the implications for eliminating recess from the school day? One possible implication is an increase in inappropriate student behavior. A 2009 study by Barros, Silver, and Stein found that providing a daily recess break for 8- to 9-year-old children in excess of 15 minutes was associated with a teacher's higher rating of class behavior scores.

In addition, eliminating recess impedes the development of social skills. Jambor (1999) recognized the playground at recess time as one of the few places where children can actively confront, interpret, and learn from meaningful social experiences. When children organize their own games, they exhibit a wide range of social competencies.

Recent evidence from the field of neuroscience (Panksepp, Burgdorf, Turner, & Gordon, 2003) suggests that the disorder known as attention deficit hyperactivity disorder (ADHD), which affects 6% to 16% of American children, may result not from faulty brain wiring or chemistry, but rather from restricting the urge to play. Panksepp (2002) has found that vigorous bouts of unstructured social play may be the best treatment for reducing the impulsive behaviors that characterize ADHD.

Further, eliminating recess harms students' physical health. Nearly one-third of children and teens are overweight or obese. According to Clements and Jarrett (2000), daily recess provides many benefits for children, such as enhanced aerobic endurance, muscle strength, motor coordination, and attentiveness. Research suggests that vigorous physical activity during recess stimulates the development of the heart, lungs, and other vital organs.

Finally, the disappearance of recess crushes the most enduring quality of our children—their human spirit. Brian Sutton-Smith (1999) sums up this idea poignantly: "The opposite of play—if redefined in terms which stress its reinforcing optimism and excitement—is not work, it is depression" (p. 254). In conclusion, as a former elementary school teacher, I will always remember the sheer joy of the screaming voices, the beaming faces, and the wild eyes of children engrossed in their unstructured outdoor play at recess. Just as striking is the deafening silence of the abandoned playgrounds that I witness too often today. Unfortunately, the landscape for many American children today mirrors that of the planet Venus from Ray Bradbury's story. Participating in child-initiated, outdoor play provides hours of unstructured fun, and such breaks play a significant role in supplying the emotional, physical, and social rejuvenation that developing bodies and minds need. Therefore, we cannot and should not stand by and let it slip away.

References

Barros, R. M., Silver, E. J., & Stein, R. E. K. (2009). School recess and group classroom behavior. *Pediatrics, 123,* 431–436.

Bradbury, R. (1959). "All summer in a day." Originally published in a short story collection titled, *A medicine for melancholy.*

Clements, R., & Jarrett, O. (2000). Elementary school recess: Then and now. *National Association of Elementary School Principals, 18*(4), 1–4.

Jambor, T. (1999). *Recess and social development.* Retrieved from www.earlychildhood.com/Articles/index.cfm?FuseAction=Article&A=39.

KaBoom. (2009). *Play matters: A study of best practices to inform local policy and process in support of children's play.* Washington, DC: Author.

Marano, H. E. (2008). *A nation of wimps: The high cost of invasive parenting.* New York: Broadway.

Panksepp, J. (2002). ADHD and the neural consequences of play and joy: A framing essay. *Consciousness & Emotion, 3*(1), 1–6.

Panksepp, J., Burgdorf, J., Turner, C., & Gordon, N. (2003). Modeling ADHD-type arousal with unilateral frontal cortex damage in rats and beneficial effects of play therapy. *Brain and Cognition, 52*(1), 97–105.

Patte, M. M. (2009). The state of recess in Pennsylvania elementary schools: A continuing tradition or a distant memory? In C. Dell-Clark (Ed.), *Play and culture studies, transactions at play,* 9, 147–165. Lanham, MD: University Press of America.

Robert Wood Johnson Foundation. (2009). *Active education: Physical education, physical activity, and academic performance.* San Diego, CA: Author.

Sutton-Smith, B. (1999). Evolving a consilience of play definitions: Playfully. In S. Reifel (Ed.), *Play and culture studies* (volume 2, pp. 239–256). Stamford, CT: Ablex.

U.S. Department of Health and Human Services, Centers for Disease Control and Prevention. (2007). *Summary health statistics for U.S. children: National health interview survey.* Washington, DC: U.S. Government Printing Office.

Discussion Questions

1. How does the story "All Summer in a Day" help support the importance of recess?
2. Does the author's evidence about the importance of recess sway you to believe it is important?
3. What are the reasons for why recess has been removed from schools?

Assignment

Come up with a campaign to bring recess back into elementary schools.

School-Wide Intervention in the Childhood Bullying Triangle

By Abigail McNamee and Mia Mercurio

For 8-year-old Connor, every day is the same. While waiting for the school bus each morning, Connor counts the seconds until Jake arrives and starts to taunt him. Jake is the school bus bully, and he has taken a special "liking" to Connor. The teasing begins at the bus stop: Jake calls Connor such names as "four-eyes" and "loser." He trips Connor as he makes his way to his seat on the bus; then Jake takes Connor's lunch money. At each stop, children enter the bus and align into three camps: the bullies, the targets, and the watchers. The bus driver hears some of the tormenting, but does not intervene, believing that bullying is just a part of growing up.

Connor's experience is not unusual. Statistics, however, vary. Christie (2005) writes that half of all children in the United States are bullied at some time in their lives; one in two is victimized on a regular basis. Thirteen percent of children in grades 6 through 10 have bullied, 11 percent have been targets, and six percent have been both bullies and targets. A 1998 Department of Education report found that approximately 25 percent of 4th- to 6th-grade students reported being bullied in the prior three months. The National Institute of Child Health and Human Development identified over three million bullies between grades 6 and 10 nationwide (Nansel et al., 2001).

Bullying today is not always done face-to-face. A recent report on *The Today Show* (2/23/07) indicated that teens are turning to technology as a means to torment. One-third of teens say that they have been mean to others on the Internet, that 25 percent of 9th- to 12th-graders know someone who has been mean on the Internet, and that 32 percent have been bullied on the Internet through gossip, rumor, and/or harmful, negative comments. In addition, the general public has become increasingly aware of school violence, in part because of intense media coverage of public school tragedies (Flynt & Morton, 2004; Lawrence & Adams, 2006; Stover, 2006).

The Problem

What Is Bullying, Anyway?

Let's be clear and state up front what might seem obvious. Bullying can be defined primarily in terms of the bully as a person: "when a more powerful person hurts, frightens, or intimidates a weaker person on a continual and deliberate basis" (Merriam-Webster OnLine, 2007; Scarpaci, 2006); "a blustering, browbeating person; especially one [who is] habitually cruel to others who are weaker" (Merriam-Webster OnLine, 2007); or "using one's authority, position, or size to undermine, frighten or intimidate another person" (Lawrence & Adams, 2006, p. 66).

Physical Bullying

- Hitting, slapping, kicking, pushing, shoving, poking, tripping
- Stealing, hiding, or ruining someone's things
- Making someone do things he/she does not want to do

Verbal Bullying

- Name calling
- Teasing
- Making insulting, deriding remarks
- Making racist remarks

Relational/Social Bullying

- Refusing to talk to someone
- Persuading others to exclude or reject someone
- Spreading lies or rumors about someone
- Making someone do things he/she does not want to do

("Bullies: What is bullying?," n.d.; Cole, Cornell, & Sheras, 2006; Scarpaci, 2006; Ritter, 2002)

Figure 1. Three types of bullying.

Bullying also can be defined primarily in terms of the bully's actions: "unprovoked, repeated, and aggressive actions or threats of action by one or more persons who have (or are perceived to have) more power or status than their victim in order to cause fear, distress, or harm" (Kim & Logan, 2004, p. 21); when students are "exposed repeatedly or over time to negative action on the part of one or more students" (Berthold & Hoover, 2000, p. 65); an action that "leaves the victim feeling afraid, powerless, incompetent, and ashamed" (Futterman, 2004, p. 27) and results in distraction and intimidation (Scarpaci, 2006). Coloroso (2005) writes that bullying is "conscious, willful, and deliberately hostile." She adds that bullies get pleasure from another's pain: "Bullying is not about anger, or even about conflict. It's about contempt—a powerful feeling of dislike toward someone considered to be worthless or inferior, combined with a lack of empathy, compassion or shame" (p. 49). It is a deliberate act that hurts young victims both emotionally and physically. In the classroom, it is disruptive, preventing students from learning and teachers from teaching (Scarpaci, 2006). Bullying involves a dynamic interaction between the bully, the bystanders, and the target ("Bully dynamic," n.d.).

Several myths about bullying exist: that it is only teasing or fooling around; that some weak children deserve to be bullied and ask for it; that only boys are bullies; that people who complain about bullying are babies, people who ask for help are wimps, and students should learn to handle their own disputes; that bullying is a normal part of growing up; that bullies will go away if ignored; that bullies have low self-esteem; that telling is tattling; that the best way to deal with a bully is to fight; and that victims of bullying should "get over it," as the situation is hopeless (Scarpaci, 2006; www.createpesse.com/bullyculture.html). These myths do not reflect the reality of bullying.

Teachers, other school personnel, and parents must recognize that bullying is a big problem that should have everyone worried. Students (even young students) are exposed repeatedly to bullying, and it can be extreme ("Dealing with bullying," n.d.; Olweus, 2003), involving not only a target, but each student, in a bullying triangle. Teachers, other school personnel, and parents must learn to recognize the indicators of bullying (Scarpaci, 2006), which can be of three types with many examples of unique bullying within each ("Bullies: What is bullying?," n.d.; Cole, Cornell, & Sheras, 2006; Ritter, 2002). Figure 1 offers an outline of the three types of bullying, with some examples. The examples are not exhaustive, however, as bullies can be quite creative.

Bullying Is a Triangle: Who Are the Participants?

The Bully. The bully has been created through genetic predisposition and/or environmental factors, and, according to Flynt and Morton (2004), bullies "have recognized characteristic behaviors ... enabling a generalized profile to be developed" (p. 331). More males than females are bullies (although both girls and boys can be very mean). Same-age peers are more likely to perpetuate bullying; teen bullies are more likely to drink alcohol, smoke, abuse other drugs, cheat on tests, and bring weapons to school (Simanton, Burthwick, & Hoover, 2000). Boys most often are physical bullies; girls more frequently bully through rumor, body language, e-mail, and sexual harassment ("Are girls meaner than boys?," n.d.; "Bullies: Who's a bully?," n.d.; "Dealing with bullying," n.d.; Whitney & Smith, 1983). The bully, in his/her life, may have experienced more than one of the following environmental factors:

- Poor attachment relationships
- Insufficient positive attention
- A distressed family situation (psychological or physically distant parents; parents who discipline inconsistently or with violence)
- Aggressive treatment
- Negative role models (seeing others get their way by being angry or pushing others around)
- Being rewarded for aggressive behavior
- Problems in school
- Exposure to a lot of media violence (television, movies, video games)
- Few and poor friendships
- Absence of being taught about, or accepting a value system of, caring for and not hurting others ("Bullies: Who's a bully?," n.d.; "Dealing with bullying," n.d.; Flynt & Morton, 2004; Lawrence & Adams, 2006)
- Sleep-disordered breathing (Toppo, 2007).

A bully likes to feel strong and superior, using what power he can muster over others to hurt. The bully may be someone other people look up to and want to hang out with ("Bullies: Innocent bystanders"), but bullies themselves are at risk. Bullying is violence and often leads to more violent behavior as the bully grows up ("Dealing with bullying," n.d.).

The Target. The target stands out to the bully as different in some way that the bully perceives as a weakness, and that the bully appears to despise. To the bully, the target looks different: taller, shorter, heavier, skinnier, older, younger, physically impaired (thus non-ambulatory or moving slower or with an unsteady gait), or a minority of some sort (by virtue of race, accent, clothing). The target might behave differently by being: a noticeably good or poor student-anxious or easily upset; labeled emotionally disturbed, withdrawn, timid, or shy; pervasively unhappy; unsure; or unaccustomed to standing up for him/herself. Students with disabilities and poor social skills have a greater likelihood of being bullied than non-disabled students ("Bullies: Who's a target?," n.d.; Flynt & Morton, 2004).

Once bullied, a target may fail in schoolwork, become disinterested in school generally, feign illness (headaches/stomachaches), be absent often from school, choose unusual routes home from school, claim to have lost things (books, money, clothing), steal to replace money, or have unexplained injuries. The effect of bullying on a targeted child is significant and may result in such mental health problems as depression and anxiety, and perhaps even suicide ("Bullies: Who's a target?," n.d.; "Dealing with bullying," n.d.; Flynt & Morton, 2004; Frankel, 1996; Heward, 2003; Lawrence & Adams, 2006; www.createpesse/symptoms/html).

The Bystander. Bullying occurs in the presence of peers about 85 percent of the time (Craig & Pepler, 1992). The peer bystander is, perhaps, the least understood aspect of the triangle of participants. Most students are probably neither bully nor victim; most are probably bystanders of bullying. What is it that motivates the bystander? Coloroso (2005) writes that bystanders of bullying are never innocent. It may be that the bystander passively connects with the bully, thinking that the bully is cool or entertaining; perhaps the bystander looks up to the bully and wants to hang out with the bully. It may be that the bystander realizes that he/she can bully vicariously. Or, the bystander could be afraid that the bully would turn on him/her. It also may be that the bystander has no expectation of being able to stop the bullying. The bystander might believe that speaking up won't help and may make things worse. He/she is not accustomed to giving an assertive response, doesn't know what to do, or has learned to stand by and be neither seen nor heard ("Bullies: Innocent bystanders"; Coloroso, 2005).

It is highly likely that the bystander feels conflicted. If he/she supports the bully, then the bystander becomes an accomplice. If the bystander supports the target, he/she may become a target in turn. Yet, if the bystander remains silent, he/she may feel guilt. The result may be a stew of uncomfortable feelings: sadness, anger, guilt, shame (Fried & Fried, 1996).

Where Does the Bullying Triangle Come Together?

In a 2003 report, the National Center for Education Statistics reported that, during the 1999-2000 school year, 29 percent of schools reported having more difficulty with student bullying than with any other single discipline problem. A 2004 report by the same organization stated that students' grade levels were inversely related to the likelihood that they would be bullied, yet these statistics seem quite low: 14 percent of 6th-graders, 7 percent of 9th-graders, and 2 percent of 12th-graders reporting being bullied at school. Overall, 7 percent of students between the ages of 12 and 18 reported that they had been bullied at school during a six-month period (cited in Christie, 2005).

Bullying is most likely to occur wherever adult intervention is unlikely (Flynt & Morton, 2004; www.createpesse.com/strike.html): in school stairwells, hallways, bathrooms, the cafeteria, empty corners, parking lots; on school buses and playgrounds; during the walk to and from school; and, most recently, even online, through e-mail and instant messaging. Thus, bullies have a range of choices concerning where to prey on their victims.

The Intervention

Who Should Intervene in the Bullying Triangle?

It is not enough for individual classroom teachers to attempt intervention in the bullying triangle. All adults in schools, certainly, should be ready to intervene. Adults in positions of authority can often find ways to resolve dangerous bullying problems without the bully ever learning how they found out about it ("Dealing with bullying," n.d.). Staff responses to bullying often fail, however, and may even encourage bullying behavior. Adults' responses may be inconsistent or fail to address bullying, even when it is known to occur. Supervision may be inappropriate, discipline may be inconsistent, and anti-bullying skills may not be taught (www.createpesse.com/bullyculture.html). Typically, the majority of effort in anti-bullying programs is teacher-directed and requires the most action from adults, as it is developed and administered primarily by adults (Lepkowski, Packman, Overton, & Smaby, 2005). School administrators, teachers, and aides must learn to recognize that bullying exists in their schools, and that bullying, when it occurs, is a serious problem for each participant. The American Medical Association (AMA) warns that bullying can damage a child as much as child abuse can (Ritter, 2002). The younger the child, the more he/she will suffer from bullying (Scarpaci, 2006). Every adult in the building must learn to recognize the indicators of bullying and to acknowledge the role of each participant. But vigilant adults in a school are not enough. Lepkowski et al. (2005) recommend instituting a student-driven anti-bullying approach, one that emphasizes the importance of students' perspectives and involvement "in dealing with such a complex student-experienced problem" (p. 546). The following checklist of questions from the AMA can be adapted, depending on the age/understanding of the children responding:

1. Have you ever been teased at school? How long has this been going on?
2. Do you know of other children who have been teased?
3. Have you ever told your teacher about the teasing? What happens when you do?
4. What kinds of things do children tease you about?
5. Do you have nicknames at school?
6. Have you ever been teased because of an illness or disability, or for looking different from other kids?
7. At recess, do you usually play with other children or by yourself? (Ritter, 2002)

Adults may be uncertain about how to handle bullying if they see it occurring. How can intervention provide the best opportunity to teach the difference between appropriate and inappropriate behavior while, at the same time, protecting a victim? First, we will focus on immediate intervention by adults and then on a school-wide plan that involves adults and students.

Immediate Intervention by Adults

Intervention needs to focus on each participant in the bullying triangle. Immediate intervention involves immediately stopping the bullying, when this seems possible. It depends on the adult being present (obviously not always a reality), and requires an adult to act quickly and understand when immediate physical intervention will not provoke violence. When the adult is present and believes it safe to intervene, the intervention could involve: stepping between the bully and the victim, thus blocking eye contact between them; referring to relevant school rules against bullying; or supporting the victim in a way that allows for regaining self-control, saving face, and feeling supported and safe. Bystanders should be included in the conversation and provided guidance on how to intervene or get help the next time. Logical consequences must be imposed, when appropriate, without requesting an apology. It requires telling the bully and his/her friends who are present that you will be watching them closely to be sure there is no further bullying and no retaliation; and it requires a follow-up meeting for the bully and target with an adult.

Next Steps in the Intervention Process

Intervention With the Bully: Introduce a New Concept of Power. Adults can defuse bullying behavior and help a child who is a bully. We believe that children who are bullies have either grown up being bullied at some point in their life, or are in need of some type of caring.

Intervention With the Target: Introduce a New Concept of the Power of One. Children who are bullied often do not wish to involve adults in the school, for fear of worse retaliation from the bully. The first step is creating a school environment in which targeted children feel safe enough to tell an adult about their problems.

Intervention With the Bystander: Introduce a New Concept of Responsibility. Children who are bystanders in the bullying triangle make up the majority of the school's population. The majority, if taught correctly, could have the most power. If teachers, parents, and administrators can teach the bystanders what to do to stop the bullying, fewer episodes may take place.

School-wide Planning for Intervention: The Power of Many

Everyone in the school—adults and students—needs to work together to establish the school and the surrounding area as a "bully-proof" safety zone, with zero tolerance for bullying of any kind, and publish it as such (Kim & Logan, 2004; The National Resource Center for Safe Schools, 1999). Together, adults and students can create a school environment characterized by warmth; adult demonstrations of positive interest and involvement; firm limits on unacceptable behavior; consistent application of non-punitive, non-physical sanctions for unacceptable behavior or violation of rules; and adults acting as authorities and positive role models. Many schools have functioning Pupil Personnel Committees involving a teacher, administrator, school counselor or social worker, school nurse, and other relevant personnel; often, however, even these committees do not know how to involve students.

Intervention should involve problem assessment through student and adult surveys to determine what is going on in the school, staff training and program development through in service workshops, preventive education with students, and behavioral and clinical intervention, as necessary (http://createpesse.com/approach.html).

The literature describes steps that schools can take in designing an anti-bullying program ("Bullies: Bully-free zones," n.d.; Christie, 2005; Cole, Cornell, & Sheras, 2006; Lepkowski et al., 2005; Stover, 2006;

Thompson & Cohen, 2005). Schools can invest in published programs designed to stop bullying, such as the National Education Association's "Quit It" or "Bullyproof," as a basis for designing a school-wide anti-bullying program. Students should be surveyed in confidence about bullying to determine what is happening both in and outside school. A comprehensive policy can be developed stating that bullying is dangerous and disrespectful and will not be tolerated, parents should be encouraged to file written reports of suspected bullying, students should be encouraged to anonymously report bullying, teachers should report bullying to administrators, and administrators should investigate reports of bullying (Thompson & Cohen, 2005). School teams should develop an intervention strategy, include a prohibition against bullying in the school handbook, notify parents (of the bully and the target) of verified bullying, and collect data on the number of bullying incidents. Additionally, students throughout the school can be trained for leadership and such skills as win-win strategies, flexibility, creativity, listening, compromise, and empathy (Lepkowski et al., 2005). The issue of bullying can be raised with a student council and the PTA, which can set up a Bullying Prevention, Student Respect, or We Care group. The school counselor can develop an anti-bullying workshop series for administrators, teachers, aides, and students, separately or in some combination (Cole, Cornell, & Sheras, 2006).

A "Conflict Wall" with steps for resolving conflicts (Phillips, 1997) can be posted in halls and classrooms, and used as a prompt for frequent discussions. The steps may include:

- Cool down
- Describe the conflict
- Describe what caused the conflict
- Describe the feelings caused by the conflict
- Listen carefully and respectfully while the other person is talking
- Brainstorm solutions to the conflict
- Try your solutions
- If something doesn't work, try another solution.

- *Follow-up with an intervention led by an adult*
- *Notify parents, when this seems appropriate*
- *Hold the bully accountable for his/her inappropriate behavior, making sure you indicate that bullying is serious and harmful*
- *Find a way to be supportive with the bully (often, bullies have lacked a caring relationship)*
- *Begin talking with the bully ("I think you've been bullied yourself ... maybe you have trouble feeling good about yourself unless you're tough ... we all have within us the ability to bully, but it can be controlled so that people won't think of us as unkind, abusive, and mean. I'd like to work on that with you.")*
- *Talk respectfully about ways of changing inappropriate behavior through building social skills: apologizing, practicing friendly approaches, developing empathy and perspective-taking abilities, feeling good about yourself without being aggressive, controlling angry feelings, using power in socially acceptable ways*

("Bullies: How to handle it," n.d.; "Bullies: Who's a bully?," n.d.; Coloroso, 2005; "Dealing with bullies," n.d.)

Figure 2. Intervention with the bully.

Classroom Planning for Intervention: The Power of Classroom "Family"

Some school districts or schools do not yet have a bully intervention program. Even so, just one teacher in one classroom can establish such a program. Often, it is the work of individual teachers to use their classrooms and the students in them to create a community in which everyone is treated with respect; an increasing number of writers indicate how this can be done (Christie, 2005; Cole et al., 2006; Lepkowski et al, 2005; Stover, 2006; Thompson & Cohen, 2005). These classrooms can be "islands of safety," with the class acting as a "family" whose members take care of each other (Stover, 2006). Such classrooms are often the only place where a target child can truly feel safe. In these classrooms, teachers talk in class about bullying in all of its parts, emphasizing that they can help and should be approached to help. They teach anti-bullying techniques: how to talk to bullies ("Cut it out!," "How'd you like it if. . ."); the skills involved in working out problems/disagreements; classroom survival skills; alternatives to aggression; and friendship-making skills. The teachers also talk about feelings by questioning and listening to students respectfully, and requiring that students do the same. They introduce the increasing number of books now available for children about bullying (Christie, 2005).

Bullying Prevention Programs That Work

Although many programs have been developed that help to address the issues of bullying in schools, no one program has been proven effective for all schools. What follows is a short list of the anti-bullying programs that appear to hold the most promise.

The Olweus Bullying Prevention Program (www.clemson.edu/olweus/). This program was created by Dan Olweus, who is considered a pioneer in bully research. A study he developed in Norway, in 1970, serves as the foundation for this program. The program is a multilevel, multi-component, school-based program designed for students ages 6–15 years old. In the 1990s, Olweus worked with two professors at Clemson University to conduct the first evaluation study of his prevention program in the United States. This Bullying Prevention Program has been identified as a model by the U.S. Department of Justice's Office of Juvenile Justice Delinquency Prevention and by the Center for the Study and Prevention of Violence (CSPV), University of Colorado. School-wide components include training for the staff, a bullying prevention committee, a school-wide kick-off event, parental involvement, and staff discussion groups. Classroom components include holding regular class meetings and consistent reinforcement of school rules against bullying.

Bully-Proofing Your School (www.creatingcaring-communities.org). This program, developed in 1996 in Colorado, was intended for elementary and middle school students. It is a comprehensive school-wide program designed to create a safe and caring school environment by taking the power out of the hands of bullies and placing it into the hands of a caring community. School-wide components include staff training, student instruction, support for the victims, parent support, and the development of caring communities.

BullySafeUSA (www.bullysafeusa.com). This comprehensive program for grades K-8 offers strategies, terminology, and scenarios for the prevention of bullying. It is intended for students, parents, and teachers. The BullySafe program contains five elements that can be offered separately or in combination: student empowerment training; in service training for faculty; seminars for parents and community leaders; conference presentations/workshops; and "Train the Trainer" institutes for school counselors, nurses, administrators, school resource officers, teachers, child advocates, and community leaders.

The Don't Laugh at Me Program (DLAM) (www.operationrespect.org). This program was created out of Operation Respect, Inc., which aims to transform schools into more safe and respectful places. Created with the intent of reducing the physical and emotional cruelty that children can inflict on each other, it contains three curricula—one for grades 2–5, another for grades 6–8, and the third for afterschool programs and camps. The program was founded by musician Peter Yarrow (from the famed music trio Peter, Paul and Mary) in collaboration with Educators for a Social Responsibility. The program consists of 14 classroom sessions that focus on developing skills and awareness and feelings, appreciation of diversity, creating a caring classroom culture, and conflict resolution.

Peaceful Schools Project/Menninger Clinic (www.backoffbully.com). Created and implemented by the Menninger Foundation's Child and Family Center in Houston, Texas, this program focuses on grades K-5 and includes a research component that looks at results of anti-bullying efforts. The Peaceful Schools Project has three essential elements: a martial arts-based program called "Gentle Warrior," which teaches a set of defensive and relaxation skills; the education campaign, which uses posters, buttons, and classroom stories to create a positive climate; and a classroom management plan, which integrates the dynamics of bully-victim/bystander into a learning environment.

Promoting Alternative Thinking Strategies (PATHS) (www.colorado.edu/cspv/blueprints/model/programs/PATHS.html). This comprehensive curriculum program promotes social and emotional strategies and helps to reduce aggression in elementary children. It is designed to be used by teachers and counselors in a multi-year format and is effective with children in both general and special education classrooms. The PATHS program focuses on: identifying, labeling, expressing, managing, and assessing feelings; understanding the differences between feelings and behaviors; learning to control impulses; stress reduction; and reading and interpreting social cues.

Safe Culture Project (www.safeculture.com). This program originated in Iowa and has been implemented in many states, including Maine and California. The project provides a tailor-made program to meet the unique needs of the school. Students in this program complete a 25-minute confidential survey, called the Inventory of Wrongful Activities (IOWA), followed by a training day for all staff and a chosen leadership group. The training helps to design a project that fits the school.

- *Allow the target time to process the experience, vent feelings, receive and feel support ... to talk about what happened*
- *Teach ways to avoid being intimidated, including reading and interpreting social signals, practicing social behavior, not walking alone, avoiding unsupervised areas, sitting near the bus driver, leaving expensive items and money at home, and labeling belongings in case they are stolen*
- *Suggest holding in anger, ignoring the bully and walking away with poise, not crying or showing frustration*
- *Suggest not getting physical, which could lead to more violence*
- *Talk about ways for a target to feel his/her best, strongest, most confident*
- *Teach ways to neutralize a bully through confident and assertive behavior, standing tall, using humor, being aware of what is going on in an area and moving away or closer to others, identifying friends who can give support, asking an adult for help*
- *Brainstorm comebacks ahead of time: "That's what you think!," "So?," or "So what?," "Stop talking to me like that!," "Can't you think of something else to say?," "Tell me when you get to the funny part!," "And your point is?"*
- *Practice "self talk" as a way of being your own cheerleader*
- *Suggest turning the bully's statement into a joke: "Thanks. I'm glad you noticed."*
- *Suggest imagining a protective "fog" that swallows up insults and allows nothing to touch or get through to the target*
- *Remind students that telling a parent and school official is crucial to stopping bullying*

("Bullies: How to handle it," n.d.; Coloroso, 2005; "Dealing with bullying," n.d.)

Figure 3. Intervention with the target.

- *Set up a bully box for anonymous reporting*
- *Teach students to take a stand, not stand by*
- *Teach students that telling an adult is not tattling, but rather is the brave and responsible thing to do*
- *Make available a list of adults whom a watcher can tell when bullying is observed*
- *Encourage students to move away from a bullying incident*
- *Encourage students to support the target privately: "That was a mean thing he did to you"*
- *Encourage students to talk to the bully privately, saying, for instance, "Leave her alone ... she's my friend"*
- *Intervene on behalf of the target (telling an adult or standing up to the bully)*
- *Institute a secret signal that a watcher can use to notify an adult when bullying is in progress*

("Bullies: How to handle it," n.d.; Coloroso, 200

Figure 4. Intervention with the bystander.

Steps to Respect Program (www.cfchildren.org). This bullying prevention curriculum is designed to decrease bullying at school and help students create positive relationships with their peers. The program is based on research showing that friendship can help protect children from being bullied. The program concentrates on elementary-age children in grades 3–6, who learn such skills as: coping with bullying, general friendship skills, emotion management, and bystander intervention. The staff and parents are taught how to report acts of bullying, how to respond to children who bully, and how to help the targets of the bully.

Conclusion

Although bullying is hardly a new phenomenon, highly publicized media accounts about bullying have raised the awareness of many people (Limber, 2003). Bullying can no longer be sloughed off as quiet, inconsequential kid stuff experienced by only a few victims who "probably deserved it any way." It can no longer be considered the rite of passage that all children go through. It can no longer be considered a children's secret that adults should stay out of. It is not up to bullying targets to "suck it up" or solve the problem on their own.

Bullying is being exposed more and more ... but children always knew about bullying. It is only the adults who sometimes forget, ignore, and deny. It is time for adults and children to get together, using the resources available, to intervene school-wide in the childhood bullying triangle.

Available Resources for Children, Teachers, and Parents

Children's Books

Move Over, Twerp. By Martha Alexander. New York: Dial Books, 1981. Ages 4–8.

Stop Bullying Bobby! Helping Children Cope With Teasing and Bullying. By Dana Smith-Mansell. Far Hills, NJ: New Horizons Press, 2004. Ages 4–8.

Stop Picking on Me: A First Look at Bullying. By Pat Thomas. New York: Barrons Educational Series, 2000. Ages 4–8.

Bye-Bye, Bully! A Kid's Guide for Dealing With Bullies. By J. S. Jackson. St. Meinrad, IN: Abbey Press, 2003. Ages 4–8.

King of the Playground. By Phyllis Naylor. New York: Simon & Schuster, 1994. Ages 4–8.

The Recess Queen. By Alexis O'Neill. New York: Scholastic Press, 2002. Ages 4–10.

My Secret Bully. By Trudy Ludwig. Berkeley, CA: Tricycle Press, 2005. Ages 5–10.

The Bully of Barkham Street. By Mary Stolz. New York: Harper and Row, 1985. Ages 9–13.

Stick Boy. By Joan T. Zeier. New York: Antheneum, 1993. Ages 9–13.

Dealing With Bullying. By Marianne Johnston. New York: Rosen, 1978. Ages 10–15.

Websites Containing Helpful Information

www.bullying.org

www.stopbullyingnow.com

www.bullystoppers.com

www.kidscape.org.uk

www.safechild.org

Numbers To Call for Additional Help

Kids Help Phone: 800-688-6868

Anti-Bullying Crisis Hotline: 877-443-9943

National Anti-Bullying Hotline: 877-443-9943

End Youth Violence: 866-89-YOUTH

References

Are girls meaner than boys? (n.d.) *Time for Kids.* Retrieved June 30, 2004, from www.timeforkids.com/TFK/magazines/story/0,6277,233883.html.

Berthold, K., & Hoover, A. (2000). Correlates of bullying and victimization among intermediate students in the midwestern USA. *School Psychology International, 21,* 65–78.

Bullies: Bully-free zones. Retrieved June 26, 2008, from http://pbskids.org/itsmylife/friends/bullies/article7.html

Bullies: How to handle it. Retrieved February 19, 2008, from http://pbskids.org/itsmylife/friends/bullies/article4.html.

Bullies: Innocent bystanders. Retrieved February 19, 2008, from http://pbskids.org/itsmylife/friends/bullies/article5.html.

Bullies: What is bullying? Retrieved February 19, 2008, from http://pbskids.org/itsmylife/friends/bullies/index.html.

Bullies: Who's a bully? Retrieved February 19, 2008, from http://pbskids.org/itsmylife/friends/bullies/article2.html.

Bullies: Who's a target? Retrieved June 26, 2008, from http://pbskids.org/itsmylife/friends/bullies/article3.html

Bully dynamic. Retrieved February 20, 2008, from www.createpesse.com/ BullyDynamic.html.

Bully-proofing your school. Retrieved February 19, 2008, from www.creatingcaringcommunities.org.

BullySafe USA. Retrieved February 19, 2008, from www.operationrespect. org.

Center for Physically and Emotionally Safe Schools, The. Retrieved February 20, 2008, from www.create-pesse.com.

Christie, K. (2005). Chasing the bullies away. *Phi Delta Kappan, 86*(10), 725–726.

Cole, J., Cornell, D., & Sheras, P. (2006). Identification of school bullies by survey methods. *Professional School Counseling, 9*(4), 305–313.

Craig, W., & Pepler, D. J. (1992, June). *Contextual variables in bullying and victimization.* Poster presentation at the Canadian Psychological Association, Quebec City.

Coloroso, B. (2005). A bully's bystanders are never innocent. *Educational Digest, 70*(8), 49–51.

Dealing with bullies. Retrieved April 30, 2008, from www.kidshealth.org/kid/feeling/emotion/bullies.html.

Dealing with bullying. Retrieved June 26, 2008, from http://kidshealth.org/teen/your_mind/problems/bullies.html

Don't Laugh at Me Program, The (DLAM). Retrieved February 19, 2008, from www.operationrespect.org.

Flynt, S., & Morton, R. (2004). Bullying and children with disabilities. *Journal of Instructional Psychology, 31*(4), 330–333.

Frankel, F. (1996). *Good friends are hard to find.* Glendale, CA: Perspective Publishing.

Fried, S., & Fried, P. (1996). *Bullies and victims.* New York: M. Evans & Co. Publishers.

Futterman, S. (2004). *When you work for a bully: Assessing your options and taking action.* Montvale, NJ: Croce Publishing Group.

Heward, W. (2003). *Exceptional children: An introduction to special education.* Upper Saddle River, NJ: Merrill/Prentice Hall.

Lawrence, G., & Adams, F. (2006). For every bully there is a victim. *American Secondary Education, 35*(1), 66–71.

Lepkowski, W., Packman, J., Overton, C, & Smaby, M. (2005). We're not gonna take it: A student driven anti-bullying approach. *Education, 125*(4), 546–556.

Limber, S. P. (2003). Efforts to address bullying in U.S. schools. *Journal of Health Education, 34*(5), 523–529.

Kim, S., & Logan, B. (2004). *Let's get real: Curriculum guide lessons and activities to address name calling and bullying.* San Francisco: The Respect for All Project.

Merriam-Webster On-Line. (2007). Retrieved February 17, 2008, from www.m-w.com/cgi-bin/dictionary.

Nansel, T. R., Overpeck, M, Pilla, R. S., Ruan, W. J., Simons-Morton, B., & Scheidt, P. (2001). Bullying behaviors among US youth: Prevalence and association with psychosocial adjustment. *Journal of the American Medical Association, 285*(16), 2094–2100.

National Resource Center for Safe Schools. (1999, Spring). *The Safety Zone, 2*(1).

Olweus Bullying Prevention Program, The. Retrieved February 19, 2008, from www.demson.edu/olweus/.

Olweus, D. (2003). A profile of bullying at school. *Educational Leadership, 60*(6), 12–17.

Peaceful Schools Project/Menninger Clinic. Retrieved February 19, 2008, from www.backoffbully.com

Phillips, P. (1997). The conflict wall. *Educational Leadership, 54*(8), 43–44.

Promoting Alternative Thinking Strategies (PATHS). Retrieved February 19, 2008, from www.colorado.edu/cspv/ blueprints/model/programs/PATHS.html.

Ritter, J. (June 20, 2002). AMA puts doctors on lookout for bullying. *Chicago Sun-Times.*

Scarpaci, R. T. (2006). Bullying: Effective strategies for its prevention. *Kappa Delta Pi Record, 42*(4), 170–174.

Simanton, E., Burthwick, P., & Hoover, J. (2000). Small town bullying and student on student aggression: An initial investigation of risk. *Journal of At-Risk Issues, 6*(2), 4–10.

Steps to Respect Program. Retrieved February 19, 2008, from www.cfchildren.org.

Stover, D. (2006). Treating cyberbullying as a school violence issue. *The Education Digest, 72*(4), 40–42.

Talking with children about violence in school. Retrieved February 20, 2008.

Thompson, M., & Cohen, L. (2005). When the bullied must adjust. *Educational Digest, 70*(6), 16–19.

Toppo, G. (June 13, 2007). Bullies more prone to sleep difficulties, study suggests. *USA Today.*

Whitney, I., & Smith, P. (1983). A survey of the nature and extent of bullying in junior/middle and secondary schools. *Educational Research, 35,* 3–25.

Discussion Questions

1. What are some myths about bullying?
2. How does this article define bullying?
3. What is the bullying triangle? Explain the parts and what research says about each part of the triangle.

Assignment

Do you think that what the authors have proposed with their bullying triangle will be useful in preventing bullying? Use evidence to support your answer. What different or original ideas have you thought of or read about that might help prevent bullying?

CPSIA information can be obtained at www.ICGtesting.com
Printed in the USA
LVOW09s2056230816

501546LV00001B/1/P

9 781621 317449